WITHDRAWN

Therapy with a Coaching Edge

Therapy with a Coaching Edge

Partnership, Action, and Possibility in Every Session

Lynn Grodzki

W. W. Norton & Company
Independent Publishers Since 1923
New York • London

For information about permission to reproduce selections from this book, write to Permissions, W. W. Norton & Company, Inc., 500 Fifth Avenue, New York, NY 10110

For information about special discounts for bulk purchases, please contact W. W. Norton Special Sales at specialsales@wwnorton.com or 800-233-4830

Manufacturing by LSC Harrisonburg
Production manager: Christine Critelli

Library of Congress Cataloging-in-Publication Data

Names: Grodzki, Lynn, author.
Title: Therapy with a coaching edge : partnership, action and possibility in every session / Lynn Grodzki.
Description: First edition. | New York : W W Norton & Company, 2018. | Series: A Norton professional book | Includes bibliographical references.
Identifiers: LCCN 2017050184 | ISBN 9780393712476 (hardcover)
Subjects: LCSH: Psychotherapy—Practice. | Personal coaching. | Psychotherapist and patient.
Classification: LCC RC465.5 .G764 2018 | DDC 616.89/140068—dc23 LC record available at https://lccn.loc.gov/2017050184ISBN: 978-0-393-71247-6

W. W. Norton & Company, Inc., 500 Fifth Avenue, New York, N.Y. 10110
www.wwnorton.com

W. W. Norton & Company Ltd., 15 Carlisle Street, London W1D 3BS

1 2 3 4 5 6 7 8 9 0

Contents

Acknowledgments   ix

Introduction   xi

PART 1: The Foundation

1   Therapy with Something Extra   3
Get better results in therapy by implementing a new model based on a coaching approach.

2   Where Therapy and Coaching Meet   13
Clarify the common ground and obvious differences between therapy and coaching.

3   Who's Coachable within Therapy?   29
Identify those clients who can benefit from a proactive model.

4   Creating Therapist–Client Collaboration   45
Apply a partnership position to promote behavioral change.

5   Results in Every Session   63
Improve client satisfaction and retention, session by session.

PART 2: Skills for Partnership

6   Skill #1: Ask Effective Questions   81
Expand therapy sessions with more "ah-ha" moments by asking the right question.

7   Skill #2: Be a Strategist with a Twist   95
         Help clients resolve big decisions by advancing client-based
            control.

8   Skill #3: Add Humor and Lightness   107
         Encourage the therapeutic alliance by being authentic and
            flexible.

PART 3: Skills for Action

9   Skill #4: Call a Client into Action   119
         Assist client readiness for forward movement.

10   Skill #5: Add Shared Accountability   133
         Support clients in accomplishing their desired goals.

11   Skill #6: Deliver a Coaching Edge   144
         Practice the art of giving direct, concise feedback to boost
            motivation.

PART 4: Skills for Possibility

12   Skill #7: Align with Core Values   161
         Show clients how to make decisions based on meaning and
            purpose.

13   Skill #8: Find the Metaphors that Matter   175
         Elicit client-driven symbols and stories that strengthen
            change.

14   Skill #9: Design a Plan for Life   189
         Invite clients to define the future they desire.

ADDENDUM

The Best Blend   209

*How to integrate Therapy with a Coaching Edge with
existing methods of therapy and counseling.*

Worksheets   219

*A quick review of checklists, exercises, and action steps
for easier application*

> Guidepost for Client Suitability
> Strategies for Collaboration
> The "Getting to Yes" Session Plan
> List of Effective Questions
> Stages of Strategic Partnership
> Therapeutic Alliance
> Client Readiness
> How to Lend a (Limited) Hand
> Steps to a Coaching Edge
> List of Core Values
> Client-Based Metaphors
> The Five-Year Life Plan

Index   253

Acknowledgments

This has been a compelling, yet challenging book for me to write. The biggest help to me in this endeavor has also been the closest to home—my husband, Tad—not a therapist himself, but a careful reader and thoughtful editor. He has been willing to think and read and talk about this manuscript with me endlessly during the past two years, through all the early and very rough drafts. Tad understands that I can be uncommunicative when I am writing, consumed with my own thoughts. When I would finally emerge after hours at my computer, we took long walks in the nearby park. He was a good listener as I debriefed, needing to assess chapters and consider changes. His genuine interest in the topic grew over time and lessened the isolation so common with writing; he allowed the book's development to be a bond between us, rather than a block. After almost 30 years of marriage, I appreciate that this venture could help us turn toward each other, as John Gottman likes to say, rather than turn away.

I also thank Rich Simon, editor of *Psychotherapy Networker* magazine, for his support in publishing an early version of this model in 2012 as "The Coaching Edge." Carol and Tom Walsh, two dear friends and savvy therapists, agreed to be early readers and gave me valuable, clear feedback so that I could make this manuscript more relevant.

This book is in your hands because of Deborah Malmud, director of the Professional Books Division at W. W. Norton, who is a gem of an editor. The publishing industry often falls victim to instability, as publishing companies rise and tumble, so I know that the consistently supportive relationship I have had with Deborah is rare. I am lucky to have had her in my corner for the past 18 years, during which time we produced 6 books (and one major revision of my first book, so really 7 books, if anyone but me is counting). It was Deborah who encouraged me to tackle this project and kept it alive as an idea. I am glad she stayed true to the need for this book. Now that it is written, I think she was right: This model seems like a natural evolution of proactive therapy, especially for the next generation of therapists and counselors who are practicing in the midst of much change and uncertainty. If this book or any of my earlier ones have been helpful or useful to you, please thank Deborah Malmud.

Introduction

In 2010, I began to notice that my normal way of working as a therapist was changing. I was curious about the change, but in no way worried. It was interesting, in the way that it interests me to walk out into my garden and see the emergence of a new plant sprouting up, a volunteer perennial that I did not add to the border but welcome as a garden bonus.

Perhaps my clinical work is undergoing a similar blossoming, I thought. As a therapist who is eclectically trained, I have gone through several shifts in methods during the course of 30 years of practice, but most of these have been intentional. This shift arrived unplanned, outside of my awareness. The good news was that client outcomes were improving. People I saw were getting better, faster. I was curious and wondered why.

By the time I talked to Rich, later that year, my thoughts had clarified somewhat. Rich Simon, the publisher of *Psychotherapy Networker* magazine, occupies a very special place in my life. He is the one person I can count on to push me beyond my professional comfort level. Every year or so, Rich contacts me to find out what I am thinking about. "Let's chat," he says, an innocent-sounding invitation by email that belies what I now know will be a fast-paced, invigorating conversation. I come to these "chats" ready to take notes. Rich is provocative, prodding me to think and then articulate what I am only vaguely grasping about my own work.

Rich knows me best in my role as a business coach, but in this particular conversation, I explained to Rich that over several years, something was surfacing in my work as a therapist. I suspected I was experiencing a synergy of sorts, based on operating two separate practices, therapy and coaching, in a side-by-side small business. My methods were blurring. Because I was working full time as both a psychotherapist and a business/life coach, my clinical skills had morphed. Without intending to, when I was doing psychotherapy with certain clients, I was working more quickly. I challenged them to have a bigger life plan. I talked about possibility instead of pathology. I focused on success factors more than symptoms. Sometimes I made big requests of clients for significant action between sessions, and they worked hard to comply. In sessions, my clients were still expressing a full range of feelings and thoughts, and we addressed difficult issues and problems. But they also seemed to be enjoying themselves more. We laughed. We bantered. This proactive persona was one I often used as a coach.

I am a master certified coach, and I teach coaching to new coaches as a faculty member for a large accredited coaching school. I knew I wasn't using a true coaching protocol or "pure" coaching skills in therapy sessions. What occurred in therapy did not mirror what I did in my role as a coach. Instead, I had developed an adaptation for psychotherapy, a way of relating that I might at best call "coach-like." I had embraced a coach-like persona and adapted some coach-like techniques and skills. The results were promising. I saw improved client motivation toward goals. Clients made results that they could identify within a single session, session after session. A faster pace in client outcomes occurred with both new and existing clients.

I told Rich that bringing a coaching style into therapy was not a singular idea. I had talked with many therapists who practiced at least some default "coaching," even if they didn't call it that. By and large, therapists today do more than listen, nod, observe, and provide a neutral "holding environment": we encourage, challenge, brainstorm and offer opinions and advice on occasion. A coaching style feels natural to many of us and reflects the shift toward cognitive behavioral therapy and other short-term, evidence-based methods that are popular with therapists and their clients. But therapists practicing some default coaching in sessions usually do this intuitively, rather than intentionally. I wanted to understand what I was doing, and why. In my spare time, I had been searching through the coaching and therapy literature for anything written about this topic, how to bring adapted coaching skills into therapy. There was nothing I could find. I started to review my case notes, pulling out examples for study. I was organizing my thoughts and tracking this change in my clinical process.

Rich was silent for a few seconds and then said, "Write me two thousand words on it." This is a very typical Rich Simon comment, which might drive fear into the heart of another therapist, but it always motivates me. I started writing.

Back and forth Rich and I went with versions of an article for another year, until "The Coaching Edge" finally appeared in *Psychotherapy Networker* magazine in 2012. It started with a case from several years earlier that described the emergence of my "inner coach" voice injecting itself into a therapy session. I included thoughts about the model I was developing. I revealed more about my coaching training and my beginning process of developing a therapeutic model. The article got a lot of response, including these comments from other magazine readers, all therapists:

"Great article. Despite years of academic psychiatric and psychotherapy training, I have always thought of myself simply as a coach in the counseling room. Thank you for your beautiful story of your development. It is always good to not feel alone. I have often wondered how to merge the directness of a coach with the tools and knowledge of a therapist. I think we can and must do this to really be good therapists."

"It is interesting to start to think of an integration. I will now be looking for times when my 'inner coach' is wanting to come out. And, I will begin to ask questions about that voice rather than squelch it in the name of 'being a good therapist'."

"This article was . . . how do I say it? Relevant! Finally, I have found something which helped me."

"You are also asking important questions about the relationship between coaching and therapy and how we can best help our clients."

"I think that clients no longer want to spend hours and years of their lives examining and recounting their woes. They want concrete solutions and action to move past the glitches in their lives. They want to function effectively even if not perfectly, but most of all, they want to feel that their life is worth living, that they can enjoy moments of happiness and feel successful in their existence. They want the tools and guidance to get them there, not just nods, empathy, and listening ears. Of course, some clients do need to have lots of that therapeutic balm initially before they can take to the edge of the nest for their first short solo flight. I will admit though that there is no 'one-size-fits-all' approach in therapy. I respect all of my colleagues in the field who are daily on the front lines providing guidance and healing to our fellow travelers on this planet."[1]

FROM HAPPENSTANCE TO HARDCOVER BOOK

After the article was printed, I felt encouraged to continue defining my process. I don't believe that good therapy occurs by happenstance, so I created a kind of handbook for myself. In the margins were questions: Where did the coaching techniques I was using come from? How had I adapted them for therapy purposes? Which clients responded well to a directive and cognitive approach? When did it backfire? What specific coaching interventions help to inspire a client to take a big step forward? What fell flat? How had I diffused normal therapeutic transference to attempt a collaborative, less hierarchical position? When did I need to stop relating in a coach-like way and resume my tried-and-true, slower-paced methods?

Slowly, I started to deconstruct what I had been doing in therapy, analyzing my case notes and observing current sessions. Then I reconstructed my process, adding in research, sources, and citations. Over time I had the basics of a working model. I started to teach the model,

---

1 https://www.psychotherapynetworker.org/magazine/article/239/the-coaching-edge

via workshops and in therapist supervision sessions, to test out my ideas. But as interesting as this project was to me, I got distracted. I had other projects to attend to: building a new house, and revising *Building Your Ideal Private Practice*, my first book on practice building, which took me a full year given that it was 15 years old and overdue for review. Other life events intervened. I could have easily let this project go, but thanks to the prompting of Deborah Malmud, my editor at W. W. Norton, I stayed involved. Both she and I felt a sense of dedication to this concept, combining the best of modern therapy and coaching. With this manuscript, I have now defined a model, complete with foundational elements and nine specific skills, that combines the strengths of therapy and coaching into a pro-active clinical approach.

Developing yet another method of therapy for a profession already filled to the brim with an abundance of methods is daunting. But the interest in this topic expressed to me by colleagues, added to the results that I see in my practice, has helped me to press ahead.

With this model, therapists can learn how to become more hands-on in sessions, using skills for leverage while still placing the locus of control within their clients. Therapists can promote behavioral change without formulaic or rigid protocols. The skills I define integrate easily into existing therapy methods, including those of psychodynamic psychotherapy, cognitive behavioral methods and humanistic-holistic approaches. The model can be used in whole or part, and can be applied in a variety of situations and settings. Perhaps best of all, as I hear from therapists who are testing it out, the skills are energizing—for both the therapists and their clients. I echo the comment from a reader of the *Psychotherapy Networker* article: Given our fast-paced world, it's time for therapists to learn how to combine the directness and action of a coach with the wisdom and experience of a therapist.

Welcome to *Therapy with a Coaching Edge.*

Therapy with a Coaching Edge

Part 1

The Foundation

1

Therapy with Something Extra

In 2008, I walk into my therapy waiting room on a Monday morning and see a heavyset, middle-aged man slumped in a chair. His body droops, elbows on his knees, head down. I can't see his face—just his round, hunched-over body and a bald spot at the top of brown, thinning hair. He doesn't move as I approach.

"Rick?" I say, and he looks up, nods slowly, and stands. His eyes are watery, and I wonder whether he's been crying.

I know a little bit about him already. His doctor, a colleague of mine who's just seen him for an emergency appointment for chest pains—which have turned out to be anxiety-related—referred Rick to me late Friday afternoon. The doctor left a message on my office phone when she made the referral: "Rick's a good man, but very stressed and worried. He has a lot of family complications that he'll tell you about. If he keeps going the way he is, he'll probably lose his job as well as his health."

When Rick sits down, I ask my standard question: How can I be of help? Rick doesn't answer immediately. He wipes a limp hand across his eyes, and I wait in silence.

"I was called into my supervisor's office last Friday. I'm on probation," he announces in a quavering voice. "It's serious. I could get fired. My supervisor put a memo in my file. I can't afford to lose my job. I thought I was having a heart attack that evening, but the doctor said it was just anxiety. That's why I'm here."

I ask Rick to tell me more about what happened on Friday. Coming back from lunch late, he'd gotten a frantic phone call from his wife, who struggles to manage complications from her diabetes. Also, Rick's mother, who suffers from dementia and lives in his home, had upset his wife in a fit of confusion and agitation. In the midst of this conversation, Rick's secretary, Anne, had walked into his office to ask about a report that was a week overdue. Distracted and overwrought, Rick snapped, yelling at Anne to get out of his office. Out of sympathy for his family situation, Anne had been covering for Rick's tardiness and work errors for months, but now he was yelling at her. Shocked and offended, she went to his supervisor to complain.

Rick fumbles in his pockets looking for a tissue, although a box is on the table right in front of him. "I can't believe I yelled at Anne. She didn't deserve that. I said terrible things to her. My supervisor was right to call me on the carpet. What a mess."

Once he's gotten his story out, I do what I usually do to try to establish initial rapport. I use some active listening and reflect what I have heard. "You were in the middle of a complicated situation, rushing because you were late, your wife on the phone crying, and then Anne came in and you were mortified that she'd overheard the scene with your wife. I see how upset you are."

Rick nods his head to signal yes, I understand him. We settle into a familiar therapeutic rhythm: he talks; I listen, nod, and make an acknowledging or validating comment. Then Rick nods—clearly reassured—and talks more. His narrative shifts away from the office to the stressors in his life: his mother, his wife, his fatigue. He continues to open up as I let the story unfold. Our conversation develops a relaxed back-and-forth rhythm.

But after 20 minutes of this comfortable flow, I start feeling antsy and begin to attend to an inner voice that I've come to hear in my sessions more and more. Instead of a calm observer of the situation, it's a sharp, bossy presence in my head. "This man is drowning," the voice asserts, "and you're letting him describe the temperature of the water and his feelings about wetness." I mentally shake my head as if to clear it of the interruption—to get back to the more pleasant cadence of listening and nodding—but the intrusion continues. "He needs to make some changes to keep his job. Get him to focus. What is his plan?"

"Okay," I think to myself, "the coach has entered the building." This coach's voice has become a familiar presence in my therapeutic work, so it doesn't take me by surprise. It often emerges when I'm with a client like Rick who needs to fix a critical problem.

My stance changes. I sit up straighter in my chair and politely, but firmly, interrupt Rick. "I'd like to shift gears now and get back to your initial problem, the one that brought you into my office today. Are you serious about finding a way to fix the mess you made on Friday so that you can keep your job?"

Rick's eyes widen and he looks surprised. I know I'm not transitioning as gracefully as I might, but the coach's edgy voice is urging me to take action now. I wait for his response, which will let me know whether this was a wise move. He begins to object, but then pauses, sighs, and looks right at me.

"Lynn, you're right. I got off track. I've been in therapy before and I know there's a lot in my life that isn't working for me. But my number one concern is that I keep my job. Everything and everyone in my family depends on me keeping my job."

"Okay," I say. "If that's your priority, then you need to make some immediate changes. Today, in the time we have left, what can we do together?"

Rick says, "Got any magic wand to make me calm down and be more productive?" He attempts a weak smile.

I smile back, genuinely. "I'm not a magician, but I sure do support that goal. I don't think you need magic to make it real. Start with specific examples: What do you mean by being calm and productive?"

"Number one: I need to hold my temper. Number two: I need to get my reports in every day. Number three: I need to remember how much I want to keep my family together and help my wife more with my mother."

I collaborate with Rick to clarify a series of action steps: Make appropriate apologies to Anne and his boss, shift his workflow to ensure that his weekly reports are complete before he leaves on Friday, and manage his time more efficiently. We role-play talking to Anne and his boss, while he makes notes on a pad of paper, which I always keep on the table in front of clients, so he can remember the key steps. One idea that brings a smile to his face involves setting up his computer screensaver to help him remember to stay calm during the inevitable interruptions of the work day, by reminding him of his favorite relaxation activity—going fishing.

With five minutes left in the session I ask, "What else do we need to discuss before ending today, so that you will feel like our session is complete?"

"I have to think about how to help my wife. She went through a lot this week. I need to find additional services for my mother. I am not sure how to fix this." Rick starts to go into detail about his mother's medical condition.

I sense that this could be another full session, and know that we are ending soon. Holding up my hands in the classic time-out position, I stop him. "That's a tall order, and we need more time to talk through this completely. We have a few minutes left. What will help you in the short term?"

Rick's eyes fill with tears. "I love my wife, and she is doing her best. I need to stay calm when crisis happens at home and keep that in mind."

I don't want to end without making even this heartfelt statement into an action step. "How will you do that, keep the best of her in mind, each day?"

"I can look down at my wedding ring. Each time I see that ring I think about the strong, caring wife I have," he says, touching the ring gently.

To end the session, I ask Rick to summarize what he will take away from our time.

"I'm amazed that I can take so many practical steps to improve things right away. This sure is a different kind of therapy than I'm used to. I thought I would leave here feeling exhausted and depressed, but I feel motivated. We did so much. I have my action plan and I have my wedding ring I can look at during the day to remind me of what's important. You sure have something extra! When can I schedule my next session?" Rick asks.

I will see him weekly and encourage him to use our sessions for accountability so that we regularly monitor on his progress at work. Once that situation is stabilized, I imagine we can shift back to a slower pace.

Rick needs insight to understand more of his reactivity and awareness of his triggers so that he can better manage his anger. I hope he can resolve his living situation and take the burden of caretaking away from his wife. There will be layers of emotion, beliefs, and history to unpack. But first things first. He needs to function as well as possible and keep his job. With a set of coaching skills in my therapeutic toolbox, I can keep him motivated and focused on his immediate goals. Later we can tackle other, more complex emotional and psychological issues.

As he leaves, I wonder, as I often do when I blend therapy with a directive persona and add in some coaching skills, what another therapist would call the process I used in this session. Rick called it having "something extra." I now call it Therapy with a Coaching Edge.

AN EXTRA EDGE

Almost a decade after that session, I have gone beyond waiting to hear from my "inner coaching voice" to alert me to shift gears to developing a working model that combines psychotherapy and coaching, based on a system of strategic principles and defined skills. After years researching the coaching literature, designing and adapting a variety of coaching skills for a clinical setting, testing out therapy interventions, reviewing my case notes, defining, and then teaching this model and its concepts in workshops to other clinicians, I now have a better understanding of how to adapt coaching skills for clinical purposes, and know why and when to bring a coaching approach into a therapy session. Using *Therapy with a Coaching Edge*, you have a map to explore the leverage and flexibility of a coaching approach, and can see how to add these skills into therapeutic treatment. I know that a map is not the territory; each therapy session must be customized for the client and situation that presents itself to us, as therapists.

I have developed this model for individual psychotherapy and counseling sessions. It is appropriate for adult clients (and mature adolescents) who meet the suitability criteria I show you in Chapter 3. Using these skills and strategies, I see how therapy clients can be more easily motivated and encouraged to take constructive action and improve their lives. Resistance to therapy treatment often softens. Client retention improves. By learning how to set goals based on what a client wants, not just needs, I watch as depressed clients become more hopeful and optimistic about the future. Anxious clients are willing to risk more, to confidently begin to identify a life plan.

Therapy with a Coaching Edge is adaptive and often used in concert with other familiar methods of psychotherapy. For example, apply a selected skill from my model to enhance client behavioral change and motivation, and then revert back to the process-oriented therapy techniques that are familiar to most therapists, to slow the pace and address the feelings that attend major behavioral changes. Knowing the techniques of a coaching approach allows you to expand the range of your effectiveness. Using the coaching skills that I describe, unlock and unblock some of the complaints about therapy that clients voice: that therapy takes too long or doesn't produce tangible results. Now you have skills to offer more to those clients who are ready to progress faster or go further.

My model is designed not only to improve client outcomes, but also to give therapists and counselors tools that energize them as practitioners. Learning to ask powerful, compelling questions, helping clients go beyond a discussion of symptoms into topics of core values, knowing how to motivate clients towards desired action, and encouraging clients to make choices based on meaning and purpose empowers the therapist, too. Having a set of specific, positive skills can revitalize the hard work of a clinician who is seeing clients hour after hour in agency settings, non-profit organizations, or private practice. Unlike other methodology, the skills offered in this book are straightforward, designed to be immediately applied by the reader without additional training programs to master the techniques. Because a coaching approach is a natural adaptation for many new and experienced therapists, this book is intended as just-in-time learning—you can learn a useful skill just when you need it, and feel confident to bring it into a session as soon as you and your client are ready. In the Addendum, a guide for integration shows you how to knowledgably blend existing methods of therapy with this approach.

One clarification for readers: Although this working model of therapy is based on adding an adapted coaching approach to therapy, this book is not intended to be a training program to teach you to become a life coach. The skills I outline are not "pure" coaching skills; the techniques, positioning, and methods are modified from those used in traditional coaching. If you want resources for becoming a life coach, two previous books of mine are geared specifically toward that career:

- *The New Private Practice: Therapist-Coaches Share Stories, Strategies, and Advice* (edited by Lynn Grodzki, W. W. Norton, 2002.) This collection of essays from therapists define how each became a successful coach. Readers gain an understanding of the most profitable coaching specialties: life coaching, executive coaching, financial coaching, and many more. Each therapist-turned-coaches offers tips of the trade to help therapists transition more easily into the coaching profession.
- *The Business and Practice of Coaching: Finding Your Niche, Making Money, and Attracting Ideal Clients* (Lynn Grodzki and Wendy Allen, W. W. Norton, 2005.) This co-authored book has been reviewed as a "voice of realism" about the coaching profession. It is widely used by new coaches entering the profession who want answers to their questions about how to become a coach, protect their practices, understand the business aspects of coaching, and find their coaching niche.

HOW TO USE THIS BOOK

This book is written for therapists, counselors, and other helping professionals who work with individual adults and mature adolescents, and are drawn to the benefits of implementing a new model of therapy, one that adds a coaching approach to psychotherapy. The book is a user-friendly, step-by-step guide, starting with an underlying foundation to describe the basics of the model and then defining a set of nine specific coaching skills that progressively build a therapist's capacity to get described results. Chapters offer case examples for the purposes of demonstration:

Client confidentiality has been protected by creating a composite case, without including any identifying client information or qualities.

Therapy with a Coaching Edge is designed to be flexible in its implementation. It can be used in whole or in part: you can select only those skills and concepts that seem right for your practice and add them to techniques or methods that you already use, or, if you prefer, adopt the complete model as it is described to have a working method of clinical practice.

The book is written in four sections:

Part 1: The Foundation explains the basic underpinnings of Therapy with a Coaching Edge, to show you how to:

- Clarify the differences and overlap in therapy and coaching, within their purpose and practice. This helps when adopting a coaching style within therapy, to understand why the essence of coaching is a logical and beneficial next step for contemporary counselors and psychotherapists.
- Assess who is "coachable" in therapy. and determine those clients who are well suited to a fast-paced, action-oriented approach within a therapy session Equally important, this chapter will help you identify clients who are best treated with another method. The chapter also has a checklist to let you confirm whether or not this model will be a good fit or not for you, as the therapist.
- Balance traditional therapeutic neutrality and client-therapist hierarchy with a more collaborative stance. Therapists using this model need to emphasize a partnership position in order to get the described results. Learn how to do this while maintaining your therapeutic and ethical boundaries.
- Implement a results-oriented therapy session plan. With this plan, you can set up each session to enhance client satisfaction and retention. Clients take ownership of their treatment from the start and feel better prepared to see therapy through to completion.

Part 2: Skills for Partnership defines three skills that further the goal of therapist-client collaboration. You will learn how to:

- Apply a set of effective questions that offer clients more "ah-ha" moments. A single question can produce new insights in a client or challenge limited existing beliefs. I show you a list of questions to use and explain how and why they work, with a case example and exercise to help you apply this skill easily.

- Become a strategist with a twist, using a coaching approach to help your clients problem-solve. This skill allows clients to feel your support while increasing their own commitment to their goals.

- Develop a lighter touch to your communication when needed to augment the therapeutic alliance. Allow clients to see you as a real and authentic person in order to develop the groundwork for the goals of the therapeutic model.

Part 3: Skills for Action focus on behavioral change, with techniques that can improve client compliance and motivation. You will learn how to:

- Call clients into action by furthering readiness and identifying desired goals.

- Combine a powerful technique of support with an action plan, so that clients can accomplish their next steps more consistently.

- Deliver a coaching "edge" when needed, a form of direct, concise verbal feedback to help clients get back on track and keep moving forward.

Part 4: Skills for Possibility offers strategies to help clients see options and choice. You will learn how to:

- Introduce the topic of core values into therapy sessions so that clients can orient their decisions to reflect both meaning and purpose.

- Explore the art of creating client-driven metaphors that resolve issues organically, often with improved outcomes.

- Help clients go beyond a treatment plan to design a prospective plan for a desirable life.

Addendum:

- **The Best Blend:** A recipe of sorts to integrate Therapy with a Coaching Edge with your existing therapy methods for easier application.

- **Worksheets:** A compilation of the checklists, exercises, and action steps from each chapter to help you easily access and implement the foundation and skills in your practice.

Ready to get started? The next chapter will clarify what coaching is and is not, to help you understand how therapy and coaching align and differ. This explanation can help you feel more assured when applying the skill set of Therapy with a Coaching Edge.

2

Where Therapy and Coaching Meet

I am at a coaching conference in Houston, Texas, listening as a group of senior coaches try to define coaching for a position paper they are writing as a group.

"How should we say coaching is different from therapy?" asks one coach.

"That's easy," says another. "Coaching focuses on the present and the future, psychotherapy focuses on the past."

"Coaching is about achieving goals, and therapy is about developing insight," says one more. I start to shake my head as others pipe up.

"Coaching is short-term and therapy takes forever, years and years."

"A coach listens and talks back to you, like a real person. A therapist is a silent, blank screen."

"Therapy deals with pain and coaching deals with pleasure."

Finally, it's my turn. "These descriptions are wrong," I protest loudly. As the lone licensed, masters-level therapist in the room who is also a certified coach, I explain that these definitions about therapy are simplistic at best, inaccurate at worst. Psychotherapy can't be compressed into a single sentence so neatly; as a profession in existence for more than one hundred years, it contains hundreds of "schools"—not academic institutions but distinct methods or models of practice—each with its own theory and knowledge base.

I make my case. "I know you want to have some sound bites to further coaching, but in doing so, you ignore that psychotherapy today can he long-term or short-term, process- or goal-oriented, insight-driven or behavioral or solution-focused. Some therapists are quiet and neutral, others are directive and talk a lot. Please stop trying to dismiss the richness and complexity of the therapy profession just to promote coaching."

Little progress got made that day. Trying to define a clear-cut difference between coaching and therapy is no easy task. Therapy is tough to define as one model, but then again, so is coaching, which now has dozens of methods and schools of its own.

Let me offer you the best explanation I can about the distinction between coaching and therapy, from a therapeutic point of view. I want to clarify the mindset and methods they share, as well as their differences. With this clarification, you can better understand the thinking behind my model, and hopefully find your way to apply its ideas and techniques. In this chapter, after analyzing the similarities and differences between coaching and therapy, you will see why and how a therapist can take advantage of a modified coaching approach and how it fits, using my model, into psychotherapy or counseling settings. I offer a brief case example, to demonstrate how easy and natural it can be to bring Therapy with a Coaching Edge into a session, to give your clients the best of both worlds: the power and flexibility of coaching combined with the depth, purpose, and treatment goals of psychotherapy.

First, let me parse out the distinctions between therapy and coaching and then their areas of overlap.

THE DIFFERENCES BETWEEN THERAPY AND COACHING

As you can see, in the beginning of this chapter, I don't believe in reducing therapy and coaching into sound bites. I think it is best to look at a broader understanding. My explanation is based on looking at the process of individual therapy and contrasting it with individual coaching, as opposed to other formulations of either or both. As a clinical psychotherapist and a master certified coach, and someone who has written a number of books examining both professions, I rely on some common criteria to clarify the differences and similarities between therapy and coaching:

- Who (professionals and populations)
- Where (sessions and settings)
- What (practice and purpose)
- How (style)

Who (Professionals and Populations)

The biggest difference between therapy and coaching starts with recognizing who is the expert in the room. Who is directing the session? Therapists are licensed professionals who have completed higher education (most commonly a master's degree plus internship, or a doctorate and beyond.) In the United States, therapists and counselors have passed state boards that designate them as equipped to diagnose and treat clients. As licensed professionals, they are held to rigorous ethical and legal standards imposed by associations and state boards. While most therapists are not medical doctors, many work within a medical model, are medically knowledgeable, and trained to work with a broad and vast client population.

The therapist-client (or therapist-patient) relationship is usually a hierarchical one, for good reason. The issues that bring people to a therapist are often entrenched and complex, and clients may present with complicated diagnoses and layers of issues that cloud important details. Therapy clients are often in treatment to address serious mental health problems. They come to us hurt, vulnerable, traumatized, addicted, or in crisis. As a result, sometimes the therapist needs to make a hard call to protect the life or well-being of the client, or to set a course of immediate action. The hierarchy also encourages the emergence of transference, one of the traditional methods some therapists use to help clients access unconscious material. Therapists take their work seriously, and most engage in years of additional training, far beyond their academic education, bolstered by close supervision to enhance clinical quality assurance.

Unlike therapists, coaches are not licensed; most are not even certified by a coach certification organization. Sadly, some are barely trained. There is no oversight by state boards. In some ways, coaching is a buyer-beware market. At this time, anyone, anywhere in the world, can claim the title of coach, regardless of experience, training, or background. A coach may have received substantial training offered by an accredited school or university, but others start seeing clients after only a weekend course, many of which are offered by unaccredited, for-profit, privately owned companies. As a result of coaching being an unlicensed profession, data about who is coaching and how they are or are not educated to be a coach, is scarce. It's impossible to know how many people consider themselves coaches and of that number, how many are actually trained by one of the approved associations.

Coaches who do become certified, most often by the International Coach Federation, go through a rigorous training and testing process, one that takes years to complete. Accredited coaching curriculums espouse a set of "core competencies"—eleven skills and requirements that must be demonstrated to attain each successive level of certification. There are three levels of certification available, and the highest level at this time, Master Certified Coach, requires that the coach has completed a 200-hour accredited training program, received 10 hours of mentoring by a senior coach, and can show evidence of 2,500 hours of paid coaching over 5 or more years. The applicant must submit two taped audio recordings and written transcripts of live coaching to be awarded this designation. A panel of assessors evaluates each candidate's application; acceptance for the highest level of coach certification through the ICF is not immediate or easy.

Some untrained coaches use the term coaching to mean that they are available for advising, consulting or teaching. This is not considered coaching, in the purest sense of the profession. Trained coaches—especially life coaches—are not normally positioned as experts or diagnosticians. For a coach, it's less about what the coach knows (via academic education, previous expertise, or career experience) and more about the coach's skill and training in the competencies of coaching to elicit what the client knows. The coach is essentially a facilitator. In a pure coaching relationship, the coach considers that clients hold the seeds of their solutions and the answer to their own problems. With good coaching skills and a level playing field, coaches optimally help clients find their own paths toward improvement and motivate clients to take action.

Given this coach positioning, it's essential that coaching clients be moderately to highly functional and managing life well enough to use coaching as it is intended. Since the coach relies on a "the client knows best" attitude, coaching clients need to be capable of setting goals, following action plans and making logical sense of the coaching conversation without undue transference, emotionality, mental health problems that interfere with logical and rational cognition, or projection.

Where (Sessions and Settings)

Most therapists agree that to provide optimal therapy they need a controlled, consistent, private setting, like an office, so that they can have confidential face-to-face sessions with a client at regular, anticipated intervals. Therapists adhere to the ethical and legal guidelines of their professions to protect vulnerable clients, finding settings for services where a client can feel safe and build trust to further the treatment and help that therapy can provide.

Coaching is notable for its elasticity in regard to setting. Coaching sessions can and do take place in a coach's office, in the client's office or workplace, in a hotel lobby, conference room, or restaurant table, in the field, on the phone, by text, or over the Internet. It's not necessary for a coach and his or her client to have ever met face to face. Sessions may be regular, infrequent, or packaged to fit the terms of a specific contract. The coach may choose to keep the professional boundaries of the coaching relationship firm or somewhat loose.

Based on just the above two categories, the who (professionals and the populations worked with) and the where (the settings and how sessions are conducted), the differences between therapists and coaches, and between therapy and coaching clients, seem obvious. But look at the next category and you will see why the public, and even some clinicians, start to scratch their heads in confusion.

What (Practice and Purpose)

In practice, the distinctions between therapy and coaching are less black and white, and more shades of gray. If we created a continuum of all known therapy methods and all known coaching methods of practice, at the extremes of the continuum, the differences are clearer than what we may see in the middle. Imagine one end of the continuum is the traditional version of psychotherapy, say psychoanalysis, and at the other end the traditional version of coaching, say sports coaching. Looking at the ends of the spectrum, one can easily discern many differences between the two methods as they are practiced. In psychoanalysis, the talking cure, there is little expectation for a patient to take action or meet goals; uncovering unconscious material and developing insight is tantamount. The analyst is a neutral presence, non-directive, and wants to help the patient weaken defenses as a way to develop self-awareness and feel repressed emotions.

Contrast this to sports coaching, on the other extreme end. There is talking in this method, too, but the feelings and inner emotions of the athlete are rarely examined; winning is the sole focus. Achieving and surpassing goals is paramount. The coach is tenaciously influential, directive, opinionated, and expressive, trying to strengthen—not weaken—defenses.

So, the extreme or conventional ends of the therapy and coaching continuum are obvious in their differences. As one starts to move toward the middle of the spectrum of methods and applications, the differences between what is therapy and what is coaching begin to blur. Cognitive, proactive therapy in practice tends to look a lot like coaching. Coaching in practice can look a lot like solution-focused counseling. In the center of the continuum, we would find even more overlap, noting all the methods of therapy and life coaching that embody personal growth and human potential philosophy, and have built on the work of Maslow, Satir, Frankl, Rogers and others.

There is also overlap in the middle of the continuum when considering the topic of purpose. Modern methods of therapy and life coaching, which inhabit the middle ground, aspire to similar purposes. What is the aim of modern therapy or coaching? Helping a client to feel happy, self-actualized, and more productive? Building a person's confidence, self-awareness, or ability to have better relationships? These goals could fit into the stated purpose of either modern therapy or life coaching.

The purpose of contemporary therapy is hard to state specifically.

Given more than one hundred models or schools of psychotherapy, trying to define one basic aim of therapy is a bit like trying to herd cats. Martin Seligman, PhD, past president of the American Association of Psychology, offered a thoughtful summary, in an article in 1995 for *American Psychologist*.[1] He defined the purpose of psychotherapy as "the improvement in the general functioning of clients/patients, as well as amelioration of a disorder and relief of specific, presenting symptoms." When therapy works, he wrote, clients report robust improvement with treatment in the specific problem that got them into therapy, as well as in personal growth, insight, confidence, well-being, productivity at work, interpersonal relations, and enjoyment of life. The purpose of therapy (removing symptoms and improving functioning) may generalize into aspects of life and work enhancement that mirror common life coaching goals (confidence, well-being, productivity at work, interpersonal relations, and enjoyment of life.)

Even if the purpose of therapy is straightforward, as using Seligman's explanation recaps, the *process* of therapy—how the therapist and client get to these goals—is rarely linear; during treatment, some aspects of a person's functioning improve while other aspects stay the same or change more slowly. When the therapy goal is broad—say to help a person gain insight, heal emotional wounds, eliminate self-destructive behaviors, or bring about characterological development—therapists must take a long view of progress. A therapist might consider the therapy successful if, after treatment, a client has made internal shifts in thinking, feeling, and behaving, even if the client is still functioning in the world in a low to moderate range. Part of the purpose of therapy is wrapped up in its developing, emergent process.

The purpose of coaching is easier to corral, in part due to the less wieldy nature of the profession. Formalized coaching has only been in existence for the past 40 years. Thomas Leonard, author of *The Portable Coach* and one of the early founders of the life coaching movement, defined the purpose of coaching as threefold, to help people: 1) set

---

1 Seligman, M. E. P. (1995). The effectiveness of psychotherapy: the Consumer Reports study. *American Psychologist, 50*(12), 965–974.

and reach better goals, 2) do more than they would have done on their own, and 3) improve focus so as to produce results more quickly. He characterized coaching as a collaborative relationship that allows clients to become self-generative and productive, and to leverage their talents. One explanation I often give those who are trying to parse out the difference between therapy and coaching focuses on process: therapy typically tends to be process-oriented (an unfolding and ongoing form of treatment that acknowledges both conscious and unconscious drives) while coaching tends to be programmatic (based on a short-term schedule with linear markers and an end point in sight.)

How (Style)

When assessing the specific skills used in therapy and its closest form of coaching, life coaching, there is, again, a lot of overlap. Most models of therapy employ talking, as does life coaching. On the surface, the verbal techniques that therapists and life coaches use are often similar. Both may rely on talking, listening, asking questions, making observations, using written materials such as surveys and checklists or formats and templates, using behavioral tools of setting and tracking goals, and both may include some non-verbal techniques of meditation, relaxation, movement, body awareness, and other skills geared toward stress reduction.

Seeing all the overlap, you may ask: Are there really any clear differences between current techniques of the many varieties of solution-focused or cognitive-behavioral therapies and life coaching? To me, the answer is yes. I have spent years thinking and writing about this distinction and I believe that the truest measure of the difference between therapy and coaching, apart from those I mentioned earlier, is easiest to understand if you consider coaching less as a methodology and more as a *style* of relating. This style is the "how" of coaching. I don't consider that there is one style of psychotherapy, but there is one, and only one, style of pure coaching. Let me explain.

A COACHING STYLE

For five years, from 2000 through 2005, I actively researched the coaching profession and coaching literature, engaged in producing two books about coaching: *The Business and Practice of Coaching*, co-written by myself and Wendy Allen, Ph.D., was specific for coaches, a look at the history, purpose, business, and application of coaching. *The New Private Practice: Therapist Coaches Share Stories, Strategies, and Advice*, was an edited series of essays written by therapists who had become coaches. As editor of this book, I found therapists who had made this professional transition to coaching and helped them articulate how and why they had become coaches. I also looked at my own clinical work, since I was actively practicing as both a therapist and a coach.

Although there is much crossover between therapy and life coaching, I finally began to define one clear difference, summed up in one word: style. I think that pure coaching, the way coaching is taught, defined, and recognized by the International Coach Federation, has its own modus operandi, a recognizable manner of interaction, a *style* of relating that seems distinct, to me, from other models of therapy or personal growth. Daniel Goleman, author of *Emotional Intelligence*, defines this style well. A coaching style, he says is "consistently positive, constructive, motivational, inspiring, and effective."[2]

This style, in the coaching world, is referred to as a "coaching approach." As I explored the meaning of a coaching approach through the coaching literature and in my position as a faculty member at one of the largest and oldest coaching schools, I began to define a coaching approach as consisting of four factors. They are interwoven and must be in place at the same time. The way they interact when intertwined constitutes my clearest explanation, the one I offer to my therapist colleagues, about what is specific and unique about coaching.

The first of the four factors concerns the locus of change. This is a spe-

---

2 Goleman, D. (2000) Leadership that gets results. *Harvard Business Review*. Retrieved from https://hbr.org/2000/03/leadership-that-gets-results.

cific difference between life coaching and many methods of therapy. For example, in therapy, the locus of change resides in many possible areas, depending on the belief system and model of therapy that is used. A therapist using a medical model relies on the change element that exists within the therapist's expertise, as well as access to a body of theory, knowledge, education, and methodology. In gestalt practices of therapy, the locus of change may be understood to reside within a relational space that is created between the therapist and the client, the liminal space between two people in a contained space, both engaged in a process of transformation. In cognitive methods of therapy, the locus of change may be understood as a combination of the protocol a therapist uses combined with the client's willingness to engage.

In a pure coaching approach, the locus of all control and change exists in only one place: firmly within the client alone. The client has the answers and is the source of his or her own transformation. Coaches merely facilitate change; clients own the results. As mentioned earlier, coaching presumes a functional client, one with less mental health issues or emotional or psychosocial complexities, one who can find inner resources to resolve problems and challenges with verbal facilitation from the coach. With a client-based locus of change in place, three more aspects define a coaching approach and all must be present:

- **Partnership:** Coaches, and specifically life coaches, use an informal, non-hierarchical position when interacting with clients. They aim to be collaborative, authentic, and in effect "even the playing field" to encourage and motivate clients by being less distant or removed.
- **Action:** Achievement is the hallmark of any and all types of coaching. Life coaches rely on a toolkit of skills to help clients do more to go faster and further, which presumes a level of client functionality. Coaching is always oriented toward helping a client get things done and take steps forward.
- **Possibility:** Coaches are optimistic. They do not pathologize problems. They exist in the realm of the imaginable. Coaches regularly engage clients in conversation about vision, purpose, mission, success, pleasure, joy, passion, and effectiveness and other future-oriented, affirm-

ing, and expansive concepts. They do this consistently, rather than occasionally, to further action and motivation.

To summarize, according to my definition, to be considered a true coaching approach, all four aspects of this style must occur simultaneously: client-based control, partnership, action, and possibility. While many methods of therapy may employ some of these aspects at different times and in different ways, I would not consider a therapy model to have a true coaching approach unless all were present, in every session. My model, Therapy with a Coaching Edge, began to evolve based on my curiosity about how, or even if, I could successfully bring a true coaching approach into therapy. As you may now understand, based on the (at times significant) differences I have explored between coaching and therapy, doing this was not as easy as it might have first appeared to me. A coaching approach, in its purest sense, doesn't translate well into therapy. This required some creative rethinking.

BRINGING A COACHING APPROACH INTO THERAPY

As I explained, bringing a coaching approach into therapy means that the essence of this coaching style, these four combined criteria, must be intact. But coaching is not therapy, and I soon concluded that a coaching approach has to be maintained in spirit, but modified and adapted in practice to protect the ethics, process, and principles of psychotherapy and counseling. It needs refinement and consideration to fit within therapeutic purposes.

This is where the real work of my process began. Although I might have tried to borrow the coaching skills I learned and taught, and insert them into my therapy sessions, coaching skills addressed a different type of client, setting, purpose and process. The upbeat language didn't always fit with my understanding of what it means to have empathy when engaged in therapy. The expectations of immediate action when I was coaching were not appropriate when treating very depressed or anxious therapy clients. As a clinical social worker, I am bound to preserve the purpose of psychotherapy, to protect susceptible clients, to use consistent and confidential settings, to apply only those methods and ways of relating to clients that adhere to the ethics and purposes of my licensure. As a result, I spent many years thinking about how to deconstruct and then adjust a coaching approach. I considered a host of coaching skills I regularly used in my coaching role, and then designed a select, specific set of modified skills to use within a therapy setting.

I have organized the book to give you the results of my adaptation so you can use what I developed to apply in my own practice. First, I offer the context of my model via an underlying foundation, some basics I want you to know and consider in order to see results. I show you nine skills focused on partnership, action, and possibility, to allow you to bring a coaching style, with all its power and effectiveness, into your therapy or counseling practice. If you naturally gravitate towards a coaching approach in your clinical practice and already apply elements of a coaching style in your work, you may find that my model, while not being altogether new for you, provides structure and validation for the way you are working with your clients. If a coaching style is new for you and this model does not reflect the way you have learned to practice, then I hope the book can function as a clear and helpful guide, one that points the way to a proactive and expansive way to work.

As I teach this model, I find that more often than not, bringing a coaching approach into therapy based on this foundation and skills can feel easy and natural for many therapists, even those who are new to this mindset. It starts with consciously shifting the locus of control a bit, to offer a client a chance to co-lead the direction of his or her therapy. Shifting the locus of control to allow the client more influence can jump-start a new aspect of growth in a client, as it did with Su-Ann.

SHIFTING THE LOCUS OF CONTROL

Su-Ann walks into the therapy room, and before sitting down in her chair, makes a tour of my office. She looks at the posters on the wall, a small wooden Buddha on the windowsill, and a book set askew on my bookshelf, which she touches lightly and then straightens. I have seen this behavior from her twice before during the past three months of weekly therapy sessions. At those times, it was a signal of delaying the start of the session because she was reluctant to bring up a topic.

At 29 years old, she refers to herself as a "lost millennial," unable to find a career or settle on a place to live. She continues to work at a Starbucks coffee shop and live in her old bedroom at her parent's house, while she ponders what to do with her degree in communications. She suffers from moderate anxiety. She says that she feels like she is floating through life without an anchor or grounding. During the past three months, Su-Ann has explored her feelings and thoughts about her family, and we have talked at length about techniques to reduce her anxiety. I wait until she is finally seated and ask her how she would like to start today.

"Well, I am pretty upset," she says. "My mother asked me what I was doing with my life, why I hadn't looked for a job in my field, and when I was going to get it together. She said she knows I am trying to figure things out, but that she is worried. The way she said it really hurt my feelings."

Su-Ann and I have explored the tension she feels with her parents. Both they and she are frustrated about her inability to find a career direction. Although I could explore the topic of her hurt feelings, I am curious about her earlier behavior, the tour of the office at the start of this therapy session. I decide to start there.

"I noticed you walked around the office when you came in, just looking at things and straightening up a book. The last time you did this, you told me it was because you were not ready to start the session because there was something you were afraid to talk about. Is that true today as well?"

"Yes, yes, it is. Here is the thing. My mother is right. What is wrong with me? Why can't I take the next step forward? I am stuck and a bit scared. I want to grow up. I need to get moving forward."

Now I am at a choice point. Some therapists would seize on the fear, go deeper into affect to explore the emotion. They might try to help Su-Ann tap further into her childhood history to develop more insight into her immaturity. I have done some of that with her in earlier sessions. But today I am going to give her a choice. She indicates an interest and a desire to move forward. Her problem of wanting to grow up is certainly one that would fit within a coaching approach model of therapy. I decide to offer her a new direction in therapy and begin to bring in a coaching approach, starting with a shift in the locus of control. If Su-Ann agrees, I am glad to hand her the reigns to let her drive this session toward a better outcome.

"Based on what you said a moment ago, we could go in two different directions today. We could explore the fear you have and where it comes from. You might understand better how it keeps you stuck and how to be less impacted by it. Or we could shift directions to focus on what it means if you want to grow up. You could begin to develop a plan to move forward toward maturity. Which would you prefer?"

I am in effect asking if Su-Ann wants to stay with a more standard therapeutic model, to focus on insight and feelings or switch to one that is more proactive. As her therapist, I am happy to work either way. By asking for her choice, I signal to Su-Ann that she is in charge. She can choose to "own" her therapy the same way she can own her life.

Su-Ann takes a deep breath. "I want a plan. I want to grow up. You know that sappy greeting card statement, that says today is the first day of the rest of your life? I want this to be the first day. But I don't really know how to do this. Can you help me?"

I have a choice now, too. I could turn this question of help, back on Su-Ann, to analyze and explore her feeling of powerlessness. I could question her statement that she doesn't know what to do and explore this for deeper feelings and thoughts. But instead, I shift into another aspect of a coaching approach: partnership. I respond in a normal, authentic tone. "I would be glad to help you do this. I appreciate what you said, that today's session could be a turning point. Are you ready to take a step forward right now?"

"Yes," she says simply. "What is the step?"

"I want you to stay in charge, even of this step of how I can help you. Can you define what would be different in your life if you were behaving more like a grown up?"

"Well, I wouldn't be so immature."

"Ok, good, not so undeveloped," I reflect back. I bring in another question to open up possibility. "What would you be instead?"

"I would be confident. I would have ideas about what I want to do. I would feel better."

"Feeling better is important." Now I bring in a question geared towards action. "What can make that happen for you?"

"I would get up at the same time each day and go for a run. I would eat breakfast."

"I like this plan, it focuses on improved self-care. You would have a routine that is healthy. Keep going, this is good. What else would you be doing if you were more grown up?"

"I would do something that I have been scared to do. I would join a job seekers club. My friend Ward goes. He says I can go along with him next time," she says.

"Now that is really a challenge, to take on something scary, but very adult. I like that you have some support from Ward if you choose to do this. Tell me more."

We spend more time with Su-Ann providing ideas and me using active listening, validating, showing my own enthusiasm as she takes charge. Before the sessions ends, I take some time to debrief with her, consolidating gains of this session to see if she can make anything actionable. I stay focused on letting her control the ideas, while I offer partnership and validate possibility. To end the session, I focus again on the fourth aspect of a coaching approach: action.

"What will you take away from our session today?"

"Well, it was productive. I guess I have a lot of ideas about how to move forward."

"I liked hearing the ideas you generated today. Based on all you said today, is there one step, even a small one, you can commit to do?"

Su-Ann takes some time to think about this. "I can call Ward about the job seeking meeting. Even if I decide not to go, I can make that call. Would that be a step?" she asks.

"I would call that a step. Is it the right step for you?

"I think it is. I can see myself doing it and it's okay."

"Great. Tell me what you see, so I can see it too."

After Su-Ann defines her plan of action, I add one more piece of partnership, one that is common in a coaching approach. "How can I best support you in taking that step?"

Su-Ann looks at me for a long while. "Well, at our next session, don't judge my result. Just ask how it went. If I did it, good for me, and if I didn't, help me understand what got in the way without making me feel like I failed. That would be support." Su-Ann is now giving me a role to play, letting me know how to help her help herself. I nod my head and agree to do this. I tell her it will go into my notes.

I know Su-Ann is scared to commit to taking action, worried she may fail yet again. Happily, since Therapy with a Coaching Edge combines the best aspects of both therapy and coaching, I have a full toolkit at hand. If she regresses and gets stuck due to fear, I can suggest that she take time to process through her emotions and feelings, using a slower-paced session or two that is focused on listening, validating, empathizing, and reflecting on her experience. When she is stabilized, we can switch back to a more action-oriented coaching approach to help her again define steps to take. With this shift back and forth, from therapy that is insightful and reflective, to a coaching approach that is directive and action-oriented, I feel confident that she can set and meet a number of specific goals. Coachable moments happen in therapy sessions every day, as long as a therapist is prepared to notice them when they emerge and offer to shift direction.

From this chapter, you may already identify clients in your caseload who would benefit from a coaching approach in therapy. But this raises an important question: How do you determine suitability for this model? Chapter 3 gives you the tools to make this assessment, using a simple process easily applied with new or existing clients. I also suggest a quick assessment to help you determine if you, the therapist, feel well suited to use this model and if so, how to take a further step in integrating it within your sessions.

3

Who's Coachable within Therapy?

I have long believed that almost everyone I have ever met could benefit from some therapy sessions with the right therapist. Although I also appreciate the value of life coaching, I wouldn't make the same claim.

Here is why: Not everyone is suitable for coaching. Life coaching is geared for a narrow population; it presupposes that a client is stable, functional, and able to follow through with a plan of action between sessions. When I was a coach in training, I heard a label for those who *didn't* fit this description: uncoachable.

"Sometimes a person seems unsteady or gets easily upset during a coaching conversation. The level of emotion in the client goes beyond what a coach is trained to handle," a teacher stated in a CoachU class, the virtual training program I attended in 1996 for two years to get my initial coaching certificate. I was new to coaching and still figuring out what constituted a coaching process. She explained that a person might be uncoachable if the presenting problem was based in a childhood upset, or if a client needed to cry or was angry, or seemed very shut down. In this case, she would consider the client to be a candidate for therapy, not coaching.

This made sense. None of my teachers at CoachU were licensed therapists, and neither they nor the other coaching students in my class were prepared to deal with complex psychological issues. I understood the need for assessing suitability when it came to life coaching. When I began to adapt coaching skills for a therapy setting, I wondered if I needed to assess suitability for therapy clients. Who was right for using my model, or in my shorthand, coachable within therapy? Given the client-focused control and directive nature of the model, I wanted a way to evaluate who would and would not be a good candidate. I wanted to create an easy-to-use assessment model, one that I could talk through with a client in a first session and then some points I could review, post-session, when I was writing my notes, to confirm or reevaluate my decision.

In this chapter, I show you the guide I developed and how you can use it to determine suitability with your existing or potential clients. My assessment tool does not take the place of a full client history, or other tools you may already rely on for treatment planning or evaluation. Use it as an add-on to determine appropriateness for this method, not to replace other formats. After I show you the guide, I explain how to use it, with case examples, and give you the questions of suitability I use when reviewing my notes. I also have a helpful checklist at the end of the chapter to help you judge if this model of therapy is a good fit for you, the therapist.

THE GUIDEPOST

When I was first starting to incorporate a coaching approach into my therapy sessions, I assessed clients unconsciously. I relied on my instincts or feelings in terms of who might benefit and who wouldn't. As I began to formalize a therapy model, I wanted data. I went back to my case notes and reviewed almost a decade of client files, trying to understand what criteria I had used and the results of my decisions over time. I see adults in my therapy practice, and occasionally some adolescents. I found that this model was appropriate for adults—at a variety of ages and stages of life—and for those adolescents who showed a level of maturity in their thinking and behaving, in other words those clients who presented in therapy as both relatively stable and functional. I tended to select those clients, for this model, who:

- Had a moderate mental health diagnosis
- Displayed normal functioning in a majority of areas of their life
- Were receptive to a directive, prospective, action-oriented approach

- Had a capacity for thinking rationally, to allow for client-based control of goals and outcomes
- Could be comfortable with a therapist who was proactive
- Could tolerate a degree of optimism that translated as therapist cheerfulness or even cheerleading
- Preferred a faster pace versus a slow unfolding of material
- Could work with less transference between client and therapist

I began to consider all the aspects of appropriateness for this model. I researched how therapists used suitability markers within other methods of therapy.[1] One afternoon, I was hiking near a lake, not far from my home, and saw a wooden guidepost at the crossroads of three dirt paths, with arrows that pointed to the various destinations around the lake: a nature center to the left, a flower garden to the right, and a playground to be found by climbing up the hill. Perfect! I need a guidepost just like this, I thought, one that would tell a therapist which way to go when assessing a potential client.

The same way the guidepost by the lake allowed me to make a quick choice and keep on hiking, the suitability guidepost would need to answer a question, right in the moment, and allow the therapy session to proceed with a clear direction. I wanted a "go" or "no go" signal to the questions I would ask—to feel assured to move ahead with a client using therapy with a coaching approach, or to stop and opt for another, perhaps more standard method.

The guidepost I ended up developing uses a series of questions in three basic categories. The questions can be asked easily when talking to a new client on the phone, or before a first session is scheduled, or early on during the first session. They are phrased in normal language without therapeutic jargon, designed to help you bring a client into the decision-making process. Some therapists to whom I have introduced the model put the guidepost questions on their website page for individual therapy, to help potential clients self-select this type of therapy.

---

1 Blenkiron, P. (1999). Who is suitable for Cognitive Behavioural Therapy? *Journal of the Royal Society of Medicine.* 92(5), 222-229.

First, let me clarify each category of questions that the guidepost evaluates. Your clients will be part of the assessment process, in a transparent and direct way, which makes the guidepost questions you use to assess them a conversation starter—not ender. You and your clients will be assessing:

- Client Preference (what your client wants out of therapy)
- Client Challenges (presenting issues, and short history of mental health problems and diagnosis)
- Client Capacity (overall functionality, and ability to work with a proactive, collaborative therapist)

Client Preference

The first category is based on knowing if your potential or existing client wants this model of therapy. Many of my clients seek out therapy with me because they see that I use a coaching approach. Coaching is a popular meme, mentioned by celebrities and on social media and in magazines.[2] It's a calling card, because life coaching seems trendy and new. But few existing or potential clients really understand what a coaching approach in therapy entails. Using these questions, you help clients understand what you are offering, and in doing so, give them a chance to affirm if this is desirable treatment, from their point of view.

Just a quick tip about asking these question, regarding preference. You need to be very neutral in your questioning, not trying to "sell" this model over another way of working. For example, some clients favor therapy that is geared toward problem solving; others want their therapist to be an interpreter of deep, complex, emotional material. Some want to work short-term, others prefer long-term therapy that will help them slowly gain insight. Some clients have no idea what they may want, and these questions can start that conversation. Remember, this is one of three categories, so these questions, by themselves, will not give you

---

2 Morgan, S. (2012, January 27). Should a life coach have a life first? *The New York Times*. Retrieved from http://www.nytimes.com.

a complete picture of appropriateness. Here is my list of questions to assess preference, to which you can add your own:

Preference Questions:

- Are you seeking short-term or long-term therapy?
- Would you prefer a slower-paced, longer-term method that would allow you to spend more time talking and processing memories and developing insight? Or would you prefer a faster-paced therapy that results in taking action and making decisions?
- Do you have trouble expressing thoughts and feelings, and would you like therapy to help with this?
- Do you want therapy sessions that focus on the present and future, or more on the past?
- Are you interested in using therapy to set and achieve goals in order to make concrete change in your life?
- Do you want a therapist who primarily listens and lets you talk, or one who voices thoughts and opinions?
- Do you like to have homework, reading, or action steps to take between sessions?

Preference Checklist:

This checklist is for you, the therapist, to help you confirm your impressions after the session. Review the answers to the preference questions above and any other assessment you have used. The client who is right for this approach prefers:

☐ Therapy or counseling that is short-term
☐ Between-session homework, reading, and/or action steps
☐ A therapist who is collaborative, interactive, and verbal during a session
☐ Session conversation that is pragmatic and optimistic
☐ To focus more on present-day issues than on the past
☐ Therapy that involves planning for the future with goals and action steps

Client Challenges

The next category considers why the client has come for help. You need to understand the presenting issues and challenges of your client in order to assess suitability. This model of therapy is designed for those sometimes called the "worried well"—those moderately functioning clients who suffer from only modest to mild symptoms of depression and anxiety or other treatable mental illness, including those who are already in recovery from addictions. It is not appropriate for use with clients in crisis, who face critical, life-threatening issues, complicated dual diagnoses, or intractable mental health conditions. It is not the model of choice for abuse victims or perpetrators, or those working through active addiction or relapse. Clients who *can* use this model well generally present with:

- *Internal struggles:* Procrastination, ambivalence, feeling stuck, and other internal struggles may prevent a client from moving forward or finding a course of direction. This model can help.
- *Cognitive distortions:* Common cognitive distortions can impede good decision making. Those who have cognitive distortions that are open to change (as opposed to other types of irrational thought disorders)[3] can benefit from this model.
- *Relationship issues:* A lack of interpersonal skills is the source of problems for many who seek therapy. Those with common relationship problems are helped in individual sessions with this model, especially in terms of behavioral change and problem solving.
- *External stressors:* The worries or fears of situational problems, such as financial indebtedness, threat of unemployment, divorce, ill health, or other real-life issues can bring people to counseling. This model helps people address issues with action-based methods.

More complicated presenting issues or diagnosis, such as those listed below, due to their complexity, are contraindicated for therapy with a

---

3 Grohol, J. (2016). 15 Common Cognitive Distortions. *Psych Central.* Retrieved from https://psychcentral.com/lib/15-common-cognitive-distortions/.

coaching approach.[4] Clients will be better served with other methods of treatment if they present with:

- *Maladaptive behaviors.* These include addiction, violence, and more severe symptoms of behaviors that could be harmful to self or others.
- *Significant traumatic experiences.* Clients who have been victims of severe abuse and trauma, including post-traumatic stress disorder (PTSD), or those dealing with traumatic loss and bereavement do best with other methods of therapy that are designed specifically for trauma treatment.
- *Biological dysfunction.* Medical issues that have psychological symptoms require biological interventions.
- *Personality disorders.* Complex diagnosis need specific treatment models, for example borderline features are not well served with this approach.
- *Life-threatening diagnoses.* This is not the best therapy for clients at risk of suicide, major depressive episodes, bipolar or emotional dysregulation, severe panic, cutting or self-injury, or other crisis-based concerns.

If you have an additional assessment tool that you regularly use to detail presenting issues, continue to use it. You can add some or all of the Client Challenge questions below to determine who is and is not right for therapy with a coaching approach:

Challenge Questions:
- Why did you decide to come to therapy now?
- Are you in danger or in a crisis that needs immediate attention?
- Are you able to make good decisions for yourself and those dependent upon you?
- Do you think your issue can be resolved by focusing on your own feelings, behavior, and/or thinking?

---

4 Lazarus, C. (2015). 9 Essential Issues Good Therapy Should Address. *Psychology Today.* Retrieved from https://www.psychologytoday.com/blog/think-well/201501/9-essential-issues-good-therapy-should-address.

- Are you interested in changing yourself and your situation?
- Do you need something or someone outside of you to change first, before you can address your own problems?
- Can you think of a possible first step that would begin to resolve one of your problems?
- What would a successful outcome in our work together be?

Challenge Checklist:

This checklist is for you, the therapist, to help you confirm your impressions after the session, from the answers to the questions above and any other evaluation you have used to assess a client. The client who is right for this approach:

- ☐ Fits the presenting criteria above and suffers from mild to moderate symptoms.
- ☐ Is not in physical danger or mental/emotional crisis, including active addiction or relapse.
- ☐ Is dealing with issues that can be resolved with a collaborative discussion, goal setting, and an action plan.
- ☐ Likes problem solving as a way to resolve challenges.
- ☐ Has access to internal and external resources to make any problematic situations (debt, living conditions, career) quickly resolvable.
- ☐ Can tolerate and participate in conversations with a therapist who is proactive and cooperative.

Client Capacity

The last category evaluates client functionality. A common denominator for those seeking therapy is that they come for services when at a low point in life. We see a broad population, from those seriously impaired to those who are moderately or even highly functional, at least in certain aspects. Therapy with a Coaching Edge requires a moderate degree of client capacity. You need to select clients who have the ability to stay grounded in reality, can talk about goals and plans, and have the facility for self-reflection. The client may have an uneven capacity, be doing well in some areas and not in others, but the clients who are best for this model tend to be employed or employable, have established routines in place, and have relationships or some level of social support— even though the connections may be weak. You need to assess if they can use straightforward therapeutic conversation to develop awareness, discuss solutions to problems, and over time, take action in order to improve outcomes.

One additional note on capacity: Many therapists have additional measures they use to determine functionality. If you regularly use one of these measures, clients who are *not* functioning well enough for this model would be on the range of 0–50 in the Global Assessment of Functioning (GAL scale[5]), or from 40 to 100 percent of disabilities in the World Health Organization's Disability Assessment Schedule (WHODAS). To assess clients, ask the questions below and listen to answers and observe nonverbal indicators. The questions also help you understand if a client can relate to you without intense transference or unrealistic projections, so that you can offer a therapy based in proactive, problem-solving methods.

Capacity Questions:

- What gives you energy and what drains you?
- What is a typical day like for you?
- What is going well?
- What is not?
- Are you worried about physical or personal safety or immediate survival?
- Of all the problems you face, which need attention immediately?
- Which are low priority that can be corrected over time?
- What are you proudest about in regards to your life and/or work?
- Where would you like to see yourself (in life, relationships, work, career) by the end of therapy?
- What would you want from me, as your therapist, to help you reach your goals?

_____

5 GAL scale (the Global Assessment of Functioning) or WHODAS (World Health Organization's Disability Assessment Schedule).

Capacity Checklist:

This checklist is for you, the therapist, to help you confirm your impressions after the session, from the answers to the questions above and any other discussion or assessment tool you regularly use with a client. The client who is right for this approach:

☐ Is struggling with only moderate or mild symptoms of depression, anxiety, loss, stress-related, relationship, parenting, or workplace issues.
☐ Has a lifeline or some type of support system in place.
☐ Has sufficient energy or vigor to stay with an approach of therapy that is faster-paced than traditional talk therapy.
☐ Functions in a safe way in the world.
☐ Can (with help) identify, set and begin to follow through on goals.
☐ Can relate to the therapist without undue projection or transference.
☐ Can allow and utilize the therapist's support to stay on track with treatment.

Ranking Categories

Ideally, clients for the Therapy with a Coaching Edge model will meet all three categories in the guidepost: Client Preference, Client Challenge, and Client Capacity. With such a candidate, it is easy to proceed with this model. But what about clients who meet only two categories, or just one? In my experience, some clients may meet only two categories and still be possible candidates for this model. The one category that *must* be in place to deem a client suitable for this model is the first one: Client Preference. Because Therapy with a Coaching Edge uses a client-based locus of control, it's essential that your clients want to work with you in this approach.

The other two categories, can be ones that seem weak initially, but using this approach might improve the situation to make a client an appropriate candidate. A client who wants this approach (Client Preference) and functions well (Client Capacity), may come up short in the area of challenges. For example, I had a client who liked the idea of a coaching approach and was employed, but in her bereavement, cried daily and felt hopeless about life, with some suicidal ideation. This was more than moderate depression. I was able to address the symptoms of grief and loss using the skills of this model, and her depression lessened quickly to a more moderate level. We continued to work together, and the model was clearly beneficial in helping her set goals for improving her situation.

You may have a client who meets preference and challenges but not capacity—does not function well—who could use this model to improve functioning quickly. One client was unable to manage his diabetes regimen and prone to having night sweats and collapses. His health seemed to preclude this approach, but I used an action plan during the first several sessions that addressed his self-care. The diabetes became manageable and I was able to then use Therapy with a Coaching Edge to treat his other presenting problems.

Even though the client weighs in on this guidepost, you, the therapist, are the expert in the therapy room. You need to make an informed determination based on your observations, information, and knowledge. Your expertise carries the day. If you start to use this model and decide it is not helpful, you can shift within a single session into a more appropriate model of treatment. One helpful aspect of conferring with a client about the choice of a treatment model is that you can always communicate if and when you need to change course.

Now let me show you how I used the guidepost with two new clients. In these case examples, you will see how to I started to ask some questions in a first session, and then how I reviewed my impressions about treatment models with the checklist after the session was over.

THE GUIDEPOST IN ACTION

Two male clients are referred to me in the same month. Ben and Shawn are the same age, 35, but have various reasons for seeking therapy. Using the guidepost, I determine what model of therapy will be the most effective offer of treatment.

Ben is referred by his physician, who is concerned about his depression. At the first in-person session, Ben tells me that he has been feeling sad and lonely for the past year. His last relationship soured. He works full-time and is able to contain his emotions and function normally, but once at home, he cries often. He has isolated himself on weekends, to sleep or watch TV. He is anxious, at times close to the point of panic.

"I was in therapy once before, in my twenties, for depression," Ben says, "and it helped me."

"What did you find most helpful about therapy at that time?" I ask.

"I liked having a set time and place each week to sort things out, with a therapist who was a good listener. I really need to think deeply about some things to figure out my problems with relationships."

"Would you like to have a similar type of therapy?" (This question starts the process of determining client preference.)

"What other types of therapy are there? What do you do?"

"I offer several methods. One is a proactive method of short-term treatment."

"I don't know that it needs to be short-term. I have had this problem of sadness and loneliness on and off for at least a decade, so it might not be easy to fix. I mean, it might not go away quickly," Ben says.

"Would you prefer a slower-paced, longer-term method that would allow you to spend more time talking and processing memories, thoughts, and feelings?"

"Yes, I need time to think, and more than anything, I want to understand why I feel this way. Why have I been like this my whole adult life? Why am I sad each day? Why can't I stay in a relationship? I know my parents were not very close to each other or to me. Is that part of this? My last girlfriend said I was cold and detached. I need to look at myself a lot more. Do you offer therapy that can help me with this?"

Based on Ben's clear description of the type of therapy he wants, he negates the first category: Client Preference. This model is not what he prefers. He says he needs to talk and gain insight, so he can be more deliberate about his life's situation. He wants to know why this problem is occurring, not how to change it right now or what to do next. Even though he might meet the other two categories, his lack of preference takes priority. I may still see him as a client, but will offer him longer-term talk therapy that is psychodynamic or narrative in nature.

Shawn found my therapy website on the Internet. He had a recent panic attack when he was traveling to a conference, feeling faint and sweaty on an airplane. He felt his heart racing and got dizzy. It resolved by the time he landed, and he later saw a doctor, who confirmed that it was anxiety and recommended therapy.

"Have you been in therapy before, for any reason?" I start.

"No, this is new to me. I really have not had much to complain about in life, I have always been a pretty happy guy. This really took me by surprise," Shawn says.

"I know anxiety and panic attacks can be very frightening in the moment. Do you know what might be causing this?"

"I think it's the situation at work. I am competing for a promotion, and it's brutal. I work very long hours. I am also stressed about my dad. He just had a heart attack, and I am trying to get to see him as often as I can. I guess there are a number of things that could be making me tense, more than usual. How long do you think therapy will take?" he asks, leaning forward.

"Are you seeking short-term treatment?"

"Exactly, that would be great."

"What else do you want from therapy?"

"I need to get control over this. I am working in a fast-paced sales industry and I have to be able to travel and stay calm. As I said, my industry is brutal. It's do or die. I don't want medication, I would rather figure out what is making me anxious and calm down."

"How would you feel about a therapist who was directive and shared verbal opinions and ideas?"

"I would like that. I am a pretty motivated guy. I like to read and am happy to do things between sessions. I don't know, like homework, do you give homework?"

"Tell me a bit about your life."

"I have a girlfriend, we have been dating seriously for a few years, we will probably be getting engaged soon. I work in sales. My boss says I am a go-getter, one of the best-earning on the team. My girlfriend, my dog, and my job are priorities for me."

"What gives you energy, and what drains you?"

"I relax and get refreshed by hanging out with my girlfriend. I see her on weekends. Work is good but draining."

"You used the word 'brutal' before to describe your job. Based on all of this, the anxiety, the pressure, your goals, where would you like to see yourself in one year?"

"I feel overwhelmed. Is there something I can do to calm down? I want to be better in my job. My girlfriend is a keeper and I would like to make that work, not mess it up. If you can help me with this, I would really appreciate it."

I hear Shawn's request for directive therapy points toward a statement of Client Preference. He has a type of anxiety that is occasional and not a major impairment, so he also fits within the presenting issues of Client Challenges. Shawn is working under pressure, but holding onto his job. He has a relationship, routines, and can set goals. He values making progress. He fits well into all three categories.

Shawn presents as a good candidate for Therapy with a Coaching Edge. He and I agree to a course of weekly therapy with a coaching approach over the next four months, during which time I will help him find ways to better identify and manage stress, find solutions to lower his anxiety, improve his relationship, and treat his depression with a series of specific, concrete action steps. He leaves the first session enthusiastic about the process of engaging in a proactive method of therapy. After the session, I use the three checklists shown above to review my notes, and am able to confirm my assessment.

SUITABILITY FOR THE THERAPIST

Now that you have a guidepost for client suitability, just one more question remains to be answered: Is this the right therapy for you, the therapist, to offer? Just as not every client prefers or responds well to this approach, not every therapist has the predilection to work within this model. Here are the criteria I would request that you consider about yourself, prior to deciding to bring it into your practice. This model is appropriate for a therapist, if:

- You naturally tend to use a proactive, personal growth, behaviorally focused approach of therapy.
- You want a model and skills to help you define and refine a way of working with clients that supports your clinical training.
- You like to work short-term.
- You are comfortable with the give and take of a behavioral method of therapy.
- You prefer tangible results, to see evidence of change, even in a single session.
- You structure your treatment to have a beginning, middle, and end when possible.
- You favor a client-based model of equality in therapy.
- You are comfortable ceding some control in a session, including veering from a strict protocol, to allow your clients to have the ability to drive the direction of a session.
- You know how to gracefully retain your expertise and adhere to a treatment plan, but still share power with a client.
- You know how to set and maintain clear boundaries in terms of session management. For example, you can start and stop a session on time, bill for sessions appropriately, don't carry a large debt of unpaid client bills, and run your practice in a professional manner.
- You adhere to ethical requirements of your licensure. You don't befriend clients inappropriately, have dual relationships, or get enmeshed with clients inside or outside of therapy sessions. (Please see the Chapter 4 to understand how to create collaboration while holding boundaries.)
- You are self-aware; you have spent time in your own therapy.
- You can recognize transference and countertransference as it occurs in a session. (It is important that you have a way to recognize and contain countertransference to promote the results of this model.)
- You are drawn to therapy with a coaching approach, but don't want to use these skills to become a life coach with a therapy client.

In the Worksheets section of this book, I have compiled the important questions and checklists from this chapter, to give you an easy way to put the suitability guidepost into action when you are ready to use this tool in your practice.

Now that you have a way to check for preference and suitability for yourself and your potential and existing clients, the next step is to shift your positioning. I want you to be able to adopt the authentic and collaborative coaching approach style of relating with clients. This positioning furthers therapy outcomes. In Chapter 4, I show you the steps to develop a therapeutic alliance that promotes client motivation and boosts action.

4

Creating Therapist– Client Collaboration

Imagine you're learning to ride a bicycle for the first time. You have asked a therapist and a coach for help. A therapist would be standing off to the side, closely observing your attempt to stay upright. She'd be empathic, compassionate when you fell, and might make insightful interpretations about why you're unstable and wobbly. She'd help you express your feelings or frustration about your struggle with learning to ride. She might explore the origins of your lack of stability. Over time your facility could improve as you developed more confidence, armed with new insight and awareness.

A coach would climb on the seat right behind you and ask, "Where do you want to go today?"

This is an exaggeration, of course, but the difference in role is clear. Having a coach right behind you, an ally guiding you and the bike as you both pedal along together, is an example of coaching collaboration, in its purest sense. The coach and the client work together through intense partnership. Rather than observing from a neutral distance (like a therapist), a coach is at your back. The coach keeps you motivated to continue riding until you can do it on your own, like a pro. You're in the steering position, and she has no agenda other than wanting you to get where you wish to go, in the fastest, most focused manner possible.

This collaborative position is the great leveler when used in many forms of coaching: Since it reduces the friction of hierarchy, it promotes faster behavioral change. You may have experienced this kind of collaboration with a personal coach who runs alongside you as you jog around a track. Or perhaps you had a tutor who sat next to you as you tired to solve a math problem, rubbing shoulders and sharing his calculations when you got stuck, to help you find the key to unlock the formula. When you have a coach at your side, or at your back, you can go faster and try harder than if you are being observed by an expert who is at a distance. I learned what this type of collaboration felt like, after hiring a life coach to resolve a problem that was beyond my grasp.

I GET COACHED

In 1998, I was working full-time as a therapist in a busy private practice. I had completed a two-year coach training program at CoachU and begun to work as a coach with a few clients, primarily as a business coach. Having a business background prior to becoming a therapist, I specialized in small business owners. I coached those I called "reluctant entrepreneurs"—people who ended up in business but had never studied business basics. My clients needed a combination of coaching and consultation; I was having fun offering this service. As time went on, many of these reluctant entrepreneurs I coached were my fellow therapists in private practice who joined a weekly coaching group I offered.

While running this group, I had a goal: I wanted to turn the manual I wrote for the group into a book, one that would help therapists master the business of therapy. I sent out a query letter to a publisher, on a lark, to gauge if there was interest in my topic. To my surprise, the publisher responded and asked me to send in my manuscript. I was totally unprepared for this response: What manuscript? I tried to put one together from the manual and found myself stuck. I had writer's block. I just couldn't move forward. One month went by, and then another and another. No change in my writing output. I'd never hired a coach for myself, but if not now, when?

I sought out Pam Richarde, a former therapist, now a life coach and director of training at CoachU. During our first call, Pam asked: "What's important about writing this book?"

"Well, it's a book for therapists, to help them build their practices. I am already teaching classes on this topic, the business of therapy, and a book would be good for my career. At least it would help me teach more classes. I'd be an author and could present workshops." On and on I went with ideas that were basically about furthering my career.

"Anything else?"

"No, that's all I can think of."

"And you're really stuck. You haven't written a word in over three months."

"Correct."

Pam took a moment to think about this. "Lynn, I'm listening to your reasons for writing and, sweetie (I learned later that Pam called all her coaching clients affectionate names), I just don't think that you have a big enough vision to get you over the writer's block. I request that you find a bigger, better reason, other than your personal career agenda, for this book to exist."

"Like what?"

"Honey, that's what I'm asking you! I can't find your answer, but I do believe it's inside you. If I was thinking about this for myself, I might start with my values. Think about this over the week and let's talk more on our next call."

For Pam, the best way to shift perception when someone was stuck was to get them to think bigger. She invited me to develop a vision for the book, so I looked at a bigger reason for writing one—beyond my capital-C Career. I took long walks and thought about what a book with this topic might accomplish for others. It occurred to me that if I could help therapists be more successful, it might keep the therapy profession alive in the world, maybe help it grow! I deeply believed in the importance of therapy and thought about all the therapists I knew who toiled in private practice—smart, generous, caring people—who deserved to earn a good living. I began to get the spirit and motivation I needed. I finally started writing, this time in earnest.

Pam was a cheerleader while I was writing, but she also brought in her expertise with publishing. When I'd completed four chapters, she outlined the next step—how to write a book proposal—and when I'd done that, she opened her Rolodex and gave me the name of a copywriter to perfect it, and a book marketing expert to advise me about how to get the world interested in it. I sent out the proposal to six publishers and got back three offers. She weighed in on the publishing responses, to help me assess them. I signed a contract and got to work, writing a book that became a best-seller in its genre.

As a coach, Pam modeled a partnership position: She sat behind me on the bike. I felt that my goals became her goals. Her interest in my success seemed real and helped me move forward faster and more easily than if I'd been on my own. But when I tried to describe my relationship with Pam to my friends, who were also therapists, I got stuck. Pam was kind of an advisor, but she worked with me, as one therapist would describe, "close-in," like a longtime buddy. She had immediate, real reactions. She was flexible and made jokes. She cared a lot about my goal. Certainly, no therapist had ever called me "sweetie" and "honey."

But she wasn't really a friend or even a colleague. We talked by phone. I had never met her face to face. And while I paid her—as I would a therapist—she was transparent and self-disclosed tidbits about her own life and her work to help me stay motivated. She'd "break the frame" to email me between our sessions to find out how I was doing and if I was making progress on a specific action. She made suggestions freely and openly. She introduced me to her publishing resources and shared her network of assistants. When my book got published, she bowed out gracefully, allowing me to take all the credit. This stood as a good example for me of the effectiveness of collaboration and the partnership position, delivered through coaching.

THE PARTNERSHIP POSITION IN THERAPY

When I began to develop the model of Therapy with a Coaching Edge, I needed to take another look at the concept of collaboration. Therapy was traditionally hierarchical, for many good reasons. But a partnership position, like the one I had with Pam or the one I might have with a personal trainer or a mentor, could produce faster change and be very motivating. Could a non-hierarchical position, being on the back seat of the bike, be adapted for a therapeutic relationship? Would the inherent aspects of a partnership position, working transparently and directly with a client, help or hurt the goal of therapy? Did partnership, in the way a coach positions herself, run counter to the integrity and realities of the mental health profession?

From my coach training, my review of the coaching literature, and my experience teaching coaching and being a coach, I saw how a reduction in hierarchy and working "close in" greased the wheels of motivation. I longed to replicate some of that leverage or ability to boost action within therapy, but wondered how to ethically translate partnership for the profession of therapy.

Was it possible? My answer is a modified yes. With careful adaptation, to respect the necessary boundaries of a therapeutic relationship, I have found ways to enhance collaboration between client and therapist that respects a therapy setting. Some, though not all, of the elements of a pure coaching partnership position can be used, in an adapted form. As I developed this adapted process of partnership and collaboration, I began to see an improvement in my client outcomes in therapy. Less hierarchy and more support results in easier action and more behavioral compliance.

In this chapter, I show you the key elements that will allow you to be more "coach-like" in your stance and collaborative positioning, while respecting the purpose of therapy, including how to:

- Take the lead.
- Use appropriate self-disclosure.
- Reduce negative transference.
- Increase the use of self.

I explain each element and offer a case example, to show you how I bring in elements of partnership to motivate a client. You will see what I needed to maintain a collaborative connection, even when I needed to

address a potential boundary issue. I will review some ethical considerations that can occur when using a collaborative position, so you can take
care to comply with professional principles and ethical responsibilities.
After reading this chapter, you will have more clarity about how to create
a client relationship with more equality and less hierarchy, for the purpose of furthering the aims of this therapy model.

As with all the suggestions in this book, you need to assess the inclusion of the techniques offered, and adopt only those that support the
clinical goals and methods that are best for your situation. I have adapted
the elements of a pure coaching partnership position for this therapeutic
model, but you may need to further adjust these elements to adhere to
your particular theoretical leanings and licensure.

First, let's take a quick step back and review therapist positioning, as it
has occurred over time. I want to remind you about the natural evolution
of the role of the therapist, so you can understand how increased collaboration between therapist and client is part of a trend line in therapy, one
that has been developing during the decades.

SHIFTING THE PERSONA OF THE THERAPIST

Therapists have been shifting their role for over one hundred years. As
therapy methods progressed, so did the positioning of the therapist.
The overarching mandate that I note as I peruse the literature about
the changing therapist persona is that the behavior of therapists and
the nature of their relationship to clients need to be congruent with the
methods practiced.

A Freudian analyst who is neutral, blank, and silent acts this way for
a reason. She wants the client to forget her presence and focus inward,
without her interference. In contrast, a therapist who makes eye contact,
shakes hands, and shows warmth and emotion does this to create rapport as a primary healing element. A shift from a persona of neutrality
and self-restraint to one that shows empathy and unconditional regard
is an example of how modern therapy methods have been developing
for therapeutic purposes over many years. Steven Johnson, PhD, author

of several classic books about psychotherapy, notes the development of what he calls "post-modern" therapy, and observes that as methods have changed in approach, therapists have too, becoming:[1]

- Natural (versus neutral)
- Proactive (versus nondirective)
- Supportive (versus diagnostic)
- Curious (versus quiet)
- Responsive (versus deflecting)
- Questioning (versus interpreting)
- Leading (versus following)

Therapy with a Coaching Edge echoes Johnson's post-modern progression. In my model, to further the coaching approach elements of client control, partnership, action, and possibility, the therapist must herself relate in a proactive way that signals authenticity. To do this, you need to be a presence in the room, not a neutral, blank slate. You need to be "real"—to talk normally, rather than with stilted or carefully worded interpretations. I urge therapists using my method to avoid therapeutic jargon. Be expressive. Allow some normal reactions to show on your face, as you would in outside relationships. Let yourself be seen as both an expert and a person. Communicate curiosity. Show real interest. Have a sense of humor. The last point in Johnson's list is also an important skill. Know how and when to go from following to leading.

Take the Lead

In my early training as a psychodynamic therapist and a social worker, I was taught that my primary role was to follow, not lead. I let the client begin a session. That meant I would start a session in silence, so as not to influence or bias the client in any way. My client could talk or not talk. I would not influence or interrupt. I let a client take the lead and watched as the session unfolded, sometimes in confusion if a client was not sure how therapy worked or what to do.

---

1 Johnson, S. (1991). *The Symbiotic Character*. New York: W. W. Norton & Company.

My model in this book is not psychodynamic in this way. Unlike the neutral, blank demeanor that I was once taught, Therapy with a Coaching Edge encourages therapists to take some leadership, at certain times, as a way to offer collaboration. Don't stay neutral and force a client to flounder. Help out the process, ensure that it goes well. Use skills to shape a session agenda, to give it structure and a dynamic flow and promote more results. (I explain how to do this in the next chapter.) Rather than allow a client to devolve into long narrative, off topic, help them follow a plan. Ask effective, pointed, even powerful questions when it would help to pick up the pace. Take responsibility to keep the session organized and relevant. Here is a short example to demonstrate how I used leadership with my client, Angela, to keep her focused on making a necessary change.

Angela is late to her therapy session. She tells me she really needs to talk about something that has come up. "I told you last time that my husband works for the military and we move a lot. We have lived in six states in four years. I am not complaining so much about that, it's something I knew when we got married. I have a young son and most of my time is spent taking care of him. I work a little part-time and I am very much into yoga, so I am a pretty calm person."

I nod my head to show that I remember her telling me this before.

"But I think I am bored or just uneasy, and when I get like this, I tend to get in trouble," she says.

"What kind of trouble?"

"Oh, you know. Maybe doing some things that don't help the situation. I guess the real trouble is man trouble. When I get bored, I start to look for a man to flirt with and then, well you know, then things get out of hand. I have started to think about getting a little friendly with my neighbor. He is awfully cute and he's single and I am home a lot by myself."

Angela looks at me for my response. I realize I have a choice to make about my therapy persona. I can stay silent, be blank faced, and just nod as many therapists do, maybe say something neutral like "Tell me more," or I can respond more authentically, using a collaborative stance. I choose the latter.

"Yikes," I say. "You sure do know how to make trouble." I smile slightly.

Angela literally sits back in her chair to indicate her surprise and barks out a laugh. "I didn't think you would say that. It sounds bad when I hear you say this out loud. But you are right. My husband really got mad the last time this happened and said if I didn't get counseling I shouldn't follow him to the next posting. It's a great posting, to a city we both love, and I want to go and live there." Angela proceeds to chat about the qualities of the city she hopes to move to. This session is starting to devolve into a tour guide.

I decide to take the lead, to interrupt, and in doing so, redirect her. "I am really curious. Are you in therapy right now so you can follow him to the next posting and live in the city you love, or are you here to save your marriage?"

There is a long pause. Angela stares at me. "That is a good question. A really good question. I guess I don't know why I am really here. Or what I really want," she says.

"Thank you for stating this so honestly. I appreciate that you don't know what you really want. If you'd like to use our therapy sessions to figure out why you are here and what you do want, I could absolutely stand behind that goal."

"I would like that, to know what I really want," she says. "That would probably change my life."

Defuse Negative Transference

In an earlier session, Angela explained that her husband reminded her of her father, who was a stern authoritarian; she rebelled as a teenager to establish her individuality. She now does this to her husband. Transference is a normal aspect of relationships. Most of us operate with some degree of idealization or demonization of those in our current lives, based on unconscious bias and family history.

But when transference, especially negative transference, is focused and projected onto the therapist by a client, therapy sessions take a turn. With the emergence of negative transference, a session needs to slow down its pace. It takes time to process. Negative transference requires a neutral, nonreactive response from a therapist; the client will benefit from having an open space and sufficient time, even multiple sessions, to work through the layers of complicated feelings and thoughts that are being projected onto the therapist.

In my model, I see that this kind of negative projection interferes with a coaching approach. Negative, erotic, or idealized transference inhibits action, possibility thinking, and even constructive partnership. While I need to stay cognizant of the normal occurrences of transference and countertransference in therapy, when negative or erotic transference occurs, I address it transparently and quickly, to lessen its intensity and get back to the topic at hand. For my model of therapy to work best, I need to maintain a collaborative relationship. When hints of a negative transference emerge, I try to observe it and talk about calmly, without reactivity or judgment. Transference is a form of client communication. I communicate back, not dodging the issue, but not trying to expand its occurrence. I address it and defuse it. Here is an example of defusing some negative transference with Angela, in order to stay collaborative and get back on track with the session goals:

Angela was late getting to the next session. She had encountered a traffic jam on her way to my office. She came in flustered and immediately asked if she would be charged for the entire session or if I would pro-rate it, so that she would only be charged for the time we actually talked. I told her that I would need to charge her for the full session, regardless of her being late.

"It's not my fault that I am late. I can't control traffic," she said, irritated. "I don't see why you can't be more flexible and work with me on this. This therapy is very expensive, and I am not getting my full session. Why can't you make an exception?"

Let's bracket Angela's question for a moment, to explore a traditional therapeutic response to this situation, so you can understand why I addressed this the way that I did. In my earlier career, using a psychodynamic model, I was trained to handle a complaint like this by doing nothing to soften the client's negative transference. Instead, I would turn the question back on her to ask, "How would you feel about me if I did make an exception?" After the client responded, I would follow up with asking, "How would you feel about me if I didn't?" and then process the responses at length to help her develop more insight about the idealized or negative feelings and thoughts, and what aspect of her history or psyche it related to. All the while, I would screen my own thoughts and feelings behind a neutral persona. Nothing would show on my face. I might explore every aspect of the issue: the meaning of lateness, the unconscious resistance to therapy, the potential lack of organization in a client's life. I would mention the issue of her statement about the expense of therapy, her feelings and thoughts about having to pay for treatment, and any and all anger or upset directed toward me.

Therapy with a Coaching Edge has a different purpose. I am not promoting insight and affect or expression of feelings to the same degree I do when using a psychodynamic approach. Instead, I am focused on action and a prospective, future-forward direction of problem solving. So I need to defuse negative transference in service of the goals of a coaching approach. First, to maintain rapport, I validated Angela's upset.

"It makes sense to me that you are frustrated and upset. I know that some of what made you late was out of your control. This is costly, not just in terms of the money involved that you feel you wasted, but also the cost of the stress you feel, trying to get here on time," I said.

Next, I chose to be transparent, to be authentic, and to allow her to see me as more than her projection. "I was a bit upset, too. I was waiting and worried about you. I am really glad that it was only traffic that delayed you."

Angela looked at me carefully. "It never occurred to me that you would be worried or wondering if I was all right."

"I was, and while I waited, I did some thinking about you. I reviewed our notes from our last session. I thought about how we could focus our conversation today, to try to make sure you got what you needed, even if we had less time. Can I share my idea of where I think we should start?" Here I collaborate to make the session successful, if possible. I take responsibility to provide value, in my role as the therapist: not just paid for waiting, but paid for working. I had a plan, given a reduced amount of time, so that she could leave the session with some results.

Angela looked relieved and said, "Yes, that would be good, thanks. I'm ready."

We were able to have a productive session. At the end, she listed the things she would take away from our time together, including what her action steps could be. At the door, she turned and thanked me for helping everything work out so well.

By opting for collaboration, I intentionally defused her negative projection, not to let myself off the hook of her anger, or to defend my boundaries, but to shield the model of therapy. I wanted to stay focused and make the session useful. I was also able to use this experience as a teachable moment in our future sessions in therapy—how to find ways to make things go better by accessing resources (in this case, the resource of me, as her collaborator, using the time to review past notes and think of a plan). I also could remind her of the attempt to stay connected to each other and to the goal of the session, even during trying circumstances of lateness.

Increase Use of Self

Throughout my training to become a social worker, I heard teachers employ the term "use of self." Use of self, I came to understand, meant that who you are, the combination of your professional and personal experience, is perhaps the most important tool you can bring into any therapeutic situation.

Therapy, at its essence, is based on a relationship. The therapist and the client sit in an otherwise empty room, without props or tools. Your ability to tap into a use of self can model "clinical wholeness"—how to collaborate by being fully present and a whole person for your clients, as family therapist Virginia Satir espoused.[2] Experienced therapists apply a use of self with ease; they are comfortable being themselves and relying on their presence as the main healing element they have to offer. For newer therapists, the need to depend on oneself is often fraught with anxiety. Newer therapists worry: "Have I said too little or too much? What if I don't know enough to be the expert on this issue? What can I say to help a client? How might I relate better?"

---

2 Satir, V., Gerber, J., Banmen, J. & Gomori, M. (1991). *The Satir Model.* Palo Alto: Science and Behavior Books.

I remember an old cartoon that showed a doctor sitting at his desk talking on the phone with a patient. Unseen by the patient was the fact that the doctor was smoking cigarettes and had an overflowing ashtray of butts, had a bottle of Scotch opened and a drink poured, and was seriously overweight. The advice he was giving the patient belied the scene. "As your doctor, I am telling you to get healthy! Immediately stop smoking, stop drinking, and drop some pounds."

The old medical mantra of "do as I say, not as I do" will not work for a therapist using a partnership position. With reduced hierarchy and less transference, when offering collaboration, clients will look to you as a model of your services. You will need to "represent"—to stand for what you provide. For example, if your therapy practice specializes in addictions, you need to be on a solid path of sobriety. If you specialize in wellness, you need to have optimized your own healthy choices. Your ability to make use of yourself, to stand as an example of the clinical results you promote, helps to forge an authentic relationship with clients. You are on view. Develop a strong therapeutic sense of self, so that when you are seen, you demonstrate a balanced, real adult in your clinical role.

One way to heighten a use of self is with appropriate self-disclosure. Studies have shown the value of therapist self-disclosure for clients; when used within suitable guidelines, it creates quite positive effects (2009).[3] Clients experience greater warmth and relatedness with a therapist who occasionally self-discloses. Showing real concern or apologizing helps to repair the therapist-client alliance when it is broken. The suggestions for this are that when you use self-disclosure, do it with intention, caution, and care. Assess whether sharing something personal about yourself would benefit or burden a client.[4] Use self-disclosure only when you feel secure that it will be useful to the client and further the treatment goals.

---

3 Henretty, J. & Levitt, H. (2009). The role of therapist self-discolosure in psychotherapy: A qualitative review. *Clinical Psychology Review.* 30(1), 63-77. doi: 10.1016/j.cpr.2009.09.004

4 Zur, O. (2016). *Self-Disclosure & Transparency in Psychotherapy and Counseling: To Disclose or Not to Disclose, This is the Question.* Retrieved from http://www.zurinstitute.com/selfdisclosure1.html.

Here is an example of how I used self-disclosure to further collaboration, and benefit Angela's sense of her own self-worth.

Angela has a lifelong tendency to diminish herself. "You probably never had this problem, Lynn," she said during a session. "You are very self-confident. I feel like I am not smart enough or strong enough to say what I think in the moment. Afterwards, I can barely stand myself, because I missed my chance."

"You seem to want to be more assertive and speak up in the moment. You feel awful when you miss a chance to be this way."

"Right. I wish I knew how to do this, it would help me a lot in life," she sighed.

I asked Angela if she thought that speaking up was a skill that could be learned, but she looked doubtful. "Either you are born with this ability or you aren't," she said.

I could have challenged this belief system by explaining that many people have overcome shyness or inability to speak up, but given her idealization of me ("you are very self-confidant"), I decided to use myself as a role model. I wanted to demonstrate, not the end result of my being assertive, but the process of its development.

"Can I share a story from my own life?" I asked. She nodded and I went on.

"I remember my first job, when I tried to ask my boss for a raise," I said. "I thought I would pass out from anxiety. I literally had to sit down to catch my breath after I got a few words out. My boss asked if I was going to be ill. You can imagine how that ended. No raise. Never got up the courage to try it with him again."

Angela laughed with delight. "You were scared? How did you get to be the way you are now?"

I paused before answering. I knew that Angela was an amateur musician, so I framed my answer as a lighthearted question, one I knew she could answer. "What do they say about getting to Carnegie Hall?" I asked.

"Practice, practice, practice," she said immediately and we laughed together.

Now I offered support. "We could practice together in a therapy session, perhaps use a role play, to help you find the right words?"

"That would be great, especially if we can make my part easy to begin with. Like playing scales first, before I have to attempt a concerto."

Angela grabbed onto the metaphor of Carnegie Hall as a way to understand how to move toward this goal of assertiveness. "Scales first" became her favorite mantra during her remaining time in therapy, one that helped her take small but important steps to achieve other meaningful actions.

The Ethics of a Collaborative Stance

Shifting to a less hierarchical, more collaborative relationship as a therapist can worry therapists who have been trained in models that are intentionally neutral to protect therapeutic and ethical boundaries. For some therapists, the elements I have demonstrated in my work with Angela may feel foreign to the way they have been taught; for example, if you are primarily psychodynamic in your orientation, any use of self-disclosure may be contrary to the methodology and jar with the purposes of the therapy. Of all the shifts and skills within my model, shifting your therapeutic persona is the one that, for some therapists, may be most complicated. If you want to adopt a coaching approach and a partnership position, and this is not natural to the way you currently work, proceed slowly.

First, adhere to all the ethical requirements of your licensure. I have sat through many ethics workshops during 30 years of practice as a social worker, and respect the rationale for keeping clear boundaries between therapist and client. But discussions of boundaries are not always black and white, or exacting in their application. There are shades of gray when it comes to situational ethics. I believe that using a collaborative stance, as I have described it in this chapter, adheres to the boundaries of standard practice, even if this last element, self-disclosure, may fall within the shades of gray for some therapists.

To better understand the shades of gray in situational ethics, when applying a new persona to your practice, I like the work of Frederic Reamer, an expert in the subtleties of the field. Another resource on ethics and boundaries, the Zur Institute, makes a distinction for modern therapists between *boundary crossings*—clinically effective interventions such as self-disclosure, home visits, client touch in the form of handshakes, or a nonsexual pat on the back—and *boundary violations*—when therapists cross the line of decency, violate or exploit their clients sexually, financially, or in other unethical ways, including misusing dual relationships.[5]

I am always attuned to the need to protect clients from any boundary violations; the last one listed above regarding dual relationships is one that can be confusing at times for a client, especially a client of a therapist who works with a therapist who is using a coaching style. We therapists get confused about what is therapy and what is coaching, and so do clients. This sets up a possible boundary issue. Here is a situation that emerged once Angela's therapy was ending, that required me to define the nature of our relationship more clearly. I needed to assert my boundary while still maintaining a collaborative stance.

Upholding Boundaries

As therapy drew to an end, Angela had decided to recommit to her marriage. She was ready to go to the next posting with her husband. She said that once they moved, she was going to start a small business based on teaching yoga classes at the military base. Angela knew that I worked as both a therapist and business coach. She asked if I could become her business coach and she could continue her work with me at a distance, by phone or using a platform such as Skype.

"Since we have worked well together and our therapy has had a coaching style, and it feels like coaching a lot of the time, can I hire you as my business coach? Would that be okay?" she asked.

Some therapists wonder whether the two roles—that of therapist and coach—can be combined with a single client. Is it possible to switch roles and be a client's therapist and then, later on, her coach? If it is sequential, or there is a break between the contracts, is it permitted? I am of the firm belief that the roles of therapist and coach for a client are distinct and need to be kept separate. Even though I use a model of therapy with adapted coaching skills, when I practice as a therapist, I stay in that role.

5 http://www.zurinstitute.com/boundaries_clinicalupdate.html

I could understand that from Angela's perspective, this boundary was not clear. For her, therapy and coaching seemed to be very similar. But I knew better. What I understood from my position, which would be hard to explain to Angela, was the concept of a dual relationship. When I work as a business coach, I explain to clients that I am part coach, part consultant. I become involved in areas of a client's business life, including their finances and debt, marketing and business planning, promotions and business strategy. It is essential, in my role as a business coach, that clients have the ability to rationally analyze what I suggest, and then freely reject my ideas. They need to rely on their knowledge and instincts, in order to do what is best for themselves and their businesses. We contract with this in mind, to balance my influence and equalize the power differential.

As Angela's therapist, I could not erase our prior therapeutic relationship to have a clean slate for coaching. Even though, as her therapist, I have tried to minimize the transference and idealization, I know that we have dealt with her vulnerabilities, emotions, and psychological issues. I have been privy to her pain, defenselessness, deep feelings, and thoughts about herself and her marriage. This would give me an unfair advantage in any coaching or consulting engagement; my words and ideas would carry extra weight, a hidden influence, because of all that had transpired before in being her therapist. That would not be fair to Angela, and would affect the balance of a coaching relationship, which requires that we have a level playing field.

So I understood why this would not work, but it was not necessary to educate her in this regard, with this level of detail. Instead, my policy, whenever I am asked to switch roles, is to say no, hold the boundary of the existing contact, and if desired, make a referral. But I do this with some care, to preserve the sense of partnership and collaboration. After Angela made her request, I took a moment and then responded.

"I am so appreciative that you would consider me for this role, to be your business coach. I like the idea of all you are planning for yourself and wish I could be a part of your circle of support. But unfortunately, I am not able to switch roles. Since I started as your therapist, I need to stay in my role as your therapist."

"I hate to leave, and wish we could still work together," Angela said. "I thought this would make sense and we could still work together."

"I have feelings as well about ending. I have enjoyed our work together, too."

"I feel sad about ending. You have helped me a lot."

"Let's spend time today talking about the sadness of ending. I can also offer a way to help you end therapy well, and consolidate all the gains you have made. When you move, whenever you are ready to hire a business coach, I would be happy at that time to see if I can suggest a few referrals. I would be glad to support you in that way, if possible."

Angela took three sessions to complete her therapy: She reviewed the progress we had made, identified next steps to maintain her new behaviors, and used time to express her thoughts and feelings about her results and our positive therapeutic relationship. She called this a good ending, again a teaching moment for her; a supportive relationship could end on a positive note.

You may have noticed that in this case with Angela, I used a structure in our therapy sessions; it's designed to increase client satisfaction and produce results. In the next chapter, the final one in this section of foundational elements, I show you how to apply this same session structure with your clients, to use a "getting to yes" framework. It can be effective for reducing client dropout, and helps clients identify their gains and results, session after session.

5

Results in Every Session

Successful treatment in Therapy with a Coaching Edge is measured, in part, by two primary indicators: client satisfaction and client retention. Do your clients feel that they get good value for the cost and considerable effort they put into therapy? Can they articulate the gains they have made as a result of treatment? Do they stay long enough to complete treatment? These are important questions for you, as a therapist using this model, to assess and measure.

This last indicator, if clients stay long enough to get a return on their investment of treatment, my definition of retention, is especially important to address. Therapy, even therapy based on short-term methods, requires time and repeat visits to be successful. We need to engage our clients session by session. It's important that you, as the therapist, know how your clients feel and think about the services they are receiving from you as the process proceeds. We know from studies that clients that are confused about or dissatisfied with services tend to leave therapy too soon, before the process of therapy yields ultimate benefit. Having a client leave therapy prematurely is difficult and can be upsetting to both the client and the therapist. You do your best to provide empathy, caring, and treatment; if a client ends treatment abruptly, without explanation or notice, it can feel like a bad breakup: You were dumped. A therapist can speculate endlessly to understand why a client left treatment, but it points to a larger problem affecting the therapy profession: Twenty percent of those who need our services leave therapy before completion. Poor retention is tied to a lack of client satisfaction.[1]

---

1 Swift, J. K., & Greenberg, R. P. (2012). Premature discontinuation in adult psychotherapy: A meta-analysis. *Journal of Consulting and Clinical Psychology, 80*(4), 547.

I have been interested in resolving the problems of poor client satisfaction and low retention for a long time, and written and given workshops on this topic.[2] When I developed Therapy with a Coaching Edge, I wanted it to include a format, embedded in its basic design, to improve these issues. I found that by using a proactive stance and a specific session format, I could improve client satisfaction and retention. In this chapter, I show you how I set up each session for these same positive outcomes.

First, I will show you my three-step session plan. This plan is integral to my model and follows the tenets of a coaching approach, offering clients a sense of control over therapy and promoting their investment in the immediate and long-term outcome. With this three-step plan in place, you remove some of the mystery from what is happening in the treatment room, so clients can better understand the therapy process and what they are receiving for their time and expense. The plan clarifies the progress that often occurs within each and every session; I will show you where and how to spot results that you may be overlooking. I also relate a case example so you can see how to apply the session plan with a client and how to track results. This plan is a tool to help you address the problem of clients leaving too soon based on being disappointed in therapy in general, and specifically in your efforts as their therapist. It helps to anticipate why clients get so disappointed.

NOTICING CLIENT DISAPPOINTMENT

Client dissatisfaction in therapy is due to several, understandable factors. Most people who need to see a therapist have mixed feelings about the need to get into therapy. Few clients calling for an appointment are delighted to be in this situation; instead, they often express some embarrassment, worry, or a sense of personal failure. Added to this is the lack of clarity, for the average client, about what psychotherapy or counseling

---

2 Grodzki, L. (2015). *Building Your Ideal Private Practice, 2nd Edition.* New York: W. W. Norton & Company.

is or does. Our profession suffers from a lack of good PR. For clients, the beginning-to-end process of being in therapy is often vague and confusing. It is expensive in terms of time and effort. Even with insurance, it can be a financial burden. Top this off with an even more damning factor: A client may demonstrate commitment to come to therapy sessions, pay money, and make an effort to get better, but there is no guarantee of results.

Therapist Steve Andreas explains the client dissatisfaction problem like this[3]: Imagine that your car is breaking down and belching smoke. You are desperate and take it to the nearest repair shop, where the manager says that his help will cost $100 an hour, and many hours are needed to address the problem. But you will need to bring it in weekly, so the car and mechanic can have a "working relationship." He gives you no assurance that he will correctly diagnose or fix the problem. Adding insult to injury, he tells you that since the "dropout rate" of cars is at least 20 percent, many cars leave no better than when they came in; some actually leave in worse shape. Still want to get your car repaired at this shop? According to Andreas, this mirrors the state of psychotherapy today.

In my early years as a therapist in private practice, I too struggled with client dropout. Like most new therapists, I felt overwhelmed and unskilled at my job. I was working hard to understand what was occurring in the moment and trying to manage not just what the client was saying, but unseen factors of transference and nonverbal cues. I was looking at everything except the one thing that could have really helped me: finding out, in the moment, what my client really wanted from me and from the session we were having, and then taking responsibility to make sure we were heading in that direction.

The problem was that, as the expert in the room, I thought I knew best. I did have a sense of the *needs* of my clients, as do most therapists, based on my ability to diagnose and my training. What a client may need is not too difficult for a licensed therapist or counselor to assess. But when it comes to client satisfaction, we must also understand what a cli-

---

3 Andreas, S. (2017). Adjusting the unconscious: Can we make quick work of lasting change? *Psychotherapy Networker*. March-April 2017, p. 47.

ent *wants*, not just needs. To keep clients engaged in returning to sessions, I had to learn the difference between client needs and wants.

Needs Versus Wants

My foray into coaching helped me understand more about the distinction between needs and wants. Perhaps because of who coaching clients are—functional, voluntary, motivated—and because of how life coaching is priced—expensive, and paid for out of pocket—life coaching, executive coaching and business coaching sessions are designed primarily to satisfy what a client wants.

In my coach training, I was reminded that the client should end each session feeling that it had been well worth the time and money spent, *and* have verbalized a compelling reason to return, all before the session ended. The structure that I was taught to make this more likely to occur was known, in coach-speak, as the "session agreement." Setting up the session agreement is a required element to demonstrate, before you can be certified as a coach. It must be done in a specific way. It is akin to setting up an agenda and may seem similar to the way a therapist might set an agenda in a model of cognitive behavioral therapy (CBT), with one difference: It focuses on wants, more than on needs.

For example, a CBT session might start with a therapist asking a client to check in on progress from the last week and then, based on the reporting of homework or other actions or issues that the client has mentioned, the therapist would ask, "What would you like to work on today?" The therapist might list items of an agenda on a whiteboard or a piece of paper. Then the therapist could help the client prioritize the items, usually in terms of importance. Then the "work" of the session can begin.

Contrast this to the way I was taught to set up a session agreement in a life coaching session: As a life coach, I might begin the same way, with a check-in on progress and a proposed agenda of things to address in the session, but it would be prioritized by figuring out, of all the agenda topics proposed, which one is really wanted by the client. As a coach, I was taught to ask questions such as these: What about that item makes it vital for you to explore and address today? What might be even more important regarding this topic for you right now? What aspect of this topic would create the biggest impact on your life or work immediately? The back and forth is a way that the client and I would both get invested in the agenda. The client needs to sell himself, and me as the coach, on which is his most desirable topic, the one he really wants to tackle. Only high-interest, desired topics make the cut. As a result of this process, the client is more fully engaged to participate in the session: The session has heightened interest and importance to him. Then the "work" of the life coaching session can begin.

Now, therapy and coaching have different purposes. In therapy, we are providing treatment, so we can't ignore what needs to be addressed or discussed. There are issues that may involve serious, life-and-death, psychological, emotional, or health-related concerns. Those needs are critical to treat and part of our mandate as clinicians.

When my goal is not just treatment, but also to improve satisfaction and retention, I try to offer a blended focus of client needs and wants in every session. In my model, a therapist's proactive role in setting up a session with a client is to facilitate a merger of both needs and wants, so that the important treatment issues are addressed, but at the same time what a client desires is also on the agenda.

Merging Needs and Wants

On my bookshelf is a well-known book on negotiation by Fisher and Ury titled *Getting to Yes*. I began to think about the process of merging needs and wants in a therapy session as a kind of negotiation. I call my session plan "getting to yes," by which I mean that if, at the end of a therapy session, I asked a client if the session met his or her needs *and* wants, I would literally get an enthusiastic Yes!

Last year, I saw an important addition to the psychological literature, a book by Joshua Swift and Roger Greenberg dealing with client retention issues titled *Premature Termination in Psychotherapy: Strategies for Engaging Clients and Improving Outcomes* (APA, 2014). To my delight, it mirrored much of the "getting-to-yes" session plan that I had developed and was already using and teaching. I enthusiastically recommend their book as a way to better understand retention.

Using my getting-to-yes session plan, I find that retention with therapy clients improves, as does their positive assessment of therapy. Resistance to completing treatment, as I knew it in my earlier years, has become a thing of the past. I began to teach this plan to other clinicians in workshops and supervision sessions, and they report back that they find the same results: better retention, improved client satisfaction, and a workable balance between needs and wants. I recommend that you use the getting-to-yes plan for each session. If it seems awkward to you at first, give it some time and practice. After a while, you will find that it gets easier and more natural to put it in place. Clients like it and also begin to prompt me in its use. The three phases in the getting-to-yes session plan are:

1. Find the purpose.
2. Work it through.
3. Consolidate gains.

1. Find the Purpose

The first phase of the session plan has a single objective: to identify the agenda for the session, one that addresses both the needs and wants category. This happens usually within the first 10 minutes of the session, sometimes sooner. The needs of your client may be familiar to you: those are the issues that the client brings in and/or the goals of treatment. The wanted agenda item may also be the one that is needed, although it may require some questions to help your client articulate how this needed topic is desired and compelling. Sometimes you can reframe a topic to do this. A needed topic might be managing time in order to get to a support group meeting. A wanted version of this same topic might be the desire to feel organized in one's life, including managing time. A needed topic may be setting boundaries with an angry spouse, and a wanted topic may be how to feel strong and grounded. In some cases, the needed topic, say staying calm before attempting to discipline a child, may be separate from an additional wanted topic, such as finding a way to take a daily walk for better self care. Of course, a therapy session can contain more than one topic to discuss, so make sure that both needs and wants get clarified on the front end of planning the session, and make time for both. As the session starts and issues or topics surface with a client, take some time to assess a good mixture of needs and wants before jumping into the work of the session by asking a few questions, such as:

> *What should we focus on or talk about today?*
> *Is this the most important topic for us today?*
> *What is it about this that would make a difference in your life?*
> *Is it vital for us to explore and address this today, or can it wait?*
> *What might be even more central to your well-being?*
> *If we resolved this topic, would you leave here today feeling satisfied with your session?*
> *What specific aspect of this topic would create the biggest impact on your life or work immediately?*

You may end up with a single focus to a session, or several agenda items. This phase of the plan is not formulaic. I want you to be flexible in discerning your client's needs and wants, and to keep in mind that most people need both to feel engaged in the outcome of the session. In the transcript offered below, my client Joan came into the session upset by a disturbing late-night phone call with her mother. This topic of upset started as a need, an issue to be discussed. I use this as a starting place to also find what she really wants, how to make the session more compelling.

JOAN: My mother woke me up last night and started in again on me. It was another drunken rant. This time she was going on about why I hadn't decided to live closer to her so I could help her more with things, and then she got into me being a bad parent to my kids. I could even hear her slurping her beer. It was 1:00 am. Really awful. After the call, I couldn't get back to sleep. I was awake for hours. I felt angry and guilty. I just feel so sorry for her, she doesn't know what she is saying.

LG: I can hear why this phone call was so upsetting. This is a very complicated situation, one full of emotion and reflecting a long history about your relationship. What part of this would you want to have as your focus today?

JOAN: I wish I knew. I would like to just be able to hang up on her.

LG: We could certainly talk about how to do that, but I wonder: With all of your complicated feelings and family history, would knowing how to hang up be the most important thing to talk about today?

JOAN: No, it's not really at the bottom of this. What would really help is not just getting off the call, but if I could stop taking what she says so personally. She's a drunk and that won't change, but maybe I could change how I hear the things she says.

LG: Changing how you hear the things she says and taking it less personally would be more core, at the bottom of this?

JOAN: Yes, that would be good.

LG: How would that help you?

JOAN: I feel like a sponge. I just absorb her wild accusations and then have to wring myself out and pull myself back into shape afterwards. If I could change how I hear her, be prepared, maybe understand more about why she says what she does, at least I would be thinking. I would not be a sponge. I would keep myself and stay with who I know I am.

LG: You want to stay alert, to stay clear about who you are, not to be a sponge soaking up her accusations.

JOAN: Yes, can we do that? I like the sound of this.

LG: We can. Let me make sure I understand exactly why this is important to you. If you can stay alert and keep your own shape and feel more solid, what difference will it make to you?

JOAN: Staying alert means not being so helpless. Thinking about what is coming next and being ready, remembering she can be mean when she is drunk, would really change how I feel about myself. Not just with her, but in my whole family. They all get this way at times, and my feelings get hurt.

LG: Thanks for helping me understand this better. I think we have an important topic for today. If we talk about this further, it can change how you feel about yourself. You might have fewer hurt feelings. You will feel more solid about yourself.

JOAN: Right!

LG: I look forward to helping you stay alert, to keep thinking about what is coming next, and to be ready. By the end of the session, if we have done justice to this topic, how will you know?

JOAN: I think I will have some new ideas and ways to think about myself. I won't be so upset. I won't feel like a sitting duck for her zingers when she is drunk. I will feel stronger, ready for the next conversation.

LG: You want to be stronger and ready, not a sitting duck waiting to be zapped. You want new ideas and ways to think about yourself. That is our focus for today.

JOAN: Exactly!

In this dialogue, I am teasing out what Joan needs and wants (from a therapeutic point of view), which is a way to stay conscious about verbal or emotional abuse from her mother during late night calls. She needs to stop the abuse and she wants to feel stronger and more solid about herself. This requires some repetition, to make sure that I clarify both and why it is important, in her own language: to not feel hurt, or like a sponge or a sitting duck, to be stronger and ready for any zingers. I might have gotten to a similar focus with Joan without asking these questions, simply by having the conversation and slowly allowing it to unfold. But by specifying her desired focus more quickly, and projecting it into the future of the session, to know what she can use as a marker of resolution of these topics, it's now possible for me to set an agenda and make sure it is clear to both of us. It will also help me at the end of the session, to assess if we have done our job together, since we took the time to clarify the direction.

If I have an item to add to the agenda from an earlier session, an issue that I think Joan needs to address, I can offer it to her and see if it is of sufficient interest, or try to reframe or change it if needed to make it more compelling, so it can be included. This process of setting the agenda with Joan took a few minutes to complete, but it was worthwhile, since it set our direction and in doing so, set up the middle phase.

2. Work It Through

The middle phase of the session is the working through and will involve your usual methods of treatment, adding skills from my model as appropriate. For example, Joan tends to speak in metaphors. ("I feel like a sponge." "I am a sitting duck.") One skill that seems natural to me to use with her is defined in skill #8: Find the Metaphors that Matter. Using that process, I can help her find a way to tap into her own symbolism to stay alert to abuse. The getting-to-yes plan is not a strict protocol. If Joan veers onto another issue during the middle phase, the plan is flexible. I welcome a therapeutic process of unfolding, allowing a client to bring up material not apparent in the beginning phase. When the session turns toward a new direction, I just slow it down to find the purpose again: the new needed and/or wanted agenda. I will make sure we both know how to judge our work at the end by asking for a marker of how to know if our work is going well. During the middle phase, I also start to track progress. I check in to make sure we are staying on the path to reach the end goal. Tracking the progress means that I am summarizing what we are doing and looking ahead to where we are going. Here is part of the dialogue with Joan as I track the work we are doing in the middle phase:

LG: I like the idea that you are exploring right now, that you are free to take a moment during a difficult phone call for a few seconds of a time-out. You might need a breath to remember who you are and what you might need to stay steady.

JOAN: Me too, I like this. It's like I am on a sailboat, the seas are rough, so from time to time I need to step back and check the sails, shift the rudder, tack in a different direction. In sailing, this is called shortening the sails.

LG: I know you sail, and this is a wonderful metaphor. Speaking of shortening the sails, our goal was for you to find a way to stay alert, think, and be ready for what might happen next during phone calls with your mother. Are we headed in that direction?

JOAN: Yes, we are heading there. It's definitely helpful to be talking about this.

LG: We have about 30 minutes left in the session. What else needs to be part of this conversation about reducing hurt, staying alert and prepared for zingers?

JOAN: I think I know why I get off course, with her zingers. Sometimes, when my mother starts blaming me, I start to get really sad. I feel guilty or I feel sorry for myself. I wish things were different. I think when I start to feel sad, I forget to stay alert. I let my guard down. Maybe we should talk about that next.

LG: Good idea. Tell me more about what happens and we can think what you can do in the moment when that sadness occurs.

3. Consolidate Gains

Just as I need to give myself time on the front end to find the purpose of the session, to clarify the needs, wants and markers of success, it's essential to have sufficient time at the end to sum up well and consolidate the gains of the session. Too often, the end of a typical therapy or counseling session is rushed and incomplete. The therapist is absorbed in the process and loses track of time. Or she keeps advancing the topic, allowing a client to open up one issue after another, without trying to shape it into a plan. If a session ends in a rush, some of the value of the session is lost because there is not time to articulate the results and note the value in a way that a client can retain. All the important objectives may have been met, but then quickly forgotten in the rush of ending or dealing with payment and scheduling.

I take leadership to end the session well. This is my responsibility as the therapist. I watch the time with a purpose in mind: I want to see if our objectives have been met and help my client identify what has been useful and helpful. I want to observe, with the client, what progress has been achieved in this session. I want to anticipate what we can expect for the next time.

When I take time to end this way, summarizing gains, it's not unusual that a client will indicate the she has already forgotten some of what has just been talked about or worked through. This makes sense, because a client is absorbing new ideas, having feelings, and integrating on both a conscious and unconscious level. Finding the right words to sum up may be difficult for a client, so I am willing to collaborate with a client in this task. I can ask if she wants me to share what I will put in my notes. I can prompt her to consider some action steps to take between sessions. Some questions I might use to help this process advance include:

- *What will you take away from our session today?*
- *What did you learn?*
- *How can you use what you learned here today in your life this week?*
- *What does this lead us to do in our next session?*
- *May I share what I think was important about today, what I observed as progress?*
- *Would you like to know what I will be highlighting in my notes about today's session?*

See how this consolidation process took place with Joan below:

LG: We have about 10 minutes left in the session and have talked about a lot today. Let's stop and review what we did. First, I'd like to get your thoughts. How do you feel at this point?

JOAN: I feel a bit relieved. Not as upset as when I started.

LG: Relief is a positive outcome, in my opinion. What about our session offered you some relief?

JOAN: I started with a situation about how I just sit and take my mother's drunken blaming me on a nighttime phone call. I understand some things I need to do. I get that I need to take a time-out, a moment to breathe, and to think, maybe then I can speak up more and not just stay silent and be a sponge.

LG: I agree that these are good actions to know that you can take, rather than staying silent and soaking up her blame. What else was helpful about our conversation?

JOAN: Umm, I'm not sure. I know we covered some other things but right this moment I can't recall.

LG: I observed some additional steps of progress you made during our session. Would it help if I share with you what I will be putting in my notes, so you know what I think is also important about today?

JOAN: Sure.

LG: You said that you wanted to end the session with having some new ideas and ways to think about yourself. I was impressed that you used a very striking metaphor about sailing and how you "shorten the sails" in rough water. You said that in sailing, it helps if you go slow, check your course, and remember that you are the captain of the boat. That was a piece of progress in my mind, that you defined a strong image of yourself, one that you can use in difficult situations like being in the middle of a drunken, late-night phone call.

JOAN: Right, I forgot, that was a good thing for me to say. I want to remember that when I am in that situation. Thanks for reminding me. I like that a lot.

LG: You also talked about why your late-night conversations trigger sadness, and we talked through the connection between this sadness and some other disappointments you have about your life right now, especially with your daughter.

JOAN: Yes, that was helpful, to see the connection between who disappoints me and why, and why my mother's zingers hurt me so much last night.

LG: I think that this is a new topic, and a big one: people who disappoint you and why.

JOAN: It relates to so much I contend with in my life and in my work.

LG: Would this be a topic for us to explore more next time? I can put it in my notes and make sure we come back to it.

JOAN: Yes, good. I also want to follow up on what we said about having control of myself. I know it seems like a small thing, but it is a new idea, that I can take control of myself no matter what is happening. I am a strong sailor and have a hardy boat to steer.

LG: I am so glad you understand this now. It is a sign of self-control, to be a strong sailor of your own boat, of yourself. How could you take an action step toward self-control between our sessions?

JOAN: I am definitely going to try it out during difficult conversations, slowing down the pace, remembering to check in with myself, to stay in control. I won't even need to tell anyone that I am doing it.

LG: I look forward to hearing how this worked and what else you might learn about yourself as you practice this step. Did you get what you wanted today?

JOAN: Yes. Definitely. And more. This was helpful. See you next week.

SPOTTING RESULTS IN A SESSION

Can therapy produce results in every session? A lot depends on how you define results and where you look in order to see progress. I define results as cognitive, behavioral, psychological, or spiritual forward movement that is of a constructive nature. I note any and all large or small steps that are heading in the direction of a desired goal. I stay attentive to these steps forward as the session develops, in the here and now. I will comment on anything that looks like a shift toward personal growth, a display of a strength, a developing skill, or improved capacity. I can take a quick time-out to give a client feedback, right in the moment. I want my clients to see and understand when therapy is producing benefits. During a session, here are things I note, that help me spot results:

- New patterns of behavior in a session. This might mean a direct comment about something I observe: (*"For the first time in our work together, you seem hopeful about your ability to tackle this problem. You are talking about it with some new energy and enthusiasm."*)
- An insight from a client that is different: (*"That sounds like a very important awareness you have just said out loud. Let's stop for a moment just to make sure both you and I are giving this its due."*)
- Demonstrated strengths, such as learning to develop some tolerance of desired behavior. (*"Today you were able to talk about the possibility of confronting your mother directly without feeling guilty. You could see her sad plight without feeling responsible for the choices she has made. That is new and important. Congratulations."*)
- Small steps of progress. (*"You took several steps today in the direction of self-control. May I list them and you can see if you agree?"*)
- Precursors of next steps. (*"I think today you sowed some seeds of assertiveness. There is more that we can talk about to make the process of being assertive easier. Next week I'd like to focus on showing you how to take another helpful step."*)
- Seeing client potential emerge. Shifting needs to include the language of wants. (*"We started with you trying to minimize hurt feelings*

brought on by a drunken late-night phone call, but you have gone beyond setting a boundary to defining what it means to be fully yourself and be captain of your own ship.")

TRACKING CLIENT PROGRESS

I track these and other demonstrations of progress in my client notes, but some therapists also like to use a pre- and post-test, asking clients a series of questions before and after a session and using this as a way of measuring client feedback. Research by Barry Duncan and Scott Miller suggests that asking clients to measure their satisfaction with therapy and the therapist actually improves therapy outcomes. They have specific ideas for ways a client can give honest feedback that is not just offered to please the therapist.[4] If you want to set up a process for formalized feedback, you can find ideas about how to do this from Duncan and Miller[5], or in an article by Tony Rousmaniere (2017) using a computer program that clients can access on a laptop in your waiting room.[6]

Beyond tracking the progress in a single session, I also like to have a sense of progress from my client's perspective, over a longer period of time. With clients in longer-term treatment, I question them to get a sense of our process and their evaluation of the arc of treatment. I do this conversationally, in a therapy session, every three to six months, using a few questions from the list below and put the responses in my notes to track progress. The questions I use include:

How do you feel about continuing to come to therapy?
Do you feel understood and listened to in here?
Is there more about you—your history or your current situation—that I should know?

4 https://www.psychotherapy.net/article/therapy-effectiveness
5 Duncan, Barry and Miller, Scott. When I'm good, I'm very good, but when I'm bad I'm better: A new mantra for psychotherapists. (2008, November). *Psychotherapy in Australia,* 15(1). Retrieved from https://www.psychotherapy.net/article/therapy-effectiveness
6 Rousmaniere, Tony. What your therapist doesn't know. *The Atlantic,* April 2017.

Do our conversations make sense to you?
Are you satisfied with the results you are getting?
Is there anything I can do better, as your therapist, to help you stay
*   involved with your treatment?*

In the Worksheet section of this book, review the Getting-to-Yes Session Plan to give you an easy way to implement it within your practice. With the completion of this chapter, you have a basic foundation for Therapy with a Coaching Edge. You have learned how to:

- Understand the distinctions and crossover between coaching and therapy and how to define a coaching approach.
- Determine suitability for those clients who can benefit from a coaching approach in therapy and how to make sure you, as the therapist, are also a good fit for this model.
- Shift into a partnership position for better collaboration by using a number of techniques while staying aligned with therapy ethics, principles, and boundaries.
- Set up a therapy session with a plan that leverages results, session by session, to improve client satisfaction and retention.

Now it's time to move forward and learn nine specific skills, the heart of this model. You will see three sections devoted to skills for partnership, action, and possibility: when combined with the foundation and techniques that increase client control, this gives your therapy the advantage of a coaching approach. After you finish reading about a skill, see the corresponding worksheet in the final section, which compiles the important points of the skill for easier implementation.

The first skills section, skills for partnership, builds on the concept of therapist-client collaboration. The section begins with a skill that is a key to being proactive and taking leadership; a refined technique of asking sharp, effective questions that can increase the pace of a session, challenge limiting beliefs, or generate an "ah-ha" moment of deeper insight for your client.

Part 2

Skills for Partnership

6

Skill #1: Ask Effective Questions

Before Leah began her first therapy session, I had a message on my voicemail from her referring physician. "Leah seems under a lot of stress. She is a young lawyer, and I am sure the stress is due to her job. You know how hard lawyers work these days, and she is still a new associate. I am concerned for her and suggested she find a new job, one that is less intense. I told her I wanted her to talk to a therapist and gave her your name."

Leah followed through on her doctor's suggestion and called to schedule an appointment. At the first session, when I asked Leah to tell me why she was coming to therapy, she said she was stressed.

I took a moment to clarify. "Your doctor thinks the stress is due to your job and suggests you find a new work situation. Do you agree?"

Leah was silent for a full minute. I let her take her time and watched her frown, deep in thought. "No, I have been thinking about this, and I don't think he is right," she finally said. "My job is actually the easiest part of my life; I like my boss and am challenged by the work. I don't think I overwork. I exercise daily. But I am in a new marriage. I waited a long time to get married and feel insecure about how it is going. I actually feel worse when I am home in the evenings and on the weekends than when I am at work. I don't want to find a new job or stop the work I am doing. That would be awful for me."

"How did your doctor get it so wrong?"

"I don't know. I have some digestive symptoms. He asked if I was stressed, but didn't ask why. When he found out I was a lawyer, he made up his own mind about what was causing the stress in my life."

Oh, the importance of asking the right questions. At the heart of therapy is our willingness to ask a lot of questions, born out of a curiosity to learn who the client is and what he or she needs and wants in order to heal. But in my training as a clinical social worker, most of my questions were passive: They didn't necessarily move a session forward. I asked questions to reiterate, clarify, and reflect on what was said. I supported the client and focused on building rapport. I rarely used a question to challenge or provoke. Sometimes, I would stumble onto a question that had a big impact in a session, what I might call a powerful or effective question. My client might go silent in response, or burst into tears, or need to think hard before answering. I could see how helpful a question like this could be. Just by dint of asking, my client might get an entirely new perspective on a difficult problem. At first, it seemed like magic. A good question would just pop into my mind. It was random, hit or miss.

It wasn't until I became a coach that I learned that there was a skill to developing and asking a question that had this type of impact. I liked honing my skill and knowing what and how to ask. Not every session needed such pointed questions, but it was a great tool to have. With this skill, the ability to ask a powerful question, I became a more confident and proactive partner for change.

In this chapter, I show you the elements of this coaching skill, which I have modified for therapeutic use. You will see three categories of effective questions. I give you lists of questions, which you can use, adapt, or add to. I also show you how to bring these questions into a therapy conversation by following up on the case of Leah, so you can see how my use of just a few effective questions helped her rethink and resolve her stressful marriage.

POSSIBLE QUESTIONS

As a therapist, my work life is full of questions, asked and hopefully answered. Similar to most therapists, I know how to ask open versus closed-ended questions and how to use gentle questions to build rapport and trust. In a therapy session, I want to create safety. I don't question like a prosecutor or interrogate. I avoid questions that are too leading, or show therapist bias, in favor of those that allow the client to answer openly and honestly.

Questions I could use with Leah might reflect what has been already been said. ("You have lived with significant anxiety your entire life, so you are a good judge of the sources of your own stress, correct?") Or they can be more strategic, to advance the conversation. ("Is there something we could discuss about the difficulties in your new marriage?")

I could use the "miracle question" often posed by solution-focused therapists. ("If a miracle happened and this problem of stress vanished right now, how would life be different?") Or a scaling question used by many trained in CBT: ("On a scale of 0 to 10, how would you rate the degree of difficulty in finding a way to relax with your husband on weekends?") Or I could ask an uncovering question used by those psychodynamically oriented. ("Why is this problem surfacing now?") Some questions buy time, such as a standard therapy question ("How do you feel about that?" or "Can you tell me more?") to help a client talk more so I can listen and think. But as I mentioned, some questions pack a punch. Coaching questions have a style of their own. They are powerful and can activate a conversation. They are often prospective, forward-facing, focusing on the immediate present and beyond, into the future. I want you to have this tool in your therapeutic toolbox, to know how to ask a question that helps a client stop and think, or gets a client to drop deeper into feelings in order to find a constructive solution.

Powerful Questions

When I started to study to become a coach, I learned how critical it was to ask questions that could give me leverage. Since coaching requires results in a single session, knowing how to use questions to move a session forward, fast, was important. In my research through the coaching literature, I found that powerful questions used by coaches fit into one of three categories, with the intention to:

- Create sudden insight.
- Challenge existing beliefs.
- Prompt new options.

As a coach, I learned to use these categories to stimulate a client to think differently in the moment. A strong question, from one of these categories, could have lasting effects.[1] The right question accelerated thoughts and awareness. I really liked having a tool that could help me "supercharge" a coaching session. I wanted to bring this skill of asking a powerful question into some of my therapy sessions. But first I had to adapt it.

A therapy session, unlike a coaching session, needs to offer a client a safe space. I wondered how I could ask a strong, even piercing question, but do it within a healing framework, while maintaining rapport. For therapy, I experimented with finding questions that could let me be proactive in a session, but respect the bond I needed to maintain with a client. When I adapted a set of questions for therapy, clients appreciated the input. They said things like "that's a good question," or "let me think," and sometimes, one single question shifted the entire direction of therapy. I began to keep a list of adapted coaching questions that seemed incisive, but also relational. Many of them energized a session. I found that the way I asked a question, not just the question itself, was one way to safeguard our bond.

How to Ask

To use effective questions in a therapy session, I do some preparation. I look over a list of questions and keep a few in mind. You will see examples of my questions in each of the three categories at the end of this chapter. When I ask a question, I do it with intention. I speak up and make sure that I have eye contact with my client. I am quiet afterwards. I listen carefully to the answer, and then use active listening to reflect or validate what is said. Only after validating a response, using active listen-

---

1 Clutterbuck, D. (2012). *What makes a powerful question?* Retrieved from https://www.davidclutterbuckpartnership.com/what-makes-a-powerful-question/

ing and letting my client have a full awareness of what has been said, will I ask another powerful question.

I resist a common mistake of therapists to "stack questions"—to ask several questions at once or in a row. Doing that dilutes the effectiveness of a single question. My suggestion is to pick one to ask, and make sure it is clear, and direct. Ask it with emphasis. Wait for the response. Don't get anxious if there is a pause. The right question causes a client to stop and think, or stop and feel. Listen to the verbal answer but also attend to any nonverbal reactions that may need to be processed and recognized, like a bark of laughter or tears.

When I use one of these questions, I don't already know the answer. This is a collaboration. I allow the question to spark new information and awareness for both my client and myself. Asking the right question is a journey of discovery for us both, another form of partnership. The question I ask may be perceived as provocative or even momentarily jarring to my client, who might respond with: "Huh? Where did that come from?" If this happens, I wait it out. I don't feel pressured to immediately respond or soften the question with an explanation. I let my client have some time to absorb the question. Using a question to fulfill the first goal, to create sudden insight, can heighten a client's awareness quickly. It can promote intense self-reflection, which studies link to an "ah-ha" moment,[2] when a well-timed, well-placed question generates a client-driven solution.

Create Sudden Insight

In her next session, Leah explains that she and her husband are newly married and arguing frequently, and she tells me she usually starts the arguments and then he accommodates her in any way he can, to keep the peace. She gives me a recent example: She was upset with her husband over a minor disagreement this week and it is still "gnawing" at her. (Note: As you read the transcript below, see the effective question I use

---

2 Danek, A. Fraps, T., von Müller, A., Grothe, B., & Öllinger, M. (2014). It's a kind of magic—what self-reports can reveal about the phenomenology of insight problem solving. *Frontiers in Psychology,* 5.| https://doi.org/10.3389/fpsyg.2014.01408

to create sudden insight with Leah, set in italics. At the end of this chapter, you will find a list of questions for sudden insight.)

LG: What troubles you the most about this particular argument?

LEAH: I don't understand why he can't just listen to me. I told him I needed to leave the house and make one stop before we met our friends for dinner. He said we could leave later if we went another way to deal with traffic. That made me mad. I told him when I wanted to leave, and I like to be on time. I don't need him to figure things out for me. I have reasons for what I plan to do.

LG: It seems that you wanted to be in control and had a plan in place you didn't want to change.

LEAH: I need to be in control. I am not a go-with-the-flow type of person. I am protective.

LG: Who were you protecting with this exchange between yourself and your husband?

LEAH: I need to protect myself at all times.

LG: (I wait a beat, to let her response above sink in for both of us. I ask this next question with direct eye contact and a bit of intensity.) *Is that really your truth?*

LEAH: (Long pause, indicating self-reflection.) What do you mean?

LG: (I stay silent, waiting. If this works as I hope, it may evoke a deeper response.)

LEAH: Am I sure I need to protect myself all the time, you mean?

LG: Yes. (I refrain from adding more questions, to let the question land.)

LEAH: Well, it feels like I do. It feels true. Let me think about this. I got mad when he made a suggestion. He immediately backed down. I keep thinking that when he asks me a question, he is attacking me. Then I feel like I better fight back and protect myself from him. I build a wall. The truth is that I build a wall with my anger. This is so sad. He is actually kind to me. The truth is that he tries to help me, I know he does. Lynn, I have been building a wall from the only gentle, loving person I have had in my life, ever.

LG: (Now I validate.) This is an important awareness. You have been protecting yourself from a gentle and loving person.

LEAH: He is on my side. He is on my side. (She starts to cry, a signal of increased self-awareness.)

LG: It's hard to recognize loving support, when you are in armor and ready for an attack. What are you learning about yourself and your marriage today?

LEAH: It's time to lay down my shield. I am safer than I understood.

This is an example of how one simple, but strong question, asked with intensity *"Is that really your truth?"* can open up an ah-ha moment of great importance. Notice my use of silence, to help respect the processing that Leah was going through. I needed to give her time to rethink the question, to find her answer. As she processed her response, I also introduced the reframe of "loving support," a new way for Leah to think about her husband's suggestions, instead of labeling them as an attack.

Challenge Existing Belief

At the next session, a week later, Leah says that she feels closer to her husband, but now she recognizes that when she is home, she is often in a bad mood. She feels put upon, that she is doing more than her share of the work at home. She seems to have a belief about what is and is not fair. I use a few questions that can challenge existing beliefs, to see if some new cognition can emerge. (Note: As you read the transcript below, please see that the questions I use to challenge existing beliefs with Leah are in italics. At the end of this chapter, you will find a short list of questions you can use for this same result.)

LG: Tell me more about your bad mood.

LEAH: I work hard and when I get home, I wish my husband would help me out more.

LG: You want more help from your husband. That makes sense. Does he work, too?

LEAH: Yes, he works the same hours that I do, but he has an easier job.

LG: You think your job is harder?

LEAH: I am sure it is. This week, we agreed about the weekly chores, you know, who is doing laundry this week, me, and who is doing shopping, him. But then the week comes and after work and the gym, I don't feel like doing the laundry. I just want to listen to music or play a game on the computer. Even though he did the shopping as we agreed, I don't think it is a big deal if I don't do the laundry. If he is so intent on it getting done, he can do it. He says he is tired too, but I am sure it is not the same as me. His job is not as hard as mine. He is a lot stronger and he has less stress. Don't forget, I had a lousy childhood and I worked at two jobs all through college and law school. He grew up in a very nice family. No wonder I need more downtime than he does.

LG: There are a lot of expectations in this situation as you describe it, about who is strong and who is weak, who should do less and who should do more, who has it harder, who had it easier in life.

LEAH: Yeah, I guess. With the chores, my husband says I am not playing fair. He says that I go back on my agreements. I explain over and over why I need more downtime and that I have had a harder life than he has. I wish he would grow up. Life ain't fair. We argue a lot about this.

LG: (I am going to challenge her a bit. I make direct eye contact and ask this in a calm, but gentle voice.) *Where did you learn to argue about who has the harder life?*

LEAH: (Silent, thinking first for a long moment.) That's a good question. I never thought about it, but I guess from my dad. When I complained about anything, he always said that I had it easy, he was raised in a much worse situation, a family of drunks and terrible fighting.

LG: He told you about his hard life when you complained.

LEAH: He didn't really make things easy for me. We moved five times in ten years when I was growing up. I never wanted to move and change schools, but my Dad kept getting fired from jobs. When I was in a bad mood, when I would come home from school, lonely and sad, he would just say to suck it up, that no one had it harder than him. He said he had a hard life and if he needed to quit his job, he still put bread on the table and deserved my total support. We argued about this, but he always won, because his life was worse and he was in charge.

LG: That sounds like a very tough situation for a growing girl to be in. You were moving constantly, starting over, lonely at school, yet having to reassure your father that his problems were the ones that mattered. This kind of thinking is what I call the "rule of worst"—whoever had it the worst, rules. Your Dad told you he had it the worst, so he should rule.

LEAH: Exactly.

LG: Now you tell your husband you have it the worst. *What do you gain by repeating this old pattern of behavior?*

LEAH: (Another long silence.) I am not happy about this, but what I gain is that I get to win, like my dad did. I get to rule. I feel like I am due for a break. It's my turn to slack off. But that's really not fair to my husband. (Another long silence.) What worries me is what I might lose if I keep doing this. I need to stop this pattern. Can you help?

With two well-timed questions, I help Leah explore a long-held belief about the primacy of self-pity. The "rule of the worst" has unseen costs for her. I am being proactive in asking these pointed questions, but also encouraging a level of partnership between us. I am direct but compassionate. I challenge her in order to strengthen her. With each client, you will need to assess your level of rapport in using these kinds of questions. For example, Leah seems to respond well to me. We have moments of nonverbal connection in these early sessions: a smile, a shared nodding of the head, a concerned look on my face. Notice that between questions, I validate and acknowledge each of her responses to preserve a relational bond between us. Using some confrontation is a bit of a risk in therapy, but with Leah, I watch to see how she receives this approach. I try to reach a part of her that is strong enough to rise to a challenge and think about these tough questions, in her desire to make a change.

Once a belief system is challenged, the right question can shift a client toward a new course of constructive action. To go from speculation ("what if?") to motivation ("how soon?") requires asking a question to promote new possibilities.

Prompt New Options

After a few weeks, Leah reports she is still working on her marriage, trying to change her behavior that is contributing to the arguments between her and her husband. She wants to make amends and be nicer to her husband to break the cycle of conflict, but she is not sure how to take the first step in the direction of being more caring. I use a few effective questions to help her think of new behaviors to satisfy her goal. (Note: The questions I use to prompt options are noted in italics. At the end of this chapter, you will find a short list of questions you can use for this same goal.)

LEAH: I wish my husband and I could do some nice things together. Like a date night now and then. We both work hard, and I try to think of things we could do together, but just can't find the right way to approach him. I wish he would take the first step and approach me.

LG: You want to have a date night, but wish he would take the first step.

LEAH: Yes, we need to have more fun as a couple to balance out the hard times.

LG: Having a goal of bringing balance to the marriage seems positive and loving.

LEAH: Now if I only had the courage to start the conversation.

LG: You aren't sure you have the courage to do this. It might help to rehearse a bit. I am curious. *What is the biggest, boldest way you could start the conversation of a date night?*

LEAH: (blushing and smiling): Well, I would never do this, but I could ask him to come into the bedroom, be in a sexy nighty, and say something like, "Hey sweetheart, want to make a plan to have some fun?" Hah! He would probably jump my bones. He always says we don't have enough sex, so if I tied this to sex, he would agree to anything. But that is not really what I want to do.

LG: So, making this a sexy request would be a big and bold way to begin, but not one that you would probably do.

LEAH: No, I really just want this to be a time for talking, not sex.

LG: Got it. Let's try it again, just rehearsing. *What is the easiest, smallest step you could take to start the conversation?*

LEAH: I could ask him if there is anything he would like me to plan for the weekend, something that would be fun for him.

LG: You could shift the focus to finding something he especially likes to do.

LEAH: Yes, I could even say that he has done so much for me lately, I want to do something back for him.

LG: You could make it even more explicit, that this is an attempt to give him a gift of your time and attention.

LEAH: Yes, I kind of like this. It takes some of the pressure off of me. It can go one way, from me to him at first. That would be kind of nice right now.

LG: Now the big question: *Are you ready to take a risk?*

LEAH: You mean really do this?

LG: Yes. (I answer with one word and then allow for some silence, to let her think and feel.)

LEAH: I think I am ready to take this risk. This is a big step, but I want to try. I will do this and let you know what happens.

By keeping the questions experimental ("what is the boldest step, what is the easiest step?"), Leah can brainstorm about this process without committing. We are just talking about ideas, and she is generating possible solutions. When I move the idea forward by asking a pointed question, to see if she is ready to take a risk, she gets a bit nervous. But the question is asked. She can't ignore my prompt. At the next session, she reports she took a risk, it was well received, and they had a much-needed date night as a couple.

Your Turn: Ask Effective Questions
Use this exercise to master the skill.

1. Below, see lists of questions below in each category to:
   - Create sudden insight.
   - Challenge existing beliefs.
   - Prompt new options.
2. Find a question you could use, or add an effective question of your own choosing to the following list.
3. Keep a question or two in mind during a therapy session to use when needed. Ask the question clearly, with eye contact and then stay silent to let the client respond. Allow the question to land and be absorbed. Listen and learn from your client's response.

4. Don't stack questions. Ask one at a time and then use active listening to reflect, acknowledge, or validate what is said in response. Maintain rapport, even in the midst of asking a pointed or powerful question.

Questions to Create Sudden Insight:

Is that really your truth?

What makes you so certain?

What might be equally true?

What or who might be missing from the way you tell this story?

Does the way you tell the story of your childhood do you justice?

In the big picture of your life, what or who matters most?

Who is in control of your life today?

Who are you when you are at your best?

Do you love yourself conditionally, unconditionally, or not at all?

If you could love yourself more, would it make a difference in your life?

If you had no fear, what would you want to accomplish before you die?

What do you need to accept, once and for all, about your life?

How do you know if you are seeing all sides of an issue?

What are you not saying that needs to be voiced right now?

What childhood story can you let go of?

What new connections are you making as we talk about this?

Questions to Challenge Existing Beliefs:

Who taught you to believe this?

Whose opinion matters now?

Is your belief based on fear or on love?

Could your belief be an excuse for bad behavior?

Why are you certain you are right?

What if the opposite is true?

Was there ever a time you took your own side first?

What do you gain by repeating your old pattern of behavior, and what do you lose?

If you were (braver, smarter, richer, etc.) what would you do differently?

Are you strong enough to fail?

Would you rather be right or be loved?

What question, if answered correctly, would help you change your mind?

Is there anyone's opinion on this issue that matters more than your own?

Based on what you believe, can you act with integrity?

How will you measure your life in 20 years?

Questions that Prompt New Options:

Are you ready to take a risk?

What is possible for you in this regard?

What seems impossible for you in this regard?

What is the easiest way to move forward on this goal?

Can you try another way entirely?

What resources do you need to make this a success?

Can you add more passion to the plan?

What is a win-win solution for all involved?

What are you waiting for?

Is this goal based on your head or your heart?

What is the biggest step you could take?

What is the safest step you could take?

What is the best possible outcome?

Who do you need to be to take this to the next level?

How can you bring more of your (essence, talent, creativity, spirit, total commitment) to this plan?

Who will you become after you have accomplished this goal?

Now that you have the steps and script for asking effective questions, let's move forward to the next coaching skill. It builds on this one. I want to show you how to take this proactive questioning technique and use it to heighten the strategic aspect of your work. Being a strategist is an effective way to offer a client collaboration and support, especially if you can do it with a coaching approach.

7

Skill #2: Be a Strategist with a Twist

How does a therapist, especially one trained to be empathic, receptive, and attuned to emotions, learn to also become a savvy strategist, one who is directive, innovative, and tactical?

Our clients come to us when faced with problems that they can't solve on their own. One collaborative role is being the person who offers strategic partnership, knowing how to help a client uncover hidden options and find good solutions to intractable issues. The challenge is to be a strategist who does more than advise or tell a client what to do: To promote partnership, you need to be a strategist with the ability to apply a coaching approach, to make strategizing client-driven, so that a client can find his or her own solution with your facilitation.

By focusing your strategizing on client-based control, partnership, action, and possibility, clients can take a big step from being passive to proactive. You provide a framework and your assistance, but they set the direction on their own terms. In this chapter, I explain how a therapist can comfortably assume the role of strategist, without imposing bias, judgment, or personal designs. I will show you the specific type of strategic listening and strategic thinking that I use—an adaptation of pure coaching that I tailored for psychotherapy. Offering clients the right kind of strategic help can be life changing for them. I should know, because I was once in need of strategic partnership myself, to help me figure out a very thorny problem. The strategic help I was lucky enough to acquire ultimately changed my life.

THE WAY OF THE STRATEGIST

Prior to becoming a therapist, I was in my first real career, and it was a tough one. I was working for my father in his scrap metal yard, as his general manager. I wore a hard hat and steel-toed shoes. This was the family business, a lucrative endeavor to be sure, and he had given me a job after I graduated college. I was late in graduating, having left home at 18 for adventure and returned at 25, broke, with a 4-year-old son in tow. I was a single parent and my dad was kind enough to hire me, after I went back to finish college. I knew I needed to make a decent income, but the rough-and-tumble world of scrap metal did not suit me well, although I learned a lot about business and management during the time I was there. After six years on the job, working 45-plus hours a week, I was exhausted and depressed. I had gone back to therapy to help me overcome my depression. I loved therapy, and privately, I longed to become a therapist. But how could I do this? I had to keep working. I considered going to night school to get my master's in social work (MSW), which would turn a two-year degree into a five-year process, requiring me to work full-time and leave my son at home many nights of the week. Given the stress and unsuitability of the current job and the many needs of my son, that was not feasible.

I let go of this goal, my desire to be a therapist. But one evening, I was reading a book about Neuro-Linguistic Programming and I came across a very powerful question posed by the author, a good question for anyone facing a big, impossible goal: "What would it take?" he asked. This was the perfect question for me. What would it take for me to get my MSW and become a therapist? I didn't know the answer. I couldn't think it through by myself. I couldn't think of a plan that was possible. However, I had a wonderful friend, someone who could help me, a professional strategic planner, Cathy Lange, now a leadership coach in her own company.

One Sunday afternoon in 1985, Cathy came to my home to ply her craft. By the end of the day I had a plan, one so bold I could never have devised it on my own. Most of it seemed like a dream. But I had it on paper so I could study it. Now all that was required was for me to become the person who could implement this wild plan. One more (small) problem: I was not yet that person, the one who could manifest this plan. My asset was that I was in psychotherapy and I was open to change. I had a therapist who was willing to help me become braver and be a risk taker. I would need all the courage I could muster.

A year later, I was successfully enrolled in a full-time MSW program. What did it take? I quit my job, which was very difficult given that my boss was my father and he had invested a lot in my training and development; quitting hurt his feelings deeply. I sold my house, a house I loved. I moved one state away, found a new school for my son, bought a cheaper house, an inexpensive car, and converted all my savings to cash. I had just enough money for one year of graduate school and living expenses. I could take classes during the day and be with my son in the evening. I was exhilarated and very, very anxious. I didn't know what would happen and how I would afford the second year of the MSW program.

Who did I need to become? Someone willing to bet on the future, to take a big risk in service of my goal. How did I do it? I stayed in therapy, made a commitment to the plan, followed the steps, and did not give up. It all worked out for me, but without the help of Cathy, a partnering strategist, it would never have occurred to me to know how to begin. This is the essence of strategizing: being a partner who can see the what, the who, and the how.

Since that time, I have looked at the process of strategizing to understand how I could adapt it, using a coaching approach, for the way that I do therapy. In doing so, I have found ways to partner as a strategist with many of my therapy clients, to help them go far beyond their limitations and realize their dreams and goals. Rather than advising and being directive, I have looked for a process where they could maintain control. I facilitate a process of strategy, but my clients are in charge of the outcome. The first step is learning how to listen as a strategist. This listening requires a mindset of calm, to listen as one of my favorite Shawn Colvin songs says, with "one cool remove away."

Strategic Listening and Thinking

To offer strategic partnership in my model, to listen as a strategist *and* as a therapist, you need to separate the problem a client is trying to resolve from the attending emotions, upset, and drama that may surround the problem. Both deserve attention, but if you get caught in the web of the emotion and the side issues of personalities and relationships that complicate the basic issue, your ability to be strategic disappears. The emotions and complications are therapeutic material and may need to be addressed, but not while you are being strategic. When you take on the partnering role of a strategist, your first attention is to listen so that the problem gets simplified. Listen to the salient facts. Have curiosity, but don't get distracted by the complexities.

I know that for some therapists, this type of strategic listening may feel cold; you might feel that it distances you from your client. If it feels like this, you are probably doing it correctly. You should be cool (maybe not cold) and at a slight remove (understanding, but detached). Sit back (literally lean back a bit in your chair). Stay cognitive. Simplify the aspects of an issue. What is the essence of core of the issue, stated constructively as a goal, in neutral terms?

For example, when Cathy was listening to me bemoan my situation at the scrap yard, instead of hearing all my feelings about not wanting to disappoint my father, my guilt, my exhaustion from long days, my worry about how my son would handle a move, or my firm belief that I was stuck forever, she heard: Lynn wants to leave her current job and get an MSW. She put aside her sympathy and caring for me, momentarily, to consider the basic goal. That made the issue easier for her to begin to examine.

With this cooler listening in place, it is easier to focus on three simple questions that form the basis of a strategic skill: defining the what, the who, and the how of any problem. As I listen, I think about the problem in this way:

1. What is the problem, stated simply and clearly in the present?
2. Who is the client, in terms of strengths, assets, and resources?
3. How can the client start to see options to get to the goal?

To bring in a coaching approach to strategy means that I also let my clients in on the process. My role is to help them find their own answers to these questions, with my support and at times, my leadership. In the following example of a therapy session with my client Valeria, another single mother feeling stuck with a different issue, you can see how I used strategic listening (to separate the issue from the emotion) and strategic thinking (to reflect on the who, what and how) to help her shift her stuck perspective. Here is each step and then the way I used strategic partnership with Valeria.

1. What: State the Problem in the Present

Seeing the "what" of a problem can be a challenge—stating it in the present, without emotion that carries over from the past (such as regret, resentment, or sadness) or worries about the future (such as fear and anxiety). Letting the problem breathe free of any and all complicated emotion can help to make the issue easier to understand and more manageable. This means that as the therapist, you need to see all that is involved, including the client's negative and positive beliefs, intentional and unconscious associations, and blame or judgment. Then put all of that to the side, momentarily. Without the "white noise" of all that surrounds the issue, a problem gets simpler. It is reduced to a basic setback or challenge.

In my coach training, this acceptance via simplification was called "making the present perfect"—giving up how things could, should, or would be better and accepting how things are, without added bias. Another formulation for thinking about the what of a problem is to use a Buddhist framework, where this type of present perfect acceptance is called "cause and condition." When standing before a flower in my garden, the *cause* is the seed that turned into the flower. The *condition* that made it possible for the seed to grow is water, dirt, and sunlight. Both cause and condition are equally true in the present moment of the flower. In the following transcript, my client Valeria explains her problem, and I help her simplify and clarify it to make it easier for her to begin to find a direction forward.

VALERIA: I want to go be with my family, back in Texas. I miss them and think about them all the time. I am lonely all the time. They miss me, too. But I have a good job here, on the East Coast. I love my work. I am on a career track and there are no jobs like this for me back home. I am divorced and have a young son. He is in first grade. So, I live in limbo. Do I stay or do I go? I want both but I can't have both.

LG: Tell me about your life as it is right now.

VALERIA: I work a lot and I take care of my son. His father remarried and he is not in the area. He is not involved in my son's life at all, so I take care of everything by myself. I live in an apartment close to my job and I have to be on call often, so I don't plan much on the weekends. My son has some friends in school, he is a sweet and happy little boy. My closest girlfriends live in Texas near my family. We chat online, but it is not the same. I am alone and this is not my natural way of being. I love family. I am proud of my work and my career. I have a good position at work, my boss supports me, I just got a big bonus. I am good at my job. I don't want to lose what I have built in my savings and financial independence. I am terrified of what it would mean if I were to let go of this job and leave. But I am homesick and miss my family and my friends. I don't see any way to resolve this.

LG: I know this must feel very complicated for you, with so much involved. I wonder if we can simplify the problem a bit, as a way to help you find your own answers.

VALERIA: Okay, you can try that.

LG: You have three big loves in your life right now: your family, your son, and your job.

VALERIA: They are all very important to me. I love them all.

LG: I like your clarity on stating their importance. Next, you spend a lot of time wishing that these three big loves could exist in the same place, within the same city, close at hand.

VALERIA: Yes, that is what I want, for everything to be together, all that I love.

LG: Good, we are understanding this in the same way. Since that isn't reality, you are currently unhappy and unsettled. Do I have this in the right order?

VALERIA: (Thinking.) Yes, I guess that is the truth of this. I like your word, that I am unsettled. I love all these things, they are separate, so I am unsettled. Yes, it seems a bit simpler put this way. One, two, three.

LG: Does it make a difference to you, to think about this problem in a simpler way?

VALERIA: I was thinking that when you said I have these three loves, that are all important to me, how these are good things to love: my family, my job, and my son And these things I love, they are all doing well. I don't have to worry about them. My family in Texas is okay, my son is doing fine, my job is very good. The only thing that is not fine is me.

LG: Given the way you are now looking at this, you see that these are good things for a person to love, and they are all doing well. The only problem, the only thing not doing well right now, is you, or more clearly, how you feel inside.

VALERIA: Yes. That is the big difference between seeing this the way you said, in a simpler way, and how I normally think about this. I normally think about all the things that are part of this. I think about others at home and my son and whether they are okay. I feel like a bad daughter for being so far away. I feel guilty when I can't go visit more often because I have responsibilities with my job. But in this way of thinking, the only problem is a smaller one. That I am unhappy. Nothing else is wrong right in this moment except what is going on inside of me.

LG: (Now I ask a pointed question geared toward the "what" of the strategy.) *What would it take to fix your unhappiness?*

VALERIA: I would normally say I can't be happy unless and until I have all these things put together, but after talking with you I see that maybe I need to think differently. They can't be put together. Maybe I could be happy in another way. I just don't know how.

LG: I appreciate that you are able to shift your perspective for a moment and see this in a new way. I also heard the beginnings of a very important idea, whether you could be happy in another way. I hope we can talk about that more.

2. Who: Identify Inner Strengths

In my experience, almost any big goal a client wants that is not yet fulfilled, usually has a missing element: The client needs to become someone slightly different, in terms of ability or personality, to accomplish this goal. The boon to being a strategist and a therapist is that you are positioned to help in both regards. You can help clients identify goals and then focus on therapy methods that allow your client to become a person who can set and meet the new goals. All of this, both strategy and inner work, is well within a therapist's purview.

I am convinced that with the right listening and questioning from me, Valeria will solve this issue herself. I listen with cool remove, and stay focused on the what, who, and how steps of strategy. I trust in her capacity to resolve her goal and ask questions and reflect her answers. She will do the rest, to determine her path. Already, without much prompting, she has shifted into the second stage, the who of strategy: When she wonders if she could be happy in another way, this means that she is poised to consider who she is and her part in the problem. My next step as strategist is eliciting Valeria's inner resources. I want to help her focus on any strength or asset that can help.

LG: Have you ever found a way to be happier about a difficult situation?

VALERIA: Yes, the most obvious is when the father of my child, my ex, decided to relocate and that meant he would not have contact with our son. I was really devastated for my son. But I realized that all I could do was try to be a good mother. I decided to make sure he had some other men in his life. I have a cousin in town, and we stay close to him. He is like a dad to my son in certain ways. When we go home, my own father is close to my son. I am happy about these two things and it consoles me.

LG: That's a great example. To help your son, you decided to provide him with good relationships with the people who were available to him. You filled in the gaps of a missing father.

VALERIA: Yes, I did. I think this is why I miss my family so much. They could bond with him more and fill in more gaps.

LG: I am curious. Who fills in the gaps for you?

VALERIA: (silence and tears) No one. I am pretty lonely.

LG: Does addressing that loneliness need to a part of your solution?

VALERIA: That would change things a lot.

LG: (Here is a powerful question geared toward the "who" of a strategy.) *Who would you need to become to be a person who is less lonely, no matter where you live?*

VALERIA: (thinking) I would need to be less shy and more outgoing. I would like to be that way. It would be a big change for me and probably help me a lot, no matter where I live. I have more to work on in therapy, I see.

3. How: See the Options

Valeria is starting to open herself to more ideas about her problem and specifically, who she needs to become: how to be less shy, find people to fill in her gaps, and find ways to be happy no matter where she is. I wonder if, between sessions, any new thoughts will surface. Sometimes these early steps in strategy—simplifying a problem and finding inner resources—can, on their own, stimulate more choices and options. At our next session, I start with a check-in, to see what may have changed in her awareness over the week.

LG: You left our session last time with some new ideas. Has anything else occurred for you about this issue, since our session?

VALERIA: I was very struck by you saying how alone I am here. I focus on work and on my son, but have yet to ever meet new friends or think about dating again. When you asked who filled in my gap, it brought tears to my eyes. It's no wonder I am so homesick. I thought about this all week and you will be surprised . . . at least, I am. I did something new. I joined the neighborhood association. I had seen the flyers before, but never joined because I felt that my living here was temporary, in my apartment. I was probably not going to be here long. So why bother to make any friends? But I decided that even if I leave, I could stand to make a friend or two.

LG: That is a definite shift from your old behavior. You took a step to be outgoing. You moved forward on this decision very fast.

VALERIA: I guess I did, didn't I?

LG: It's good for me to know you have this ability, to see something that is missing and then take a step forward right away. That is a real strength, to see it and do it. From this place of strength, are there any other helpful options you can see?

VALERIA: To be happier?

LG: Yes. To be happier.

VALERIA: I was thinking of one other thing I could do. I am scared to say this out loud, it feels so big. Okay, here goes. I want to buy a house, one that would have several bedrooms, and then ask my mother and father to come and stay with me for a month each year. I miss them a lot. I don't have room for them now—we are in a small one-bedroom apartment. I never owned a home, and it is a big financial risk. I don't know anything about real estate. But the idea that I could make this city a second home base for my family, maybe it could be the family base in the summer, when Texas is terribly hot. Anyway, I am very excited and scared and thrilled that I could even think to do this, to claim that this is my home and they could come here and share it with me. What do you think?

LG: I think it is a big, important goal. I can see how it could make you happier.

VALERIA: Do you think I could do this?

LG: I would like to turn the question around for you to answer. But I wonder: Which part of you will answer? Could we hear from the strong Valeria who joined the neighborhood association?

VALERIA: Oh my gosh. That part of me would probably say yes. I could see a way to actually do this. I might need some help to figure it out fully. Could you help me think it through?

Over more sessions, Valeria and I spend time defining her plan. Our conversation moves back and forth between what needs to happen next in the plan (finding a loan) and who she needs to be in order to take the step (able to calm her anxiety and talk to a mortgage lender). After each session, I always ask a question, to further the "how" of the strategy, for example "How easily could you take the next step?" By using a coaching approach, I make sure that my role as a strategist gives Valeria the ultimate control over any plan. She develops and writes a plan, using a simple format of S.M.A.R.T. goals: specific, measurable, achievable, results-focused and time-bound.[1] I stay involved, as a strategic partner, by asking questions, tracking her answers, and encouraging her to consider the full level of change that might be needed to see new possibilities. My role is to remain constructive and positive, to model making the present perfect. When Valeria's difficult emotions surface, we process them. When she needs to slow down, we stop and review, so she can find her place and get reoriented to so much change. Step by step, she moves forward and in the process, becomes a more proactive, confident person regarding this issue of consolidating all she loves.

Your Turn: Be a Strategist with a Twist
Use this exercise to master the skill.

1. *Listen strategically.* Detach slightly from the emotions and complications of a difficult client issue to hear its basic elements.
2. *Think strategically.* Think about the what, who, and how as you talk with your client:
   What is the problem, stated simply and clearly in the present?
   Who is the client, in terms of strengths, assets, and resources?
   How can the client start to see options to get to the goal?
3. *Use a coaching approach.* Make sure that your role as a strategist continues to give your client sufficient control over any personal plan. Don't get ahead of the client or get overly attached to any aspect of the plan. Be encouraging of any and all small steps heading in the right direction. Use therapy sessions for accountability as needed, to support next steps.
4. *Ask effective questions geared to strategy.* See a list of additional questions below that can help a client become more proactive. Use the question-asking process outlined in Skill #1 to allow the questions to land well and have an impact.
5. *Encourage your client to use a written goal-based format for tracking.* Use a format to track and measure goals such as Doran's S.M.A.R.T. goals.

---

1 Doran, G. T. (1981). There's a S.M.A.R.T. way to write management's goals and objectives. *Management Review*, 70(11). 35-36.

Questions for Strategizing

If you rise above the emotional complications, what is the truth about your present situation?

How can you state the problem at its core?

Now that you see the heart of the issue, what do you really want?

What would it take to make this happen?

Who do you need to become to make this happen?

What are five existing opportunities you can spot?

Which of those opportunities hold the most hope for you?

What are five brand new possibilities you could imagine?

If your goal was already true and present, how would you live, from this moment forward?

Who, besides yourself, would you be helping or benefitting with this goal in place?

How long would you be willing to persist to see results?

How can you confidently and happily take the first step?

The next chapter shows you yet another skill for partnership: how to bring humor and lightness into a therapy setting to further the therapeutic alliance.

8

Skill #3: Add Humor and Lightness

The subject of therapy has long been the butt of many jokes. Have you heard this one?

A man has a heart attack and is brought to the hospital ER. The doctor tells him that he will not live unless he has a heart transplant right away. Another doctor runs into the room and says, "You're in luck, two hearts just became available, so you will get to choose which one you want. One belongs to an attorney and the other to a social worker." The man quickly responds, saying he will take the attorney's heart.

The doctor says, "Wait! Don't you want to know a little about them before you make your decision?"

The man says, "I already know enough. We all know that social workers are bleeding hearts and the attorney probably never used his. So, I'll take the attorney's!"[1]

Humor has another role in connection with therapy, not just for the purpose of jokes. Whether to use humor or not within therapy for healing has been written about since Freud. It's controversial.[2] Some argue that

---

1 http://www.workjoke.com/social-workers-jokes.html
2 Lyttle, J. (2015). Catching the joke: Evaluating the use of humour in therapy. *New Therapist*, 97, no. May/June: 8-21.

humor builds rapport and presents the therapist in a more approachable light. Others argue that therapists are not trained to use humor and that it can have unintended consequences, harming a client.

In contrast, the coaching profession condones the benefits of humor and lightness within coaching. Humor aids partnership. It adds flexibility. Humor reveals the coach as a real person, who smiles and laughs and gets a joke. Humor and lightness are core competencies that every coach must demonstrate to receive certification from the International Coach Federation. As I was developing this model, Therapy with a Coaching Edge, I wondered: Could I add some of this flexibility into therapy, to aid partnership? How can humor and lightness fit within a therapy session? While I believe that humor can enhance therapy and build a therapeutic alliance, there is much to consider first, to make sure it is used well, to respect the purpose and integrity of psychotherapy. You can add a bit of spontaneity, flexibility, and even humor in a therapy session, if you know how. Humor and lightness, as well as flexibility and spontaneity, are important tools to have in your toolkit to promote a coaching approach in therapy, especially when you want to augment the therapeutic alliance.

In this chapter, I review the ability of humor to heal; I reflect on the pros and cons of using humor in therapy, and why it factors so strongly in coaching. Then I pull this all together, to offer you a step-by-step, skill-based application for knowing how and when to use humor in therapy. I include a case example that shows how humor can build partnership and develop an essential client connection when all else fails.

HUMOR AND HEALING

For many years, I ran ongoing, weekly psychotherapy groups. One adult group was held in an office suite I rented for this purpose, with therapists working in the offices on either side of mine. The walls were not well insulated. One morning, the therapist in the next office stopped me in the hallway.

"I heard your group last night through the wall," she said. "There was a lot of laughter going on. That's not my idea of how therapy should sound."

I thought back to the night before. A client in the group shared that his mother had died a week earlier. He told the group about his upset and shock at her death. The group members were quiet, empathizing with his pain. He told the group that he gave her eulogy in a small service at the gravesite. He was nervous and not really sure what to say to honor her. Standing at the cemetery under an awning, in a gentle rain, he talked about her nurturing qualities. She was an immigrant and a single parent. He was her only child, and they had been very, very close. When he went off to college, she moved into an apartment in the same town so she could make sure he was being well fed. When he graduated, and found a good job in another city. She again looked for and found an apartment close by. "She really wanted us to stay close. Her job was to look after me," he told my group sadly. "Maybe it was too close and too much, but that was her way."

At the gravesite, he told us that he had an uncomfortable moment. With tears running down his face, and the rain getting more intense, he took another step back under the awning to get out of the rain and stumbled, almost falling into the grave.

"What happened?" asked a concerned group member.

"I had this immediate thought: Damn it, Mom, this is one time you are going to need to stop insisting we do everything together," he said, wryly.

The group understandably burst into laughter; he laughed as well. Then he continued to share, talking through a range of his feelings including the sorrow, gratitude, and even some uncomfortable relief he felt for now being able to take a step toward autonomy.

Contrary to what my neighbor thought, for me, this had been an evening of serious, valid group therapy. The client thanked the group for letting him share. He said that after dealing with his mother's mortality, the group felt true to life. The group had supported him, he added, with both their laughter and tears.

Adding humor and lightheartedness does not mean therapy has gone astray. It may signal something quite different: that counseling or therapy is reaching a greater level of closeness and warmth. Humor can be experienced by clients as cathartic, welcome, and have a liberating effect. It provides comfort, and helps to relieve the pain of misfortunes, thereby enabling them to deal with situations in a mature, intelligent, and constructive fashion. Most importantly, for our purposes, it can promote a collaborative, therapeutic relationship and help to broaden perspective.[3] Humor in therapy can be a valid communication tool for a therapist, much like empathy and genuineness. According to Rod Marin, Ph.D., author of *The Psychology of Humor,* when humor is used in this way, it can contribute to a therapist's overall effectiveness, regardless of theoretical orientation.[4]

Humor is not indicated for seriously depressed individuals, or those who would find it unwelcome or irrelevant to the issue being discussed in therapy or counseling. It shouldn't be used by a therapist to avoid dealing with a client's difficult topics or emotional expression. If the use of irony, sarcasm, teasing, or puns by a therapist is intended to be veiled insults or to discount a client in any way, of course that is highly inappropriate. If used inappropriately by a therapist, humor could inhibit a client's ability to feel safe in therapy and express important conversations or emotions. The risks of humor include offending clients, interrupting their progress, wounding them, and/or sending them away permanently from the therapy.[5] For this reason, therapists need a careful approach to the inclusion of humor.

Compare this to coaching, which sees humor as less threatening, to understand how it can be an advantageous tool for change.

HUMOR IN COACHING AND THERAPY

When I started training to be a coach, I was struck by the importance given to the use of humor in a coaching conversation. From the first day of my first coaching class in 1996, all the way through to graduation two

---

3 Dziegielewski, S. (2003). Humor: An essential communication tool in therapy. *International Journal of Mental Health*, 32(3), 74-90. .

4 Martin, R. (2010). *The Psychology of Humor: An Integrative Approach.* Salt Lake City: Academic Press.

5 Lyttle, J. (2015). Catching the joke: Evaluating the use of humour in therapy. *New Therapist*, 97, no. May/June: 8-21.

years later, I was asked—well, maybe it's more accurate to say I was directed—to lighten up.

We new coaches were instructed to consider appropriate use of humor and lightness as a tool for achieving "coaching presence"—having an ability to create a spontaneous relationship with the client by employing a style that is open and confident. One additional cohort, "dancing with the client," meaning a willingness to be flexible in terms of leading and following, describes the complete competency. With this ideal, and clear markers about humor and lightness from the coaching profession, I became more alert to the way I was relating to clients as a coach.

As I thought about transferring humor to therapy, I wondered if there were markers that should be applied to think of humor as a skill for a therapist. When humor is desirable in therapy, it needs to be intentional. Bruckman's *Handbook of Humor: Clinical Applications in Psychotherapy* offers several directives to boost understanding about how to make a use of humor appropriate.[6] Here are some thoughts and tips that make sense when bringing humor and lightness into a therapeutic setting:

- Build rapport first. Get to know the client before using humor in a session.
- Use humor in a timely way. Wait for an opening or the right moment. Let your client initiate humor when possible.
- Enjoy a laugh with a client as an expression of a healthy defense mechanism.
- Let an appreciation of the occasional expression of life's normal absurdity be part of an ability of you and your client to also accomplish the painful work of therapy.
- Allow the things your client says and does, the natural incongruity of humans, to surprise you.
- Cultivate "thoughtful spontaneity," a willingness to think about being more flexible in a session.
- Remember this formula: humor = pain + distance.

---

6 Buckman, E.S. (ed.) 1994. *The Handbook of Humor: Clinical Applications in Psychotherapy*. Malabar, FL: Krieger Publishing.

- Consider nonclinical resources to help you develop more expressions of humor: listen to comedy; take an improv class; find a way to laugh every day; learn to tell a funny joke.

Here is a case when I relied on humor and lightness to develop an alliance and rapport with a client whose presenting issue was the trouble he had connecting to others.

How Humor Builds Connection

I had a phone call from a colleague who was referring Jered, the adult son of her client, his mother. "I don't know if this referral is right for you, but you are my first call," she said on my voicemail. "According to his mother, Jered is high functioning. He is 26 years old, an engineer, employed, and independent. He has social anxiety. She says he has a very hard time communicating and making friends. He may have some Asperger syndrome. Jered said he might be willing to give therapy a try, and I thought about you. You have a very natural way of relating to clients and I think he could benefit from someone who can be flexible."

Jered's first session confirmed much of what my colleague had suggested. Jered was tall, and thin. He made little eye contact and fidgeted in his chair as he sat. He spoke with a flat affect and talked in short sentences. I tried to ask questions to build rapport: I asked about his job, where he lived, how he spent his time. All I got back were brief answers, until I asked about his anxiety.

LG: Tell me about your anxiety.

JERED: I have a lot of anxiety. Anxiety restricts your ability to lead a normal life and to make friends. It leads to worry and fear, which are constant and overwhelming, and can be disabling. It's considered a serious mental illness. There are several types: generalized anxiety disorder, panic disorder, and social anxiety disorder. Did you know that?

LG: (taken aback with the rush of information) Well, actually yes, I guess I did know that. Have you been researching anxiety a lot?

JERED: Sure. I need to know what I have. It helps if I have all the information. There's a difference between anxiety and panic disorder. Did you know that?

LG: Yes, I did know that.

JERED: What's the difference between anxiety and panic?

LG: Well, panic is usually considered to be a more extreme expression of anxiety.

JERED: No.

LG: No?

JERED: Anxiety is what a guy like me feels, when he is with a girl, and for the first time, you can't do it the second time. Panic is what a guy feels, when for the second time, you can't do it the first time.

LG: (startled, then laughing) That's a pretty good joke.

JERED: I read it on a chat board about social anxiety. LOL.

LG: You have a good sense of humor.

JERED (still no facial expression): It's one of the best things about me. Most people don't get me, they don't realize that I am often joking. I say "LOL" to let them know it's a joke, but they still don't get it.

LG: I appreciate a good sense of humor. I hope that you will continue to use it in here. I like a good joke.

JERED: I will have another one for you when I come back next week.

I was taken by surprise by Jered's joke. Because I was willing to laugh freely and naturally at his attempt at humor, he began to bond with me. I was heartened that he considered coming back to one more session.

Thoughtful Spontaneity

Humor became one way for me to connect with Jered. Like Scheherazade in *One Thousand and One Nights*, each week he approached the session with one more joke, to be delivered when I least expected it. Jered liked to catch me by surprise and make me laugh. The jokes were corny and most, he admitted, came from the Internet, but that was not the point. For a man who had struggled with social anxiety and other issues his entire life, it allowed him to have a nondefensive form of communication. My willingness to welcome humor and lightness in a session offered Jered a rare experience of connection.

As treatment progressed, we focused on his isolation. I looked for ways to help him engage in a stressful conversation, with the help of some humor. One session started with a check-in about his previous week's goal to call a friend and ask him to meet for lunch.

LG: Did you follow up with your goal of asking Ralph to grab some lunch?

JERED: No. I told you I would talk to him by leaving a message on his phone, but I got nervous. I couldn't do it. I am not sure I can talk on the phone. It might not be possible.

LG: I was thinking about this goal and wondering if it would be one we would need to talk about more, as a way to make it easier. I found a joke about making phone calls. It's a long one, so I shortened it a bit, and wrote it down for you. I heard it on *Car Talk*, the radio show, and found it on their website.[7] Want to hear it?

JERED: Yes.

LG: Here it is. (I read this out loud to Jered.)

Hello, and welcome to the mental health hotline.

If you are obsessive-compulsive, press 1 repeatedly.

If you are codependent, please ask someone to press 2 for you.

If you have multiple personalities, press 3, 4, 5, and 6.

If you have a nervous disorder, please fidget with the pound key until a representative comes on the line.

If you have short-term memory loss, press 9. If you have short-term memory loss, press 9. If you have short-term memory loss, press 9. If you have short-term memory loss, press 9.

If you have low self-esteem, please hang up. All operators are too busy to talk to you.

JERED: Ha. That's pretty good. LOL. That's funny. I think one of these is me, which is why I can't call Ralph.

LG: I am curious, which one feels like it is you?

JERED: The low self-esteem.

LG: Can we talk more about that?

JERED: Okay.

---

7 http://www.cartalk.com/content/mental-health-hotline

Humor = Pain + Distance

Ultimately, therapy is going to involve serious conversation, and some of it will be difficult. Jered needed to talk about his anxiety and loneliness, in order to find a way to address these lifelong issues. He was worried that he would always be alone, and although he was smart and had landed a job in a field that was suited to his personality, he wanted more in life. He wanted friends.

In one session, he talked about a particularly difficult time in his life, his first year in college. He was desperately lonely, and said that he could go weeks without talking with anyone except his teachers. His roommate shunned him as being weird. I listened and asked questions to help him develop insight and validate his struggle. This was one session when we did not share a joke. The conversation was important, but painful for him. But the next week, Jered came into the session, ready to connect again with humor.

LG: Did you have any thoughts or feelings after last week's session?

JERED: I thought more about what happened that year in college. I am really glad I could be an engineer. I wanted to tell you something. My mother said I should mention it.

LG: Oh, what is it?

JERED: I think this therapy is helping me. My mother thinks it is also. She said I am more willing to talk. I use some jokes with her too, and she laughs.

LG: That is a very big result. Thanks for telling me.

JERED: Remember when I came in the first week and could barely talk and looked away a lot?

LG: Yes, I do. We discussed your difficulty making eye contact.

JERED: Yes. I was an introverted engineer. I only looked at my shoes when I was talking to someone. Now I am an extroverted engineer. Know how you can tell an extroverted engineer?

LG: (getting ready for the joke) No, how?

JERED: They look at *your* shoes when they are talking to you.

LG: (laughing) That is very funny! I like it!

JERED: But actually, I do better than that. I make eye contact when I can remember. I look at a person's face.

LG: You have become an extra-extroverted engineer.

JARED: Ha. Good one. LOL.

Your Turn: Add Humor and Lightness

Use this exercise to master the skill.

1. *Build the therapeutic alliance.* Use humor to aid partnership. Don't immediately judge a client's attempts to bring humor into therapy as resistance or obfuscating. Humor may be a valid way of communicating. Consider how it can be used to develop warmth and trust, as appropriate.
2. *Be thoughtfully spontaneous.* Think of the metaphor of dancing. Be on your toes, by allowing your role as a therapist to have plasticity. Be flexible. Be prepared to listen, brainstorm, question, celebrate, and even bring in a joke or funny story. Respect all ethical boundaries and principles of your licensure so that humor is healing and helpful, not harmful.
3. *Remember the formula.* As Bruckman suggests, Humor = Pain + Distance. Give difficult issues and memories a chance to fade first, before bringing in humor.
4. Track your results with this skill and notice what it provides in terms of increasing therapeutic alliance.

Now you have three skills for aiding partnership: how to ask a powerful question, using a strategic form of listening and thinking, and bringing in humor and lightness to secure a therapeutic bond. The next section of skills hones your ability to promote action, how to help clients achieve desired behavioral outcomes more quickly. First, I show you a skill to enhance readiness, so you know how to call a stuck client into action.

Part 3

Skills for Action

9

Skill #4: Call a Client into Action

One major distinction between coaching and therapy is the necessity for action. Action is the hallmark of any and all types of coaching. If you are a coach, you need to get your clients moving toward their goals and keep them on track until the goals are completed. Of course, many models of therapy also promote behavioral, action-oriented change, and you may already be using some method of behavioral therapy in your practice. But not every model of therapy requires or desires that clients take action, at least not in the way that coaching does.

I learned a lot of techniques to promote and sustain client action during my many years as a coach. I have modified some of these skills for my therapy model, to make client-based action easier in therapy. A common challenge for therapists is how to help clients who are stuck or resistant take a first step forward, when they have identified a needed and wanted goal. You can help a client take action faster, without difficulty, if you only know how.

This section of *Therapy with a Coaching Edge* offers three skills for promoting behavioral change. You will learn how to:

- Call a client into action—help a resistant client get ready to act.
- Add shared accountability—use the secret ingredient to help clients stick with goals until they are accomplished.
- Deliver a coaching edge—give direct feedback, useful for motivating clients who need to pick up the pace, change direction, or get back on track.

In this chapter, I start with the concept of readiness. I show you a skill, inspired by a sports coaching strategy, that I later adapted for psychotherapy to help overcome normal client resistance. This skill is a gift for clients who tend to procrastinate or have trouble starting a desired and needed plan of action. Understanding what gets in the way of readiness is useful, so I want to briefly review the stages of change. Then I show you how to help a client shift focus to begin to move forward faster, with therapeutic support and a coaching approach.

CONSIDERING THE STAGES OF CHANGE

One of my favorite rock songs is by a group called Little Feat. The lyrics are voiced in the words of an exhausted truck driver, who sings that despite battling the weather, fatigue, and weariness, he is still willing. We often underestimate the sheer effort that outward success requires.

Being willing to act, despite hardship, fear, rejection, anxiety, or depression, is the essence of successful behavioral change. As a therapist with a coaching approach, part of my role is to help clients, especially resistant clients, become willing. But various models of therapy have many differing ideas about how to do this.

For example, in my early clinical practice, I was trained in a psychodynamic approach and cautioned by a supervisor that clients couldn't and shouldn't be hurried. Even when it was obvious that getting my client to just take a step toward a desired goal would benefit his or her mental health, I was urged to be patient. If the client wasn't ready, then the client wasn't ready. I learned to wait, sometimes through many years of weekly therapy sessions, until something inside the client would shift. I was told that with enough time and with sufficient insight and awareness gained in therapy, the client could indicate a state of readiness. Willingness couldn't be rushed.

I also studied methods of cognitive behavioral therapy (CBT). I learned that it was acceptable to rush, or push, or at the very least encourage, my clients to get moving. I used protocols to direct clients to identify and set a goal; then I assigned homework. But here, too, I could be defeated by a client who just wasn't willing. Homework did not get done or even started. Client readiness, with a resistant client, is hard to overcome.

Most therapists interested in readiness gravitate to the work of Prochaska (1994), and his Stages of Change model.[1] The model identifies early stages of resistance. Using his model, I could recognize when a client was in the stage of precontemplation ("Problem, what problem?") or had shifted to contemplation ("I agree to *think* about doing something in regards to my problem.") or on to preparation ("I might want to do something, but I don't know what to do or how to do it."). But knowing what the stages were called and how to recognize them in my clients did not mean that the work of readiness went any faster.

After trying additional techniques during my two decades of practice as a therapist, I finally had a breakthrough. It occurred when I had to confront my own lack of readiness, my inability to move forward with an important goal. I knew the goal and needed to take action. But I was unwilling. I was resistant to making a start. This was a case of "therapist with resistance, heal thyself first," in order to learn how to help others be willing to change.

My Path to Action

In 2006, I confronted an unexpected health issue: I was diagnosed with early breast cancer that required bilateral mastectomies. I recovered well but had some complications with scar tissue that meant that I had trouble raising my left arm. I went to physical therapy. My doctor also prescribed upper body exercise to increase my range of motion. I agreed that this was a good idea, but I found reasons not to comply. I would start an exercise routine and then stop. Much of my resistance was emotional. I felt self-conscious and anxious about my

---

1 Prochaska, J., Norcross, J., DiClimente, C. (1994). *Changing for good: A revolutionary six-stage program for overcoming bad habits and moving your life positively forward.* New York: Quill.

surgical scars. Each time I looked down at my flat chest, I was sad. My scars healed, but I still felt vulnerable. I was upset with my body's lack of resilience and grieving the loss of my breasts. I also had a list of rational excuses for not lifting weights or doing other things to build arm and chest muscles. I was busy, I was writing, I had days filled with clients. Exercise was boring, and lifting weights was uncomfortable. I talked about this to others, but talking did not help. The bottom line: I could not get myself to start an exercise program to make my upper body strong again.

One day, I saw Andrew Weiss. He lived in a house with his family across the street from me and was playing with his dog, a fetching Basset hound, on his front lawn. I went over to pet the dog, and we chatted. Andrew was a 20-year-old sports coach who worked at the local YMCA, running a basketball camp for kids. I had attended a local stretching class he offered a year earlier. When he asked how I was doing, I took a breath and told him about my surgery. I said I was a "couch potato" and asked if he had any ideas how I might get into better shape. Andrew took a long look at me and then said that he could help. "I will train you to be a basketball player," he said, seriously, to my disbelief. I had never watched a basketball game or even held a basketball. He explained that the training that could help me play basketball would be optimal for my upper body. I was not sold.

"Walk with me," he suggested. We took a walk around the block. I got winded and felt embarrassed. But Andrew told me I did fine on the walk, and he was sure we could make strides forward together. His encouragement was unexpected and in great contrast to the negative messages I had been giving myself for my lack of physical effort. I hired him to be my personal trainer, and we started that week.

I came to the session expecting to work hard, but Andrew had other plans. He went slowly with me. We walked around the block. He gave me a basketball to bounce on the sidewalk. We played catch on his lawn. We walked to an outdoor basketball court a block away, not to shoot baskets, but to skip from end to end. I laughed a lot, between some huffing and puffing. Andrew asked me to purchase my own basketball, and to name it. (I chose Darlene, much like Darling.) He wanted me to relate to it and keep it with me, even when I wasn't working out. I realized that, given his coaching of youngsters at the YMCA, he was working with me the way he would with a 10-year-old child. I told him this and he nodded, with one correction.

"A four-year-old child," he said.

He was right; I had a long way to go. Andrew took a very purposeful approach. Every exercise we did related to basketball. Each request for me to do a sit-up, a push-up, a wall sit, was framed as a building block for the body I would need to play on the court. I went along with this, but didn't think I would ever play an actual game. It was just a metaphor, one that had more meaning to him than it did to me. After a few months of meeting each week to walk, stretch, lift light weights, and bounce a ball, he asked if I had any training goals. I had started watching some basketball on TV to better understand the moves he was asking me to make, and said that I wouldn't mind knowing how to do a lay-up.

He nodded, a small smile on his face.

At the next session, he drew steps on the court with a piece of chalk. I just had to follow the steps, like learning a new dance, and then I would know the basics of a lay-up. Making the shot did not matter. My lay-up was a long process of learning. I often fell asleep thinking about the lay-up steps. The day I could take the steps and get the ball in the air and even into the net was one of celebration. I made a lay-up! I had barely noticed that I had shifted beyond readiness, into actual action. My action had a purpose. It felt so natural and easy. As best as I could discern, Andrew relied on this strategy:

- *Start slow.* For Andrew, small, even baby steps, were a valid start. He watched for any sign of effort. All forward movement, whether done well or poorly, counted as progress.
- *Tie small steps to a larger vision.* Andrew had a vision in his mind, that of me becoming a basketball player. Despite my protestations that this would never occur, he trained my body, from head to toe, to support

that vision. Every conversation we had, and exercise or drill we did built to a larger purpose. His vision became contagious. I wanted this vision, too.

- *Make it all a game.* Andrew often told me "We are just here to play." We played games, but games that required me to think, work hard, and stay in action. I got winded and red in the face, but I laughed, too. The framework of playing a game helped me suspend judgment and stay engaged.

I am going to explain how I translated Andrew's sports coaching strategy into a skill that I use to help my therapy clients achieve readiness. But first, one more story about the value of Andrew's coaching approach.

After a year of meeting for weekly training sessions with Andrew, a surprising shift took place within me. I began to get interested in basketball. I watched it on TV. I could recognize moves like fakes and crossovers. I couldn't do these moves, but I now knew their names. "Look at that ball handling!" I would yell out to the TV. My husband, watching with me, sat there mystified at my transformation. I now followed a sport. I increased my sessions with Andrew, and we started going to a gym regularly. He taught me to play one-on-one basketball with him, which was both terrifying and a total hoot. I next found and joined a senior women's basketball class, also known as the "granny league," to learn how to play on a team. I went to a "not too late for basketball" summer clinic in Maine for a grueling weekend with 50 other senior women, from 50 to 78 years of age, who all were much better players. They had "game"—were committed ballers. I didn't have game, but I was getting a very strong physique. I was no longer a couch potato. I worked out hours every week, and it was all due to a new interest in a sense of play. This wasn't boring exercise, it was basketball.

Then Andrew and I took our workout one step further, into the community. This coaching strategy had been so successful for me in my physical recovery that we wanted to offer it to others. We designed a monthly free clinic for local breast cancer survivors we called "Healing with Basketball." We combined social support, using my social work skills and exercise, using Andrew's basketball-themed exercises to build upper body strength. After a year of offering the clinics ourselves in a number of venues, I found a sponsor. The George Washington University Cancer Institute Office of Survivorship brought our program to inner-city women in Washington, DC. For the next three years, I watched Andrew repeat the same process he had used with me with dozens of other women. They went through the stages of change rapidly, from contemplation ("I don't know if I can do this") to preparation ("Okay, show me how") to readiness ("Watch me shoot"), in a *single* two-hour clinic. He started slow, tied our exercise to a vision of basketball and always made it playful. The participants came back again and again. Just like me, they got stronger and more confident. Andrew's strategy worked for me and with others on a larger scale, equally well.

I finally understood readiness, in all its complexity. I began to modify Andrew's strategy to use with my clients in therapy. I only had words to work with, not basketballs, but the essence of his work helped guide me in developing another Therapy with a Coaching Edge skill. It was an important skill to have for working with my client, Linda, who was facing a crisis of her own making.

Readiness within Therapy

At her first session, Linda sits in my office, scowling. "I've got a problem, but I doubt that therapy can help me," she says. "Here it is. I desperately need to get back to work." Linda, a former associate lawyer at a high-powered firm, was laid off seven years earlier. She has not gone back to work, despite knowing that she needed to earn a living. Instead, she has been spending down the money she has in savings. Now she and her family are at a critical point: Linda has enough money for one more year of living expenses, and then they are broke. Her home life is chaotic. Her husband is disabled with back problems and not currently working. The house is in disrepair and needs some attention. Her teenage son is in recovery from a drug addiction and attends a pricey boarding school. Linda says she feels like a rubber ball, bouncing from one crisis to the next.

"So, you must see why I can't decide what to do or how to get back to work, when everything else is falling apart," she says.

"What did you hope we could do together in therapy?" I ask.

"I heard you are good with issues like this. You are some type of thera-pist and coach. I need to bring in some income. I have to get back to work, or figure out a direction to go in. But I feel paralyzed. I don't want to go back into the law, I hate it. But I don't know what else I can do."

"That seems difficult, to be at this place in life, with these pressures," I said.

"Just for you to know, I have tried therapy before and it didn't get me anywhere," Linda told me. "The therapist I saw before said I am depressed, no surprises there. I spent a year with that therapist and am still as stuck with this problem as I ever was. I figure I am either too lazy or too crazy for anyone to help me. I lost my drive about work. It's my own fault. I got used to not working. I don't want to go back to the law, and I can't figure out what else to do. I need to make money, but I don't have the will or the energy I need to work at anything."

Next, I ask what ideas Linda has thought about and rejected, or tried without success. This is an important line of inquiry, with someone as stuck as Linda. I want to know what she has taken off the table. Some-times a person who is depressed and stuck can only be clear about what she doesn't want or is convinced won't work; she can't think about what else might be possible. Linda gives me a list of what she won't do to find a job: networking, answering job ads, volunteer work, hiring a headhunter, joining a jobs group, updating her resume, going back to her old place of work, changing careers to something else. Her list is long and com-plete. It seems to eliminate anything I would think to suggest. I am glad I asked, prior to making any suggestions. I change the direction of the conversation a bit. I am looking for another way into action.

"Tell me about the rest of your life. What do you do with your days?" I ask.

"Well, I tend to my husband. He has a back condition; he can walk and help out around the house, but he has pain and sleeps a lot. I make our breakfast and lunch. Then I think about my son's situation. He is actually smart and a good student. I am trying to figure out what he can do when he gets out of the boarding school this year. We have so little money for his college education, so I spend hours at a time on the computer and chat boards, looking for scholarships or grants or anything that could be of help."

"You spend hours a day researching funding for his college education?"

"Yes."

"Let me understand. You are not stuck when it comes to researching options for him?"

"No."

"Do the hours you spend researching options count as a form of work?"

Now Linda is very quiet, thinking. This is a new thought for her. I have stumbled onto a powerful question, one that reframes her view of herself as lazy. "What are you saying?" she finally asks. "You think this time on the computer counts as me working?"

"I am saying that you are spending several hours a day doing research. That does indeed count as work, in my book." I have lowered the bar in regard to what work means. For Linda, work meant going to an office and working long hours, being a lawyer. Now I have suggested that work means another serious pursuit that use her skills.

"It doesn't bring in any money," she counters.

"Not directly, I agree. But it might save money. Sometimes work generates income, sometimes it reduces expenses."

"I guess that's true. Work is work. Maybe I am overlooking the work I am doing. That's a very different thought." I request that Linda continue to do her daily research, with one slight change: I want her to be more intentional.

"What could you do, while you are conducting research, that would recognize this as a valid, serious, worthwhile task?" I ask.

"I work on the computer in a bedroom we turned into a home office. I could close the door and could leave my phone turned off and not look at my email. I could put myself on a schedule, to do this while my husband naps so I won't be interrupted. I could start a file and print things out. I can do this, but Lynn, remember, I also need to find real work," she reminds me.

"I understand your bigger goal. But for this week, please treat the research as the real job that it is." I am starting slow, with small steps, building on her existing strengths. Just as Andrew had me walk around the block at our first session, I am looking for a way to support her in what she can do, not what she can't.

As we close, I ask Linda to sum up her session: What will she take away from our time? She says it was useful. That is a start. She agrees to return the next week. By lowering the bar, I have found a way to move her from contemplation ("I guess I can think of my existing research as work.") to preparation ("I can make it more formalized and scheduled."). Next week, I will build on her momentum, to show her that her current actions can be part of a larger vision of readiness.

Make It Relevant

Linda's next session starts with a check-in about her research. She has gone farther than she (and I) had expected and found a program for her son. She called and got an application and made a submission. To do this, she needed to advocate for her son's attendance to a program for students in recovery, and she planned what to say and made sure she used a calm, professional delivery. She did this while her husband napped and with her office door closed. She is proud of her accomplishment. I validate her progress, with praise, the same way that Andrew validated any and all forward movement with me.

"What's next?" she asks.

"I can see you have strong research skills. What is another project that appeals to you, perhaps one that stays on the expense reduction side of the work equation, but requires research?"

We spend the session brainstorming things she might want to research at home on her computer. I am not invested in the content of the research, but want her to expand her ability into new areas. Linda decides that she could do some research about her husband's medication regime, to make sure that he is being well treated and not over-medicated. She also likes the idea of researching how to start a home business, although she has no specific ideas. She can research how to replace storm windows, one of her home repairs. Again, I suggest that all of this constitutes work. She is building muscles and skill sets that will be needed when she moves forward to generate income and find a paying job.

In this session, I also ask about any other skills that Linda has, ones that she relied on when she was a lawyer. She says she liked writing briefs and considers herself a good technical writer. "That is very interesting to hear," I say. "Anything else I should know about you?" Linda warms to the acknowledgment and tells me a long story about a case she worked on at her firm, her "shining moment in law," she calls it. She sits up straighter as she talks. This is a shift into a working persona, and one that I attend to, and again validate.

"This was a good moment for you in your career," I acknowledge, and she agrees.

By talking about the positive memories of work and encouraging her to use her researching and writing ability for personal projects, I am rebuilding Linda's professional sense of herself. Even though she lost her job, she did not lose her skills. In future sessions, I will continue to look for more capacity, anything that can contribute to the larger goal: generating income.

It's an Experiment

After two months of doing home research and some writing about what she is learning from her computer searches, Linda has started to research one more area: she is looking for local jobs. She has stayed active and is writing a new résumé that includes a focus on her preference for research, writing, and advocating. It's time for a big next step: applying for a job. Linda is ready to submit her résumé and then gets stuck. Her activity comes to a halt. Her anxiety causes her to regress. She gets resistant, and at a session retells me her beliefs about her laziness and the demands at home as reasons why she cannot go forward. I have anticipated some pushback. It's not unusual that at every stage of change, a client needs to confront some fear or anxiety before proceeding.

When I was coached by Andrew, if I got scared, he would remind me that this was just a game we were playing. It helped lighten up the situation. I can't use this same reframe with Linda, because we are not on the basketball court and her next step is not a game. We are approaching her stated goal of finding a job, a goal that carries a lot of weight. But I need to find a way to lighten up the action or she will not be able to take the next step. To reframe the situation with Linda, I like a concept I read from the work of a leadership coach, Robert Hicks, who writes about "action experiments" (2014). Talking about action as an experiment, rather than as a step in a plan, can reduce pressure. To make an action experiment successful for a client, Hicks suggests to focus less on outcome and more on the process—the experience of the activity.[2] After taking a few steps toward a goal, process questions to use in therapy to debrief an action experiment can include:

What did you learn?
What do you need to do more of? Less of?
What will be different the next time?
How was this experiment useful?
What are you most proud of?
Was any of this fun or interesting?

Linda needs to think about her next step, submitting her résumé, as an action experiment. "Thomas Edison supposedly made a thousand tries to invent the light bulb," I say to Linda. "How many tries do you think you deserve to have, in order to find the right job?"

"I may need a lot. I hate the process of trying. It feels like rejection."

"I know, this is a tough experiment to undertake. Let's set a number of tries. Is one thousand too many?"

Linda laughs. "Yes, way too many. Okay, let me think. I could agree to 15. Fifteen tries, then I need to reassess. After 15 tries, if I am no further down the road, I will probably stop coming to therapy."

"Fair enough, thanks for the warning. Fifteen is a good number. Let's treat all 15 as Edison experiments. You submit the résumé, we see what happens. If you get an interview, you follow through, no matter what you feel about the possibility of it working out. Just go and do the interview, as an experiment. Then we debrief together. We can unpack each experiment with a few simple questions. We both learn from your brave efforts. Each experiment is a chance to talk and maybe refine and improve the next time."

---

2 Hicks, R. F. (2014). *Coaching as a leadership style: The art and science of coaching.* New York: Routledge.

"Okay. I agree to 15 experiments," she says.

With this approach, I let Linda set the rules, but I offer a reframe and my partnership as her therapist with a coaching style. I will debrief with her to help her handle any feelings or cognition that prevents the next experiment. This was indeed a tough experiment to take on. Linda had to handle dashed hopes and rejection. The benefits of being a therapist with a coaching approach was the ability to have the skills of therapy, to help her process feelings and thoughts about the dashed hopes, while also having a set of proactive, strategic coaching skills to keep her motivated and moving forward. During the next several months as she began job hunting, I used all my skills, shifting back and forth depending on what Linda needed. It took her 12 separate job interviews over four months before she got the first call back for a second interview. Then she had a job offer. She was very pleased to finally say yes. After a total of six months in therapy, Linda was no longer resistant to doing whatever it took to move herself forward. She told me she valued the help that therapy had provided.

"I didn't think this would happen, Lynn. I guess I am no longer lazy or crazy. I am going to be working again. It's kind of phenomenal," she said. She was smiling.

I appreciated her excitement. "One of my therapy teachers used to tell new therapists that they should accept praise when their services offered results. He said we could take credit for all local miracles, so I will take some credit," I said, smiling. "But I give you the bulk of the credit. You showed willingness, resilience, and courage. You got moving and stayed in action. This was tough. But you were tougher."

Privately, I was also thanking Andrew, for helping me understand how to work with resistance and get to readiness. He helped me understand the mechanics of a call to action, from the inside out.

Your Turn: Call a Client into Action
Use this exercise to master the skill.

1. *Lower the bar.* Find a way to make the action easier to begin. Small steps always count. Build on a client's existing ability or interest as a starting place.

2. *Make action steps relevant.* Don't forget the overall vision as a motivator for action. Any and all forward movement can be relevant to the end goal. See action steps as building blocks that are helpful in developing a person's capacity.

3. *It's an experiment.* Help a client stay in process while they are taking action. Ask questions that put the focus on learning and improving, instead of on the outcome. Debrief by asking:

   What did you learn?
   What do you need to do more of? Less of?
   What will be different the next time?
   How was this experiment useful?
   What are you most proud of?
   Was any of this fun or interesting?

Now that you have a therapeutic strategy, one based on sports coaching, to overcome client resistance and inspire client readiness, I want to go further with the skills of action. In the next chapter, I show you how to help clients achieve a goal more consistently by offering a helping hand, the type of therapeutic support that can be highly motivating.

10

Skill #5: Add Shared Accountability

Bryan has a clear goal and a deadline: He needs to make his home more welcoming for his preteen daughter, who will visit him for a month in the summer. "I am a Disneyland dad, without the Disney part—I don't have much that entertains or interests her," he explains. "I want my daughter to feel comfortable when she visits. Last time she was bored and unhappy, and a lot of it was my fault. I didn't make an effort to think about what she wanted and needed. One thing she said was that I should set aside a real bedroom for her. That stuck with me."

Bryan explains that cleaning out his office is harder than it might sound. It's full of years of unfiled documents and will take him a few months to work on, since he only has time during the weekends. He finds it hard to stick with a plan that requires months to complete; he gets discouraged and distracted. "I know some of this is based on my feelings about the divorce and how hard it is to be so distant from my daughter. I am not really part of her life anymore. I am mad about that. But it's not my daughter's fault. I am worried I won't follow through in getting her room ready. Maybe you think it is a small thing, but it's big to her. I need to do this for her. The problem is that I know what I need to do, but I also know myself, and to be honest, I am not sure if I can stick with it. I may have some ADD, but mostly I have trouble with things like this. I am really worried. I could use some help."

The more I have come to study the issue of accomplishing goals, the more I can understand how and why Bryan may get stuck. Studies show that 80 percent of people who set a goal, even a very desirable goal that would improve their lives, will fail in fulfilling it.[1] Bryan's task is complicated with emotional issues about loss and a longing for more attachment. Therapy is good at sorting out emotional issues, but not always effective in helping people accomplish their goals. As a therapist who promotes behavioral change, I am glad he sought me out. I want to help Bryan develop insight about his divorce, but I can also help him stick with his goal of getting a room ready for his daughter.

To enhance goal accomplishment in therapy, I look to the role of accountability and how it is used in the field of coaching. I have developed a skill to bring accountability into therapy, in a way that works well for my clients. In this chapter, I first explain some of the existing problems of goal setting in therapy and the limits of relying on a client's willpower. Then I show you a "shared accountability" strategy that I designed to help my therapy clients stay motivated and on task. It supports them in achieving their goals, and at the same time, enhances personal growth.

THE LIMITS OF WILLPOWER

When I ask Bryan what he thinks is missing, why he can't meet his goal of cleaning up his office, he grimaces and says, "I need more self discipline." I hear this a lot from clients, who say that if they only had more discipline, they could be successful. But relying on self-discipline is not always the best strategy for every goal. For example, Bryan has plenty of resolve in some areas of his life. He is disciplined when it comes to paying his monthly bills. He rarely misses a day of work. But as for finding the will to spend weekends cleaning up his old files and turning his office into a bedroom for his daughter—he would rather be doing anything else. I don't believe that willpower can be transferred easily. Based on what I have come to understand about self-discipline, thinking

---

1 Luciani, J. (2015, December). Why 80 percent of new year's resolutions fail. *US News and World Report*. Retrieved from http://health.usnews.com/health-news/blogs/eat-run/articles/2015-12-29/why-80-percent-of-new-years-resolutions-fail.

that Bryan can bring a reserve of willpower from one task—like paying bills—to use in another task he dislikes and delays is a dicey proposition. Willpower is fickle.

Researcher Roy Baumeister has written extensively about self-control. He finds that willpower is much like a set of muscles. Some aspects of a person's willpower may be well-formed and strong, similar to an arm muscle that you may use every day to do push-ups. But some aspects of willpower are like an unused muscle, and these get easily fatigued with any effort.[2] Willpower consists of circuitry in the brain that runs on glucose, and as such, unused neural networks that correlate to willpower have a limited capacity and short staying power. Imagine if Bryan was a weekend walker and he had strong walking leg muscles for his strolls in the park. But say he wanted to be a marathon runner. "I can walk for hours," he might think. "Why can't I run for hours, too?" We might see him running hard for 30 minutes and then watch him collapse, panting, legs burning. He needs a different set of muscles for running.

Neural networks take time to develop. Building willpower in an unused area of the brain could take years. It requires a plan to build a neural pathway and then strengthen it over longer and longer timeframes. Bryan has a deadline for his task. He needs it to be ready by summer. He doesn't have the time to build a new neural pathway and rely on willpower for this task.

Instead of building his own reserve of self-discipline or willpower for this goal, he needs to *borrow* willpower from someone else. He needs to be accountable for his actions to someone outside of himself. Borrowed willpower, also known as external accountability, is a better strategy, one more likely to help Bryan accomplish his goal in the time he has available.

As a therapist, the more I understand about the types of accountability available and how to help clients select and use the right type of accountability, the easier I find it to help clients, like Bryan, who need some extra help to stick with a goal.

---

2 http://www.nytimes.com/2011/09/04/books/review/willpower-by-roy-f-baumeister-and-john-tierney-book-review.html

Understanding Accountability

Accountability means taking responsibility for one's actions. Accountability is a loaded word, one that implies personal trustworthiness. Are you as good as your word? Can you answer for what you have or have not done? Therapists who use methods of behavioral therapy often rely on accountability like this: I assign you a task, then I give you homework. You do the homework. Next session, you report on your progress. You are accountable to yourself and to me.

But a problem is that any letdown in accountability feels, to a client, like a personal failure. As Bryan said to me in a session when talking about this goal, "I have started and stopped this task several times during the past year. I feel very badly about myself when I don't follow through. I am worried that if I start it again, and don't complete it, you will think badly of me, too."

I don't want to repeat this sense of failure, so I will not be using accountability in this way with Bryan. There are two kinds of accountability, internal and external. Internal accountability, another term for self-discipline or willpower, is the resource that Bryan lacks when it comes to this particular task. He doesn't have it inside of him to tap into. If he did, he would already be using some basic behaviors that are inherent in internal accountability, like time management, having a daily routine, and defining a plan with measures and markers. If I try to give Bryan homework that depends on these internal accountability behaviors, he will fail. He will judge himself and probably think I will be judging him, too. I don't need Bryan to feel worse about himself than he already does in regard to this goal.

Now you can understand where some therapists fall down in methods of behavioral change. They assign tasks, with homework, that require internal accountability behaviors, even though these are the exact areas of the client's brain that are not accessible to internal accountability. The client's failure, not doing therapy homework, becomes one more area of self-doubt for an already struggling client. David Burns, author of *Feeling Good: The New Mood Therapy*, acknowledges this problem has dogged some practitioners of CBT.[3] He suggests that client unwillingness with CBT homework may be due to either *process resistance* (when clients don't want to do what's requested by the therapist) or *outcome resistance* (when clients are ambivalent about the basic concept of getting better). Either way, it's complicated. The end result is that client noncompliance with homework becomes a reason to stop therapy.

So internal accountability with Bryan is out. But accountability is still needed to help him succeed with his goal. He needs the other kind of accountability, external accountability. Bryan tells me that he does better when he has someone to report to: a boss, his parents (when he was young), teachers, anyone who has some leverage and influence to make him feel compelled to complete his goals. The problem is that external accountability, this kind of reporting, is also a poor fit for therapy.

Gretchen Rubin, author of *The Happiness Project*, looks at habits that promote happiness. She finds that when people who want to develop better habits try to get help in therapy, they run into the problems I describe. "In some psychotherapy models, the therapist wants to help you hold yourself accountable. But for many people, external expectations are far more effective in getting people to act. I think a lot of times people get frustrated with therapists because they want them to provide external accountability, but they won't: They don't see that as their proper role."[4] As Rubin suggests, most therapists shy away from taking on the role of external accountability. Most therapists don't want that level of projection, to be seen in therapy as a client's boss, teacher, or worse, demanding parent. To summarize, external accountability is very effective in achieving behavioral change, but it's not good for the therapeutic alliance.

What a dilemma. In coaching, the use of external accountability is really helpful. It is a prime aid for me, as a coach, to help my clients reach their goals. It's so highly valued in coaching that it is considered one of

3 Burns, D. (2017) When helping doesn't help. *Psychotherapy Networker*. pg 19-21.
4 https://www.psychotherapynetworker.org/blog/details/625/helping-therapy-clients-learn-habits-for-happiness

the 11 "core coaching competencies" that coaches must demonstrate to attain certification. I am a master certified coach, and I had to demonstrate my ability to manage external accountability in written and verbal exams, as well as demonstrate it in live coaching, to become certified. The methods that I regularly use as a coach for accountability vary, but usually involve a lot of hands-on effort: frequent prompts or reminders to a client; checking in on progress between sessions; constant encouragement; occasional insistence. All this is accepted and even expected within a coaching relationship, but as explained, these techniques are not often appropriate or useful within therapeutic treatment. Coaching is not therapy and the client expectations are different. Often in coaching, clients pay to be pushed, but rarely is this pushing relationship optimal in therapy.

So, a challenge: As a therapist, my work is not just to motivate my clients; I am also hired to help them heal psychologically and emotionally. Clients who are stuck with a goal and don't have the willpower to see it through don't need the extra pressure of me expecting them to use internal accountability, when their brain won't comply. Like Burns, I have had clients drop out of therapy rather than admit to not making progress with homework. I no longer assign homework this way, and I don't want to be in this position with Bryan.

Fortunately, I have found another way, a third type of accountability, one that combines a skill from coaching with the purposes of psychotherapy. I am going to offer a bit of myself for some borrowed willpower and partnership, while attending to his emotional and psychological process. I call this combination "shared" accountability. It's a way of me extending Bryan a helping hand without incurring the complications of negative transference and more resistance. Here is how I set this up with Bryan, and the results that developed.

Shared Accountability in Action

At the next session, I ask Bryan to help me understand all the steps involved in getting the room ready for his daughter, Sharon. He thinks hard and lists out every task, including clearing out file cabinets, emptying the room, painting it, replacing the carpet, buying a bed and other bedroom furniture, and adding some decorative touches that she would enjoy. Together, we write up his list. Together, we craft a plan. Then Bryan alone decides on his first step: consolidating files. Bryan says he will set aside several hours on the upcoming Saturday. He will start on the first file cabinet (out of eight file cabinets) in the room, to look through files and make decisions about what to keep and what he can throw away. So far, this goal-setting process is similar to what many therapists offer in methods of CBT. Now comes the difference, as I offer shared accountability for this first task. I start with checking in about his feelings.

"How do you feel about this first step?" I ask.

"I can do this and get started, but I know it's going to be hard and not much fun," Bryan admits.

"I would like to help you with this as much as I can, to make it easier."

"Want to come over and go through files with me?" He smiles.

"No, I am stuck with my own tedious filing to do," I reply with a smile, using Skill #3: Humor and Lightness, to aid partnership. "But I wonder how else I could support you in this difficult task. Let's think together. What part of this is yours? What part could be mine?"

Bryan is surprised, almost taken aback, that I would offer to think about any part of this goal being mine. "You mean that you think that part of this task, this goal of getting my daughter's room ready, is your responsibility?"

"I am invested in helping you be successful. I am curious about how I might share some of the effort. What could I do, apart from coming to your house to file papers with you, that would be of help to you?" I clarify.

Bryan gets teary and then starts to cry. He covers his face with his hands as he sobs. This embarrasses him and he is confused, but I have seen this reaction before, when I offer shared accountability. Just offering to help is a big point of contact for someone as isolated as Bryan. Bryan explains that he feels very alone in his life and in trying to be a better father for Sharon. I listen quietly and let him talk. I acknowledge his sadness and loneliness. He wipes his eyes and asks me what I meant about helping him.

"Let's look more at what you will do in order to consolidate the files on Saturday. Is there anything I could do that you would feel was supportive?"

Bryan said that it would mean a lot if he knew that I might think about him at his task, even once during that day. He takes some time and then says that he would like to be able to email me when it was complete. He is shy and uncomfortable with this request. He tells me that I don't need to answer his email, but if I want to, he would appreciate it.

I am glad to agree to his requests and clarify our two roles: Bryan will do the work, taking the time and effort to empty and consolidate the first of his eight file cabinets. I will keep him in my mind at some point during the day, thinking of him. If and when he emails me, I will respond briefly, with a virtual pat on the back, by saying something akin to "good job."

I ask about how I can support him when I see him the next time, to set realistic expectations so he will not feel judged or a failure if he doesn't accomplish all he hoped. Bryan says it will help if I check in with him at the next session, not by asking for a progress report, but by asking how he felt about Saturday's task. I agree again. Bryan says he is very touched by this shared plan, and says it makes him feel almost eager to get started. He says the biggest change in our session, his takeaway from our time together, is a recognition that he is not really alone.

Using this strategy of shared accountability, Bryan is able to stay on track with his task, week by week. He does not always need my support; some weeks he is feeling motivated and fully capable to accomplish the next step. Other weeks he has feelings to unpack, and worries about his progress. Because we are working within a therapeutic (not coaching) session, I can shift back and forth, between emotional processing that often comes with tears and regrets about the loss of time with his daughter, and a look to the future of his next step in his plan. Throughout our session, I allow Bryan to consider me as a source of limited support. This elicits conversation about his need to feel less isolated and to be connected to others, including to his daughter.

I am unfailingly curious each week to learn what he has done, not done, learned, or become aware of, all without judgment. I am glad to think of him at his task. I send the occasional email response when requested. I take responsibility in sessions to move back and forth between the big picture of where he is heading, what it means to be moving ahead on this important goal, but also to be sensitive to his feelings and growth as he takes each step. I also ask questions of Bryan, session by session, task by task, to consider how he may want to use my support including:

What is my role in this task and what is yours?
What will you do and what will I do?
What can help this week to keep you on track?
What should we do if you fall off track?
How would you like me to check in with you next time?
How can I support you?

The Therapist's Limited Role

Shared accountability is not an invitation to set up dependency with a client. It's not designed to break the frame of therapy or to overburden a therapist with more work, especially uncompensated work, between sessions. Instead it is a stance, based on partnership and the desire to further behavioral change. It can help certain clients stay on task with important goals, when they need borrowed willpower or external accountability without the complication of added transference or resistance.

When I use this skill, I offer only small, easy-to-deliver expressions of support that fit within my ethical and professional boundaries. I am clear to decide, when asked, what I can and can't comfortably agree to. Can I keep Bryan in mind once during the day on Saturday? Sure. Will I initiate a call to Bryan and see how he is doing? No. Will I initiate an email to check in with Bryan during the weekend to see if he completed his task? No. Can I respond to Bryan's email with a short, virtual acknowledgment such as: "Good going, thanks for the update!" Yes.

In cases of shared accountability, I only offer support that feels appropriate and natural to me and my style of therapy. I stay within my normal therapeutic persona. I don't offer or agree to do or say anything that would make me feel anxious, uncomfortable, resentful, or that I am being taken advantage of. It's important that shared accountability be a model for my clients of appropriate responsibility. I am responsible to myself and my professional ethics, purpose, and boundaries. I model the concept of support, having clear boundaries, the ability to say yes or no, and agreeing to take on only those tasks that are realistic and appropriate.

What is most interesting about this strategy of shared accountability is that when I offer it to therapy clients who have goals they very much want to accomplish, but struggle with finding the willpower, they are generally quite respectful and careful not to overstep my boundaries. Often, these clients have little experience in asking others for help. This becomes a teaching tool: how to ask or request support. Raising this topic helps clients think about finding additional sources of support, beyond me, for accountability and more significant help.

Over several months of therapy, the issue of needing support became more central for Bryan. He could see how important and motivating the minimal support I offered was to him. One of our goals, in addition to getting the room ready for his daughter, was that he begin to build a community of support. He joined a church that offered a divorced dads' support group and met other fathers whom he could talk to. When Sharon finally came to visit, her room was ready and lovingly decorated. During her vacation, Bryan invited a few dads from the support group and their kids for a barbecue at his house. Sharon congratulated him on making a life for himself; he felt proud of his ability to heal from the divorce and be a better parent to her, even at a distance.

Your Turn: Add Shared Accountability
Use this exercise to master the skill.

1. *Clarify the goal.* Ask your client to define the goal, tasks, and action steps. Participate in this conversation so that the parameters of the goal are well understood by your client and yourself. Be strategic in your listening, using Skill #2: Be a Strategist with a Twist.
2. *Extend limited partnership.* Offer some shared accountability, with appropriate limits, in the process of a task. Ask:
   What is my role in this task, and what is yours?
   What specifically will you do, and how can you be accountable to me?
   What can I offer to keep you on track?

What should we do if you fall off track?
How would you like me to check in with you at the next session?
How can I support you to succeed?

3. *Check your boundaries.* Find an expression of support that feels appropriate to you, as the therapist, and meaningful to your client. Follow through with your end of the agreement. Don't promise or agree to anything that is not within your ethical principles or that would jeopardize your licensure. Get supervision or advice, if needed, to maintain your boundaries.

4. *Focus on process, not just progress.* Check in each session with your client, not just about what has been done, but what has been learned, experienced, and opened up in the process of committing to a goal. Continue to extend shared accountability as appropriate until the goal is complete.

In the next chapter, let me show you another skill to promote action. You will see how to give a direct feedback, also known as a coaching edge, when needed and appropriate to further action or help a client change direction quickly.

11

Skill #6: Deliver a Coaching Edge

Most therapists walk their talk—by this I mean that we spend time going to therapy ourselves. I certainly spent decades in my own therapy, with several different therapists. One noted time was a year I spent in couples counseling with my husband, after we had been married for about five years. We had a stormy marriage at that point—one filled with a lot of arguments. This was a second marriage for both of us. My husband is Italian and Polish, raised in Argentina. I am Jewish, raised in the suburbs of Maryland. With this mixture of divergent cultures and belief systems, everything in our marriage either felt very stimulating or like a battle for control. At one point, we seemed to be in a never-ending power struggle, so we sought therapy with Skip. Skip had become a therapist after a long, successful career as an engineer. He was smart, strategic, and no-nonsense in his approach.

In one session, my husband and I were retelling our latest argument. Of course, my husband and I saw what happened very differently. I made my case and then he made his. Some therapists try to stay neutral, assigning equal culpability to both members of the couple. Not Skip. When he thought you were wrong, he said so, openly and bluntly. In this case, Skip must have sided with me because he looked at my husband and said, "For being such a smart man, you can sound really stupid."

I was a bit shocked. Unlike the way most therapists talk to clients, softening their statements with active listening or balancing opinions with a show of empathy, Skip just let it fly. Skip and my husband had a good prior rapport, and my husband took the feedback well. Our marital argument got resolved quickly in the session. With Skip's tough love, my husband was able to see his part of the problem more clearly than anything I had been able to communicate on my own.

Sometimes a therapist needs to know how to make a point and challenge a client, to give frank feedback without softening the message. The ability to deliver a no-nonsense, strongly worded observation is a powerful skill to have. Strong feedback is a skill coaches use, too. When a coach delivers a direct, no-holds-barred message, it's known as using a "coaching edge." I learned to develop this ability, this edge, during my coach training; then I adapted it for use in therapy, so that I could have it as a tool, one to use judiciously, only when needed.

In this chapter, I want to offer you a how-to in delivering a coaching edge. Think of this as the art of using straightforward, direct feedback with a client, similar to a confrontation, but not used in anger or in fear. With some practice, you will be able to use it in the moment, and again, only when necessary, as a wake-up call. I will explain the different situations when this style of delivery is helpful and useful, and give you some specific wording examples, as well as case anecdotes so you can understand how it might work in the therapy room.

AN EDGE, NOT A DAGGER

Some therapists, like Skip, are very direct. They have a coaching edge as part of their personality, and use it naturally. Other therapists need to learn to do this in order to employ a specific type of therapy. As I looked for models of therapeutic directness, I watched therapist Terry Real, a proponent of the "full throttle marriage" style of couples counseling, deliver his brand of blunt feedback to a couple during a workshop. Real is very unswerving in his feedback, and it's quite effective with his clients. He takes sides and labels some of them "blatant" (egregious contributors to marital problems) and others "latents" (seemingly more benign). Both blatants and latents are fair game for his strong interpretations. His clients seem to like his confrontative nature, and I have seen it delivered by Real with what I could best call affection. Other models of therapy use confrontation with good results as well, such as Intensive Short-term Dynamic Psychotherapy, with an intervention called a "head-on collision," that works to help a client confront resistant defenses. I believe that any method of therapy that includes confronting or challenging a client requires intentional skill and practice.

Perhaps your style of therapy does not consist of you confronting a client or being this direct. If so, you may find this chapter's skill to be challenging, but also a little anxiety-provoking. If you are going to offer therapy with a coaching approach, and if you like the idea of furthering action with clients, you will want to have this tool available. It can prove very beneficial. As mentioned, it's best as a wake-up call, when a therapist needs to get a client's attention. It's an edge, not a dagger. This is not designed to hurt a client. Don't use it to cut or draw blood. It's to get attention, not to shame someone who has come to you for help. Use it sparingly and appropriately.

You can soften a coaching edge. For example, you might ask permission before giving a client feedback in this way. This style of feedback can be phrased as a question or delivered as a simple, clear statement. If you have a strong rapport with a client, you can be like Skip and just say what you need to say, without softeners. As with Terry Real, many of my clients appreciate that I have this ability, to be straight and direct from time to time. I certainly don't use it in every session, and some clients, especially those vulnerable clients dealing with difficult emotional issues, have never heard me talk this way. But for coachable clients (as described in Chapter 3: Who's Coachable in Therapy?), for those with sufficient ego-strength who want to work short-term and see results, it is a handy tool to have if needed. It can promote better or faster action from a client who is stuck, help a client go further and accomplish more, or even keep a client from harm.

Let me show you some examples of when a coaching edge can be of great advantage to a client. For example, you may need this edge when you start to feel concerned about something occurring with a client in the moment, to quickly address some type of acting out behavior that needs attention.

Step Over Nothing

Do you address problematic issues with clients as they occur? In my early years as a therapist, if I noticed something a client said or did in a session that bothered me, I did not speak about it. I was not very confident about what I was seeing or hearing. Instead, I would silently observe it, put it in my notes, and talk about it in supervision. I would wait to deal with it in a later session, sometimes much later. Sometimes, never. I was trained to work psychodynamically and saw clients long-term, in weekly sessions, for many years. The issue or behavior was bound to resurface at some point, I would rationalize. The truth was that I didn't feel ready to address an issue like this as it occurred. I didn't know how. I didn't have the words or the courage to call a client on an issue or destructive behavior that I observed, even when it signified something deeper that really needed recognition from the therapist.

Currently, I tend to work in shorter-term therapy sessions. I can't wait years to address troubling issues or behaviors, because I don't have the time. Instead, as the sign in the airport cautions, if I see something, I need to say something. In coaching jargon, I don't "step over" (ignore) anything. I address all that I can, when I can. This is a faster way to process a relational experience with a therapy client. Issues that I no longer step over can include:

- A client reports a situation that sounds risky, unrealistic, irrational, or is worrisome to me as I am hearing about it.
- A client casually makes a statement signaling a limiting or negative belief that impedes progress or stops balanced behavior.
- A client acts out in a session by repeatedly coming late, not paying on time, or coming into a session and wanting to keep texting or taking phone calls.
- A client stays on the surface of the conversation, or starts to express an emotion, like tears, and then chokes it back to keep telling a story, and never allows the emotion full expression.
- A client mentions a projection about me, or some transference surfaces that can become an obstacle to this model of therapy.

If any of these situations occurs, and I want to address it in the session, I will use wording that has some edge to it. It might be a stated observation, or offered as feedback, or a direct, pointed question. My purpose is to clarify what has just happened or just been said. I am metaphorically holding up a stop sign to slow down the session with my comment, to deal with something that concerns me and needs further comment from my client.

Wording examples:

I think you are planning to do something risky. Am I correct?
Hold on, back up to what you were just saying. Say it again, clearly, so I can understand it.
This is the third time you are late for your session. What is this about?
That doesn't work for me.
Tell me what we should be talking about today to get you more invested in this session.
You are running out of time and are at a critical point.
Please don't take that next step until you think hard about the consequences.
What you do next could change your life.
I think you are better than what you are demonstrating.
Each time you show a real emotion in here you dismiss it. What can I do to help you allow the emotion some air-time?
You seem to have me confused with someone else you distrust, like your mother.
I don't think that you should make any changes in the frequency of your therapy sessions at this time, and I want to tell you why.
What you are saying does not make sense to me.

Case example:

Jeff juggled therapy with his many other work and life commitments. He often asked to change his time to accommodate his work schedule, and lately had decided to fit therapy in during his lunch hour. This meant he relied on traffic being light in order to get to my office on time, although in our traffic-congested city this was not usually the case. He often came in and had trouble getting focused, distracted by the traffic and rushing, or other demands of his workday. At this session, he came late. Then, before we could establish a session agreement or a topic for the session, his phone began to buzz. "I better get this," he said. I watched while the time ticked away. He put the phone down, got back into his issue for today, and the phone buzzed again. Again, he picked it up, read the text, and began to type away to reply. I decided to speak up and interrupt his texting. "Jeff, your phone is interrupting our time together," I said.

"Sorry, sorry," he said, still texting. "I just need to get this."

"That doesn't work for me," I said. This was edgy, and I hoped he would put the phone away and focus on therapy.

Instead, he turned to me, irritated. "If it cuts into our time, I will still pay. After all, it's my session."

Ah-ha, I thought, a chance to use a bit more directness, for his benefit. "No, Jeff, it's *our* session. I am not willing to have a session today without you being fully present."

"Do you want me to leave?" he challenged.

"If this is the best it gets, I would say yes. Can you do better than this?" Then I added an interpretation, to give him more of a perspective on my confrontation. "What is happening right now is similar to what you say goes wrong at home, with your spouse. I am glad you are showing me this firsthand, so I can help you with it."

Now I had his attention. He later told me that this was a session where he felt he got his money's worth. He liked that I could be direct and not be intimidated by his own confronting nature. He said his wife usually backed down when he got angry or irritated. But he needed to learn how to stop, pay attention, and talk differently, in order to sustain a relationship—even one with me as his therapist. I was glad I had been able to be frank and honest. I took a risk to challenge him in the moment. There was no guarantee that he would stay, rather than walk out in a huff. We did have some rapport established from our time in therapy, and it turned out that my ability to be straightforward and stand up to him was the right approach, and helped him confront a difficult piece of his own behavior over time.

Ask for More

I had a savvy teacher in social work school who told her students that if we were working harder than a client in a session, something was out of balance. As a therapist, I have learned that there are times when it is necessary to ask a client to do more. I use some coaching edge to make a request. I am not shy about making a strong request for the client's benefit. Reasons to ask for more include:

- Lack of commitment from a client.
- Superficial communication about an important topic.
- A need for more self-reflection and self-awareness.
- Wanting a client to start a new behavior immediately, or stop an old one, to stay safe.
- Not seeing the results of what a client had wanted from therapy in terms of progress.

I do this by making a request. Sometimes my requests have an edge to them, but sometimes they are just a challenge to take another, bigger step. When I make a request like this I am, in effect, asking my client to help me to see a return on the considerable investment he or she is making in therapy. In every case, I use a calm voice, make eye contact, and speak normally and naturally.

Wording examples:

Can you take a bigger step in that direction?
Your efforts are a good start, but you will need to do more to get where you say you want to go.
I'd like you to double that goal, how about it?
I request that, instead of self-care, you add extreme self care to your action steps.
What can you do to have more self-respect this week?
Like the Nike slogan, I want to challenge you to "just do it!"

Case example:

Addy started the session with a story about interpersonal problems she was having at work. She was criticized unfairly by her boss, and rather than speak up in her own defense, she simply nodded her head and stayed silent, even though she felt the complaint was undeserved. "Afterwards, I think endlessly about what I could have said," she told me. "I rethink it dozens of times, what would have been good for me to say. But the moment has passed. It's too late to go back now and talk to him."

"In my experience, after the fact still counts," I said.

"What do you mean, go back afterwards to address it with him?"

"Is that an option you are willing to consider?" I ask.

"That's a good question. I am not sure, let me think," she said. We spent the rest of the session unpacking this idea, exploring all of Addy's longing and fear about being more assertive with her boss. It was a difficult session for her and she was uncomfortable. Finally, she rejected the option of talking to her boss. "I don't think I can do this yet."

I agreed that it was too much of a stretch, given her lack of practice. Instead, I made a request that she practice this type of assertiveness with me. I started with a review of my earlier intervention.

"I don't think I did as well in this session as I might have. I think I rushed some things and didn't understand all you were saying. I request that for our next session, you practice asserting yourself with me. Tell me what I did incorrectly and how I could have done it better. How about it, would you help me with this?"

This request was framed in a way she could accept. It was still a stretch, asking her to be more assertive with me and share her opinions of my work directly. It was a skill-building exercise. It helped to take pressure off her, and respected her need to protect her job and go slowly before deciding to talk to her boss. After this kind of practice, in subsequent therapy sessions, Addy learned the skill and language of being appropriately assertive. Talking to her boss about her performance still felt too risky, but she began to find opportunities to be more assertive in other settings.

Expect Evidence

My model of therapy is not "evidence-based" in a clinical sense, because it is new, just being articulated and written about in this book, and as such does not have a body of evidence to support it. But given that it is a model reliant on results, I look for and appreciate tangible evidence of progress. The evidence I seek is defined and determined by me and my clients, and we make it explicit, part of the conversation. In Chapter 5: Results in Every Session, I showed you how to do this, to look for, identify and share results of progress with clients, session by session. But sometimes I have a client who has high expectations and wants bigger goals or more evidence of progress, or faster results. For this type of client, I can use a coaching edge to set out a challenge that produces more change. Examples of when I might use this edge include working with clients who:

- Feel that a desired goal is not progressing fast enough.
- Find that their progress is not significant to them.
- Like challenge and want to "up their game" and go further.

Having a coaching edge in this case can be offered as a serious challenge or a playful competition. Some clients in therapy delight in moving quickly, and for them, I need to stay on my toes and keep pace. Others want progress, but need me to push a bit so that they can spot evidence of outcomes.

Wording examples:

Please rate your progress this month.

I am eager to celebrate any and all wins with you today, where do we start?

What you regard as a small step seems huge to me. I request that you appreciate what you have done before you go further.

How will you top this?

Do. Or do not. There is no try.[1]

---

1 Yoda, in *The Empire Strikes Back*

Case example:

Ethan is anxious about his studies. He is a very bright student in a demanding science program. He says his biggest need in therapy is to find ways to be organized in order to pass his courses. After his first session, he leaves with an action step: to organize his lab reports. In this second week, he tells me about his progress.

"I did the lab reports," he says.

"How did it go?" I ask.

"Okay, I guess."

I decide to push him a bit, using some edge. "I think you deserve better than a guess. Be a scientist for a moment about this. How would you know if you really made any progress?"

"Well, if therapy was really helping, I should be able to complete my assignment this week 20 percent faster than it usually takes."

I press on. "Hmm, evidence based on time. Are you up for a challenge?"

"Okay," he says, intrigued. I have his attention.

"I request that you design an experiment that would help both of us really know if this organization plan we are developing is benefiting you. It needs to include a clear path of evidence. You are a lot smarter than I will ever be about designing experiments, so I bow to your expertise. Are you willing?"

Ethan liked this approach, especially my willingness to concede his superior intelligence in this regard. He designed an experiment with a graph that kept him engaged in the task of organization. This was the first of many challenges I used to help him progress quickly in the time we had, to give him a model of ways he could tackle issues that made him anxious: setting a goal, designing a plan, and testing it out as a scientific experiment. After issuing the challenge, I was happy to stand by the sidelines to cheer him on.

When Health Depends on a Coaching Edge

As I was refining my coaching edge as a therapist, I began to see a new client, referred to me by her nutritionist who was worried about her recovery from illness. Not only was Nancy, who was 32, young to have breast cancer, but as in many who become ill at that early age, it was an extremely aggressive form. She'd completed her surgery and chemo, but was being watched carefully by her medical team. Her oncologist had strongly encouraged her to lose weight and exercise, to become as physically healthy as possible. But, depressed and angry about her illness, Nancy was stuck in a rut of watching endless hours of TV and being preoccupied with her rotten luck. She was already in couples therapy with her husband, but had decided she wanted some individual sessions with a therapist who understood what she was facing with her cancer treatment. The referring nutritionist and I had shared referrals of several past clients who were in cancer treatment or recovery.

In our first therapy session, Nancy said she couldn't get herself to stay on her exercise program, and she knew why. "Part of me just wants to give up," she admitted in a little girl's whining voice. She was grieving. Bitter about getting the disease so young, she also worried about her two young children. What would become of them? She took out her worry and anger on everyone and everything—her treatment team, her husband, her friends. She repeated several times that it was so unfair, that no one really understood how awful this was for her. I listened silently for about 15 minutes, nodding my head, saying little other than a few validating comments. Then I switched gears.

"Do you have a jacket?" I asked.

"Yes. Why?"

"I want to do the rest of this session outside while we walk. Would you be willing to walk with me?" Nancy was surprised, but she followed me outside. My office adjoins a public school with a beautiful outdoor track next to some woods. At the school, I set a medium pace and we walked alongside each other. We talked or we walked in silence, but we kept moving. I was modeling action: Rather than telling her to move, I'd move with her, as a partner. After 30 minutes, I stopped and we sat on the steps near the track.

Nancy was winded. "That was different," she said. "Is that how you usually do therapy?"

"You're the first," I said. "You did well on the walk. Good going!" She continued to catch her breath, so I talked. "Here's the thing. I can't be your personal trainer or your dietician. I can only be your therapist. I work with words. But I can walk and talk at the same time, and so can you. I know you're going through a very rough time."

Nancy nodded and took my empathy as a signal to start complaining. She said, in a small voice, "You have no idea how hard this is for me—no one gets it."

I held up my hand in a *stop* position. Here came the coaching edge. "Nancy, let me finish. I know some of what you're facing. I know that you have some decisions to make about how to live your life. To do that, you need more than my pity, or your own."

Nancy gave me a sharp look and started to tear up, which embarrassed her. I stayed silent until she composed herself. Finally, she took a deep breath. "I thought therapists were supposed to be nice," she started in that small voice. I still stayed silent, watching her. I wondered if this experiment—treating her as a cancer survivor the way I'd learned to treat myself—would help her reach inside and find some of her own inner strength.

"What do you think you can do for me?" she asked.

"I don't know what I can do *for* you, but I can tell you what I can do *with* you. I want you to have a place and a time, each week, with someone who knows what it means to have to fight for better health. I'll hang in there with you, week after week, while you find your own answers about your next steps. And I'll take some of those next steps with you, literally." I smiled now and glanced back at the track.

Nancy and I worked together for close to a year. Sometimes we walked on the track; most times we sat in my office. To my surprise, we laughed a lot; once she lost her little-girl voice, it turned out she had a wicked sense of humor. Nancy began to live for the future. She created a series of short- and longer-term plans. She changed her diet, found a trainer, and got into a routine at the gym. She reveled in getting stronger and told me about her reps on the equipment and her ability to do squats. She took an art class and discovered that it was a positive outlet for her grief and anger. She saw a lawyer and made a will with provisions for her husband and children if she died early. We were walking on the track during that session. When she told me about that, she walked fast, with tears streaming down her face. I came to admire her tremendously and even though, as her therapist, I wanted to be more nurturing or empathic at times, I understood that she needed me to relate to her from a position of mutual strength, speaking to the part of her I believed could step up to the challenge.

A coaching edge can be a gift to a client when it is used with a specific therapeutic purpose, for respectful helping and healing.

Your Turn: Deliver a Coaching Edge
Use this exercise to master the skill.

1. *Speak up to benefit the client, not yourself.* Giving strong feedback is not an ego trip, to make the therapist look good or strong in a session. It can be done to benefit a client who needs honest feedback, a strong message to start or stop an action, to highlight a critical moment in therapy, or as a caution about what is needed to survive or succeed. Be clear about why and what you are going to say. Examples of direct statement to give a wake-up call to a client include:

   That step is too small to get you where you say you want to go.
   You need to do more and do it this month.
   You are running out of time and are at a critical point.
   Please don't take that next step until you think hard about the consequences.
   What you do next could change your life.
   I think you are better than what you are demonstrating.
   This is the most important thing you have ever said in a session.
   What you are describing is a very good way to lose a job (or a spouse, etc.)
   Like the Nike slogan, I want to challenge you to "just do it!"

2. *Use a neutral tone of voice.* You are not a drill sergeant, barking out orders. You are a therapist, and it is best to use a coaching edge from a place of calm confidence. In my coach training, this was called "charge neutral"—no positive or negative charge, just a natural tone of voice without judgment, anger, fear, or bias in the statement.

3. *Step over nothing.* Address what you observe. Don't hold back on what a client needs to know or hear. If you don't have the courage to say

what is needed to your client, who will? As one of my social work teachers used to say, ironically, about the need to be honest and direct with a client, even when the topic was uncomfortable: "This is why we therapists get paid the big bucks."

4. *Make strong requests.* Establish that a client has the right to say yes, no or maybe to any request that you, the therapist make and then ask for what you would like to see. Look at the wording that is offered in this chapter to make sure that your requests fit within appropriate bounds for your session and your therapeutic relationship. Examples:

   Please rate your progress this month.

   I need you to pick up the pace. Are you game?

   I request that, instead of self care, you add extreme self care to your action steps.

   Can you stop and recognize what you have done so far, before you go further?

   How will you top this?

   I'd like you to double that goal, how about it?

   Do. Or do not. There is no try.[2]

5. *Validate and acknowledge all forward movement.* Once a client responds to your coaching edge, it's important to appreciate any and all willingness to correct the situation.

You now have three skills geared toward action: You can help therapy clients 1) shift into readiness with a call to action, 2) increase their progress using shared accountability, and 3) have a way to motivate them with a verbal challenge, using your coaching edge.

In the next section, Part 4: Skills for Possibility, you will see three skills designed to help clients think bigger and more expansively, to develop more potential for change. First up, learn a skill to help clients align with their core values, a way to let clients bring more meaning and purpose to their decisions.

---

2 Yoda, *The Empire Strikes Back*

Part 4

Skills for Possibility

12

Skill #7: Align with Core Values

Maxine, 80, isn't sure if she belongs in therapy. "I am a widow and retired from a long teaching career. I have plenty money to live on comfortably. I have family and grandchildren and friends. I don't know what is wrong with me. Maybe I don't have the ability to be happy. The best way I can explain it, mostly to myself because I am embarrassed to talk about this with others, is that I feel disappointed with the way my life feels now," she says. "This is not really the life I want to be living. It sounds dramatic. I don't mean I feel really depressed, I am okay. I guess I would say that I am just not content."

Maxine adds that she was in therapy in her 40s and wants to try therapy one more time while she is still in good health and feeling fit. "Maybe I am just old and irritated. Do you think these thoughts and regrets are going to be with me forever? Maybe this is how old age feels. Do you understand what I am describing?" she asks.

I assure her that I do. Her thoughts and feelings are not unusual in my experience, nor age related. Feeling bored, wanting something more, being disappointed in life may not fit into a mental health diagnosis. I work with many highly functional adults who, like Maxine, are doing well, yet want more. They feel depressed or anxious and fall into a loose description called the "worried well"—people who are very functional in many areas of life, but unsatisfied and unfulfilled in other areas. Many complain of feeling a lack of happiness. Most benefit from the Therapy with a Coaching Edge model of treatment because it goes beyond a medical model and a focus on pathology, to look at possibility: how clients can define larger, more ideal goals, see opportunities for extended personal growth and enhance their current quality of life.

In this chapter, I want to show you how to introduce a therapeutic conversation about meaning, purpose, and potentiality—topics that enrich the reach of a traditional therapy session. I give you a basic tool to start a discussion with clients, a survey for identifying core values. Then I explain how to guide clients to align their values with their goals and actions, so they can resolve personal challenges based on the ideals that they hold dear. First, I want to clarify the shift from a medical model of treatment toward one that is inherent in my method of therapy, based on personal growth.

BEYOND A MEDICAL MODEL

If you are a therapist working within a traditional medical model, you are required to diagnose, treat, and perhaps cure a patient's issues and illness. In a medical model, problems are often viewed as pathology. Your role as a health provider is to be the expert and know the answers to effecting better health. When you shift from a medical model to Therapy with a Coaching Edge, your role becomes less that of a medical expert and more that of a partner in holistic healing. While you may still diagnose and offer treatment, you see a client's problems in a larger context to encourage a coaching approach: client-based control, partnership, action, and possibility. You not only offer services designed to help people resolve immediate issues, but also to assist self-actualization.

Gerald Celente, author of *Trends 2000*, correctly predicted a major trend more than a decade ago, by recognizing that our aging, relatively affluent Baby Boomer population is focused on high-quality longevity. We want to live well and age well. We yearn for long-term physical and mental health—to stay interested in life until the day we die. This trend pointed the way for an expanded role for the therapy profession. We saw the emergence of mind-body therapy, energy therapy, mindfulness meditation within therapy, and an overall focus on wellness. Bringing skills of possibility into therapy helps you lead the way in allowing clients to develop optimal lives.

Returning to the idea of a continuum between therapy and coaching that I explained in Chapter 2, the personal growth or human potential movement is right in the middle of the continuum. It is the common ground where therapy and life coaching share a basis of theory and thought. One theory that defines personal growth is that of psychologist Abraham Maslow, the father of humanistic psychology. Maslow organized human development through his famous hierarchy of human needs. Maslow reasoned that needs take a stair-step approach: Until the lower needs get met, we humans can't address the higher ones. According to Maslow, meeting these levels of needs also organizes a therapeutic approach, as each one follows the next:

1. *Physiological*—the biological needs we humans require to exist
2. *Safety and security*—the need for shelter, protection, and other survival needs
3. *Belonging*—the need to have relationships and be part of a society
4. *Esteem*—the need for respect from self and others
5. *Self-actualization*—a state of fulfillment and high personal achievement[1]

In 1970, Maslow expanded the list of self-actualization to include the universal needs of knowledge, harmony, and life balance. He suggested that it was the job of therapy to help clients reach their full potential rather than end up with unfulfilled longings. Near the end of his life, Abraham Maslow expanded his thinking yet again to define what he called "metavalues and metaneeds"—core, timeless principles like truth, beauty, and goodness that motivate people to greatness.[2]

---

1 Maslow, A. H. (1954). *Motivation and Personality*. New York: Harper and Row
2 Maslow, A. H. (1964). *Religions, Values, and Peak Experiences*. New York: Penguin.

Understanding Core Values

During my coach training, I learned about the benefit of identifying core values—the ideals and principles that are personally meaningful and relevant to a client. Consideration of a coaching client's personal values often preceded a conversation about personal goals: In order to make goals relevant, a goal needed to be value-based. Once values were in place, a goal became part of a larger vision, one that was now filled with meaning and purpose.

The more comfortable I became with an open-ended conversation in coaching about transformational topics, the more I began to test out raising these topics within a therapeutic setting. As with a coaching session, I found that a starting place was to introduce a conversation about core values. I often define the idea of core values, for those therapy clients who are unfamiliar with the term, as personal beliefs, or basic and central ideals about life. I explain that often we make decisions based on these beliefs unconsciously, without thinking. By being more conscious about our core values and applying the values to our decisions, we tend to feel more satisfied about our results.

As I asked my therapy clients about their values and wondered with them, how their core values factored into their choices, therapy conversations took an interesting turn. Sessions became more spacious and abstract. No longer did we just talk about symptoms or problems. Now we also discussed:

- The reciprocal nature of relationships.
- Learning to create a reserve (more than enough) of time, energy, love, money, peace, and community, to shore up any missing areas and prevent future crisis.
- How to start or deepen practices of spirituality, meditation, or contemplation.
- Sustaining pleasure and having a playful outlook on life.
- Appreciating nature and using time in nature to restore a sense of well-being.
- Nurturing oneself in healthy ways.

- Enhancing social interest, social justice, compassion, and ties to humanity.
- Maintaining good physical health and other life-giving techniques.
- Practicing forgiveness, to have peace of mind.
- Loving and being loved.
- Opening doors on life's further possibilities.

In our conversations, I helped clients find a way to shape these lofty topics into relevant and pragmatic goals or as part of treatment plans. For some therapists, this kind of personal growth or values-based conversation is easy and natural to initiate. For others, it is unfamiliar and can even be a bit anxiety-provoking. If it is unfamiliar, I can offer you a concrete way to begin. You can use a core values survey that many of my clients find helpful and interesting to complete.

Bringing Core Values into Therapy

Maxine, who says she has no serious issues, still wants a therapist to talk to. She is looking for someone who won't pathologize her concerns, but instead can be trusted to help her consider what else is possible in life as she ages. Research shows us that the best way to stay strong and vibrant into old age is to continue to learn and grow at all ages and stages of life. Maxine is an example of a client who wants to talk about her life, going beyond a medical model of symptomology, to explore overcoming past regrets, setting current life direction, and looking at future opportunity.

Maxine and I contract for short-term therapy, a package of five sessions. At her request, we focus the first session with the goal of getting better acquainted. Maxine wants time to tell me more about her current feelings and thoughts. She reiterates her goals for therapy, including that she wants to find out how to feel happier with the life she has. As the first session comes to a close, I introduce the core values survey:

LG: Maxine, I appreciate that in this first session you have helped me understand more about yourself, your past life, and present-day current concerns. I understand that you want to resolve your feelings of emptiness and wondering if there is more for you, at this age and stage of life.

MAXINE: Yes, that is what I am feeling and thinking, although I don't understand exactly why. Can you help with this?

LG: I have a process that I would like to offer, starting with some homework. As a former teacher, how do you feel about homework?

MAXINE: I loved teaching and I always gave homework. It was really helpful as a way to move students further, to have them think about what they heard and learned in my class. I was always an excellent student myself, so homework is fine with me.

LG: Okay, that is good to know. Here is a list of almost one hundred core values. (See the list at the end of this chapter.) I would like you to look through this list as your homework. Then before our next session, your task is to select your three top values, those that represent principles you hold most dear now, at this stage of life. They may be the same or different than those at an earlier stage. Here is one request from me. Please try not to judge what you select. Don't pick those values you think you should hold dear; instead, find those values you already stand for, ones that are significant to who you are and how you are naturally wired.

MAXINE: Just glancing through this, it's a long list. Many of these seem like good standards to live by.

LG: I agree, but I would like you to narrow this to just three. For example, if fairness is one of your core values, you are fair, regardless of whether anyone else notices or cares. You are naturally drawn to listen to both sides. You give others the benefit of the doubt. Your evenhandedness is reflected in all your relationships and the way you try to live your life. No one has to tell you to be reasonable; you already are. You get upset or angry when this value is violated, when someone is unfair.

MAXINE: Okay, I get it. I will have three picked out by next session. Thanks. This is interesting to think about.

Prioritizing Values

At the next session, Maxine comes in with three core values circled: *nurturing, honesty,* and *learning.* We spend a lot of time talking about these values in the session. I ask questions, she talks at length. I ask her to tell me how each has influenced her life.

Maxine shares anecdotes, some that she has not thought about for many years. I listen, acknowledge her experiences, and basically enjoy the conversation, getting to know her now based on her principles and core beliefs. I watch her body language and facial expressions as she recounts the memories tied to each value. Then I help her prioritize just one value of the three, for our next step together.

LG: Of these three values, which would you say are still central for you today?

MAXINE: I was thinking about that myself, after doing the homework. I am still very much a part of my family, so nurturing is part of my life. I spend time with my daughters and grandchildren and enjoy the contact and being part of their world. I am not as necessary to my daughters as I once was when my children were younger and my husband was alive, but I do see them all regularly. I like doing things for them, like baking pies, and of course I talk with the grandchildren about their school and what it going on in their lives.

LG: You are still involved in the nurturing of family and it is meaningful to you. What about honesty?

MAXINE: Well, that is one that has been with me for my whole life. I abhor lying in any form. I have always set things up to be honest as I could be, in my work, with my family. I am in a book club and I give my opinion, even if others aren't agreeing with me. I think it also shows in the way I vote for politicians. I put a lot of weight into who is telling the truth and who is not. So that is still with me.

LG: Honesty is at your center, it seems. What about learning?

MAXINE: This is what I think I am missing. I used to feel like I was always thinking. My mind was active and engaged with so many things. I was teaching, and you know, we always had to take courses because the schools changed their methods over time. I traveled with my husband and loved to see places. We had guides on some of the trips, and that was wonderful and exciting. I was always a big reader, both of fiction and nonfiction.

LG: You had a life filled with learning and travel adventure with your husband. That must have been very special.

MAXINE: But right now, at this point in my life, I am not interested in travel. I don't have a travel companion and really, with my arthritis, it's not a pleasure. I try to read, but often nod off in the quiet of the room. I see my women friends, those who are still alive. Mostly we just play cards and talk about inconsequential things. A lot of gossip, to tell you the truth.

LG: That is important to understand, that one of your core values is no longer central to your life. It seems like the lack of learning has changed the current quality of life for you in many ways.

MAXINE: Without mental stimulation, I am bored. I worry that I am boring as well.

LG: Are you more concerned with being bored or with being boring?

MAXINE: Is there a difference? You ask hard questions, Lynn. Let me think. (I sense I have hit upon an effective question. She takes some time, and I see sadness on her face.) The truth is that I am bored with myself, so it's the worst of both.

LG: That takes honesty to say. I can only imagine how it must feel, after a lifetime of being so engaged in learning, to be bored with yourself. I hope you can take more time to think about this lack of stimulation, and we can talk about it further next time. What will you take away from today's session?

MAXINE: It is making things much more clear to me. I am bored, and I am boring myself! I am stuck in old routines. How can I get engaged in my love of knowledge when I am so old? Can I ever find life interesting again? I will think about this a lot more.

Aligning Values and Decisions

During the next session, our third, I suggest that Maxine talk about a way to bring her value of learning front and center into her current life. I ask if she has any ideas. Maxine reviews the things she had done in her past, but none of them fits for her now. She is not interested in traveling, nor joining another book group, nor learning to play a new type of card game. I listen to the long list of things she does not want to do. Some of these rejected ideas are based on being alone, a widow without a partner; some are due to her age and feeling more fatigue and less healthy than in the past.

In this session, I hear her sadness and depression, how uninterested she feels with the life that she has right now. Maxine has spent many years unintentionally making her world smaller, with set routines and reasons for not doing things. I stop myself from offering any solutions. I feel she would just reject my ideas, as she had rejected her own. This is a situation in therapy where some therapists err, in their desire to be helpful: to try to suggest or advise or brainstorm before a client can be receptive to anything new.

Instead, I validate her feelings. Each time she raises an idea herself, I ask gentle questions, several of them in the variety of "tell me more" or "how might that work?" She then talks it through, and rejects her own idea. I validate her rejection, saying something like, "that makes sense, it is not much fun to take a walk when your knees are bothering you." I want her to find her own ideas. For now, she has run out of options. She looks dejected. I believe that the best ideas will come from Maxine herself, but as her therapist and collaborator, she might need me to frame a question or two in order to prompt her. By anticipating her frustration and not rushing in to find an answer for her, I am able to make a decision in line with her value of learning. See how I did this in the transcript below.

LG: I know you have exhausted your ideas right now, and you seem very sad that there is no obvious solution.

MAXINE: It's hopeless. This is why I came in to see you. We are not getting any further. You charge a lot, but you're not doing very well as a therapist. I will give you a report card when we are done.

LG: (Not taking the bait or feeling defensive) I look forward to that evaluation. I do have a question: What activity from the past do you feel helped you learn the most?

MAXINE: Oh, that's easy. Becoming a teacher. I loved getting that teaching certificate, it meant everything to me. I learned so much by teaching. I was most alive when I was teaching others, because I had to read and study and observe. I really miss that. I enjoyed every school year, can you imagine that? Everything was interesting to me, all the funny stories the children brought in, who they were, how they grew and developed, and even the subjects I taught. It was really lucky that I chose to be a teacher.

LG: Being a teacher was a wonderful education for you.

MAXINE: Yes, it was.

LG: Here comes another one of my hard questions: Are you willing to take a risk and teach again?

MAXINE: (in a small voice) Who would want to learn anything from me now?

LG: Maybe that's the wrong question.

MAXINE: What is the right one?

LG: Who is someone *you* could learn from now, in the process of teaching?

MAXINE: (Silent, looks at me with intense stare.)

LG: I can see that this is hard. I think you might be in the process of learning something new right now, in this conversation. It is not always easy to learn.

MAXINE: You are making me think about a lot of things. You are right, it's not easy, but I want to give all of this some thought. I hope I can figure out the answer to this last question.

LG: As do I. The answer might change your life. It is a very big question to consider.

MAXINE: It is. I am really immersed in this question.

LG: Given we are at the end of our session, what will you take away from today?

MAXINE: I am going to think more about this, that's my homework. I might talk to a good friend about this. That's the best I can say right now.

LG: That seems productive, thinking more about this and maybe talking with a trusted friend.

A Value-Based Plan

Maxine leaves the session unsettled, but she is thinking and, I hope, starting to learn something about herself from the process of therapy.

I know she leaves with some anxiety from my questions. I will trust the process of therapy—that what has emerged is going to be useful. I think that someone who loves the value of learning may be open to my reframe, that even in the process of discomfort in therapy, she may be learning something new. You may recognize by now, after the skills I have described in this book, that being a client in this model of therapy can prove to be disquieting. You and your client need to accept the rocky sea at times. When a client is in the process of changing a belief or an old and set way of thinking, it makes sense to see their disturbance expressed, even if it means that the client seems disturbed or irritated. If you can stay calm and centered, it allows a client to have a chance to continue to process a change, and ultimately opens the possibility of new thinking, feelings or behaviors.

I later learned that Maxine thought about her question all week. She talked to her good friend and came up with a plan. That Sunday, she went to church and took a big risk. She reached out to a church member who organized a tutoring program for homeless children. In spite of her limitations of age and health, Maxine asked if she could be of help. Did they need another volunteer tutor? The church member was delighted and relieved; she had children in great need of help all the time. Maxine was immediately matched with a nine-year-old girl. We spent her fourth session anticipating the tutoring, which for Maxine involved feelings of excitement and anxiety. The next week Maxine comes to her fifth session. She is smiling.

MAXINE: Lynn, I have your grade. You get an A-plus as a therapist. I can't believe it, but I am teaching again! This little girl is the smartest, dearest thing. She really wants to learn, and she thanked me and shook my hand when we were done. I felt alive again. I told my daughters and my women friends. I couldn't wait to tell you all about it.

LG: Tell me everything!

MAXINE: I want to tell you about the tutoring—my preparation and lesson plan, getting to the neighborhood after-school center to meet my student. It feels strange to be back in a classroom, but good. I had a conversation with the girl's mother, who came to pick her up and meet me. Oh, Lynn, the feel of the child's hand in mine as we said goodbye. The tutoring will be a weekly contract for the rest of the school year, and maybe into the summer if I am available. I am ready.

LG: I am very impressed with all you did.

MAXINE: I think this was a missing piece, to have a sense of going back to my roots and teaching again.

LG: Might you also be getting educated in this process?

MAXINE: Well, of course, you would ask another one of your questions. Yes, I am learning a lot myself. I am teaching reading to an elementary-age child. I haven't done that since I was a student teacher, more than 50 years ago. I needed to find a book we could use. Thank goodness for the Internet, which I never had much use for before except for email with my grandchildren. I found a lot about the way reading is taught now, quite different from my early days. It's fascinating.

This is a very different Maxine: engaged, curious, active. By aligning herself with this forgotten core value of learning, she finds a renewed purpose in life at age 80. Given that this is our last contracted session, we end with an open-door policy: Maxine can return for more therapy as desired, but for now, she wants to see if this new activity will be good enough.

Your Turn: Align with Core Values

Use this exercise to master the skill. If you have not taken time to identify your own set of core values, please use this exercise on yourself first, before using it with clients.

1. *Identify core values.* To bring the topic of values into therapy in a concrete way, offer a client a core values list similar to the one offered below. Ask a client to target no more than three core values for this process.

2. *Align action with values.* Use therapy sessions to help your client talk about his or her top three values. Allow your client to talk about how these values have influenced earlier choices and decisions. Ask questions, hear stories from the past. Listen, acknowledge, and be curious. Suggest that your client select one value to focus on now. Then ask

your client to consider how to orient some problem, challenge or desired goal to highlight this core value.

3. *Design a value-based plan.* Help your client orient a goal based on furthering the selected, specific core value. Talk about a plan to resolve the goal. Ask:

> *How does this plan honor the core value?*
> *What steps will bring this value into play?*
> *Is there a way to make sure that the solution to the problem, challenge, or goal allows this value to shine through?*

4. *Map out the plan with measurable action steps.* Once your client is satisfied with a plan that is based on the selected value, commit the plan to paper. Track progress toward the goal in subsequent sessions. Check that the core value remains at the forefront of the plan as it unfolds. Celebrate any wins. Use sessions to overcome obstacles. Continue to process how a plan based on the core value changes and improves the level of meaning and purpose in your client's life.

Here is a sample list of core values that you can share with your clients; ask them to supplement with any that they hold dear that are not listed.

Core Values List

accomplishment	duty	influence	power
action	economy	inspiration	quiet
adventure	encouragement	integrity	respect
advocacy	enlightenment	intuition	risk
altruism	excellence	invention	rules
assurance	experience	joy	sacredness
awareness	expression	justice	safety
beauty	fairness	kindness	security
diversity	faith	leadership	sensuality
optimism	family	learning	service

challenge	freedom	literature	attraction
change	friendship	love	spirituality
children	frugality	loyalty	stability
cleanliness	fun	mastering	strength
community	goodwill	nature	support
compassion	grace	novelty	trust
connection	gratitude	nurturing	truth
contribution	growth	openness	understanding
courage	happiness	organization	vitality
creativity	home	partnership	wholeness
daring	honesty	patience	winning
decency	honor	peace	wonder
democracy	humility	persuasion	youthfulness
discovery	imagination	perfection	playfulness

Feel free to use this list or develop your own. Other lists of core values can be found at:

- http://www.taproot.com/archives/37771
- *The CoachU Personal Development Workbook and Guide,* John Wiley & Sons, 2005, pg. 141.
- VIA (Values in Action) Strengths Survey at https://www.viacharacter .org/survey/account/register

I will return to the idea of aligning a plan with core values in the last chapter in this section, to show you the skill to help a client learn to design a plan for life. But first, see the next skill that builds on the topic of personal growth and furthers possibility. Help clients resolve difficult, personal problems by tapping into their internal resources, including the wisdom of their imagination.

13

Skill #8: Find the Metaphors that Matter

"Therapy is a mountain to climb. Think of me as your guide," the therapist said. "I have climbed many mountains with others, but this one, your mountain, is unique because it is about you. From time to time, I will be a lookout, to spot a ledge we can stand on. We can look out over the valley below, to see how far you have come."

"What happens when I get to the top?" asked the client, who was, in fact, an outdoor enthusiast.

"That's up to you. You can stop and enjoy the view and celebrate, knowing that you reached your goal. Or you can look for the next peak to conquer."

This metaphor about therapy was offered by a therapist during a workshop I taught years ago, when I asked for creative examples from therapists to demonstrate how they describe the work of therapy. Words can paint a picture for a client. If you talk to clients in a way that conveys a deep awareness of their experience, you probably make use of some metaphors. Well-crafted metaphors—analogies or comparisons that make abstract concepts more concrete—offer clients helpful perspectives about intangible situations.

Starting from my earliest days, working as a psychotherapist, I liked to use metaphors. They offered new possibility to clients, new perspective. I borrowed the style my therapist demonstrated. I prepared stories with embedded messages and suggestions, or I offered an anecdote from my own reading, training, or personal experience. Developing Therapy with a Coaching Edge, I changed my thinking about metaphors. I now prefer primarily to use metaphors that are client-based. When a client is stuck with a problem, I co-create a story or symbol that is specifically relevant to his or her inner thoughts and feelings. In the coaching literature, I was interested to see that a specific client-based process of using metaphors is often mentioned; I now use this process, with some adaptation, for facilitating the creation of client-based metaphors within a therapy setting. Anytime I can help clients find their own solutions this way, it is empowering: Clients see more possibility for themselves, knowing that problems are not as intolerable if they have the healing solution inside their own mind.

In this chapter, I teach you the skill I modified to elicit client-based metaphors in therapy. You will see how it helps clients begin to find a hidden resource for resolving their problems, one that exists within their own memories, associations, and imagination. Solutions to big and small issues can be unearthed inside a client's everyday language. This process is also useful in that it motivates client behavioral change. When clients create their personal solution in this way, they seem eager to take immediate action steps. They now "own" the solution, since it emerged from their internal symbols, in a way that a metaphor I might have imposed can't match.

First, let me explain how metaphors work. Then I want to explain the difference between the power of a metaphor you might come up with and offer, versus one that a client invents. I will show you the steps to co-create a client-based metaphor, including a case example. You can see how a client-based metaphor flows from a simple therapy conversation to an actual solution, in an elegant and memorable way.

HOW METAPHORS HELP

Since its inception more than a hundred years ago, psychotherapy has a history of using metaphors for healing purposes. Psychotherapists listened to their clients and noted the analogies and symbols that clients hinted at through their language. Freud and Jung delved into symbols to explain deeper motivations. Adler followed, seeing metaphors as a window into a whole brain process, a way of understanding how his patients thought, reasoned, perceived, imagined, and communicated.[1]

In contemporary therapy, it has commonly become the role of the therapist to be the one to supply a metaphor in a session to help a client develop insight or change behavior. This can be very effective and sometimes the metaphor is part of a hypnotic induction. An effective example of a therapist-constructed metaphor for this purpose is described by marriage and family therapist Ron Soderquist, in a case about a father who wanted therapy for his 13-year-old daughter with a disturbing habit: she picked her nose, in private and in public, and ate the mucus.[2] The father said this was a long-term, seemingly unconscious habit from childhood, but now that his daughter was being teased by other students, he wanted therapy to help her control the behavior. When Soderquist met with the daughter, he used a metaphor to remove judgment for behaving in an antisocial way. "[Bad] habits are like a virus in a computer," he told the daughter. "Would it be okay if we updated your software today?"

A metaphor can immediately shift perception and reduce sticky emotions like blame. Using this analogy, Soderquist lifts the judgment of the girl's peers; she is not culpable, it's just her brain acting like an infected computer. A metaphor can override the conscious, resistant mind and offer a more workable perspective on an intractable problem. The difference between telling a teenager: "Don't pick your nose all the time," versus "Let's update your software," removes embarrassment and in doing so, makes other interventions possible. With Soderquist's metaphor, a problem becomes a puzzle, ready for the solving with some additional clinical or hypnotic interventions.

According to one classic work on metaphor, we respond well to metaphors because we are already primed for thinking imaginatively, espe-

---

1 Mueller, C. L. (2015). *We are metaphor: How client-generated metaphors relate to Adlerian Theory. A master's project.* Paper presented to The Faculty of the Adler Graduate School. Retrieved from http://alfredadler.edu/sites/default/files/Mueller%20MP%202015.pdf

2 Soderquist, R. (2016). Upgrading the software: A one-session cure for an obnoxious habit. *Psychotherapy Networker.*

cially about ordinary issues.[3] Our brains naturally combine reality and creativity as a way to make sense of a perplexing world. Since metaphors are part of common speech, they can be heard in daily expressions ("It's a tug of war with my sister when we argue."), or deeper ideas with additional levels of meaning ("My family life was a circus, so now that I am an adult, I tend to favor a little craziness in my love life."). Some are embedded and partially unconscious ("I take on a lot of responsibility for my friends, always propping them up, then this week for no reason, my back gives out.") Your clients are continually using metaphors in their speech; we all do.

Since your clients are already speaking, at times, in metaphor, consider two important questions:

- *Can you hear the metaphoric language?* It may take some intention to listen for it.
- *Can you find the solution within the metaphor?* Once you learn to listen for symbolic language, you can use it to help your client resolve important problems.

Let me show you how to do both, to listen for client's symbolic language and then use it to further a client's goals, by applying a method that favors client-based control.

Client-Based Metaphors

When my clients discover that the solutions to their own problems may exist within themselves, I find it boosts their self-esteem. This process took me some time to understand. At first, in therapy sessions, I could hear that my clients were often associating certain symbols and stories to communicate their issues. I heard common expressions like: *That hit me like a ton of bricks. I'm dead tired. I nipped it in the bud.* I also heard more unique, even poetic expressions: *Love is a lemon, bitter and best in small doses. Cancer and time are both thieves, stealing from me.*

---

3 Lakoff, G. & Johnson, M. (1980) *Metaphors we live by.* Chicago: University of Chicago Press.

His anger is a thunderstorm that busts out the windows and breaks my dishes and my heart. I could hear the symbolic language, but the idea that their symbols and language could be an effective and creative way to heal issues was new to me, until I began reading the work of psychologist David Grove. His work began as a process for therapists and evolved into a variety of methods. I first learned of it through the coaching literature.

In 1980, Grove was studying how to reduce traumatic memory and post-traumatic stress disorder (PTSD). He found that traumatized clients, lacking the words to describe their difficult symptoms, often explained their distress with the use of metaphor. When he reflected back the clients' imagery and words to them, his clients began to shift their subjective experience about the trauma. Symptoms began to change as well. Grove, a native of New Zealand and Maori culture, wanted to facilitate these stories and symbols, but not intrude on the elicitation. He introduced a technique of "clean language" to help his clients identify and claim their own highly personal and meaningful symbols, without the interference of a therapist's retelling the story and bringing therapist bias into the meaning.[4]

Clean language is a very specific protocol that requires some study. The therapist is trained to eliminate bias, the unconscious inflections that can show up in syntax or wording. In this way, as the therapist prompts the story, every sentence the therapist utters is "cleaned" so as to not interfere with the client's own symbolism. Over time, Grove's technique of clean language became its own method, called symbolic modeling, now popular in some models of therapy and coaching.[5]

I appreciated Grove's theory as developed for trauma reduction, but in practice, I was not comfortable with Grove's rigorous protocol for symbolic modeling. It felt too constraining and stilted for me to be able to use in a talk therapy session, and still maintain a natural, collaborative alliance. When I saw how clean language was used in coaching, I espe-

---

4 Grove, D. & Panzer, B. I. (1989) *Resolving Traumatic Memories: Metaphors and Symbols in Psychotherapy.* Irvington Pub.
5 Lawley, J. &Tompkins, P. (2000). *Metaphors in Mind: Transformation Through Symbolic Modelling.* London: Developing Company Press.

cially liked an adaptation of Grove's process from Marian Way.[6] I began to experiment how to keep the essence of Grove's model, as I understood it, and as Way had interpreted it, but speak more normally to stay in rapport with my client. Let me explain how this model of Grove's works within my adaptation for Therapy with a Coaching Edge.

When my client has a difficult decision to make or problem to solve, I listen for my client's unique language and symbols. I honor the client's personal symbolism by matching or mirroring his language. I facilitate to expand the client's story and help to elicit the symbolic solution. Going from a story to a plan of action becomes easier, because it is so entwined with imagination and creativity.

It begins during a session. A client is troubled with a problem. If he or she begins to talk about it using an analogy, or symbolic language, or a metaphor, I stay alert: I focus on the metaphor as a way to enter the client's world and use a few specific techniques. My therapy sessions with my client, Larry, show how I used this client-based metaphor process to help him tackle a critical issue he faced: How to stop feeling abused by a tough boss.

Listening for the Metaphor

A year after the death of his partner from AIDS, Larry moved, with his young son, to a new city to begin working as a project manager in a large nonprofit agency. He was excited by the job, which paid well. He hoped the move would give him and his son a chance to start over and build a new life, one without all their painful memories confronting them each day. Larry is still grieving and tells me that he feels very tired. Tiredness is a common symptom I hear in therapy, one that often masks other issues. We have been meeting weekly for two months. I start the session wanting to find out more about his tiredness. (Note: My responses that show me listening for the metaphor are in italics.)

LARRY: I am tired after a day in the office. I am still trying to figure out the hierarchy and dynamics that go on there. It's so political. Most

---

6 Way, M. (2013). *Clean Approaches for Coaches.* Clean Publishing.

of the people there have been in their jobs for a while, and the old-timers have the influence. They stake out territory. I am constantly trying to figure out not just what I am supposed to do, but how to get along with others.

LG: (I hear two metaphors: *work is political* and *co-workers stake out territory*. I am not ready to elicit more about them yet.) This all sounds hard. I can understand you would be tired at the end of a day. Tell me more.

LARRY: One of the bosses, a manager assigned to oversee my team, is always criticizing me. She doesn't mean to hurt me, I think she is trying to help me take off the brakes and get up to speed. I guess. She wants me to do more and do it faster. (Larry sighs and pauses for a while.) But I end up feeling bruised.

LG: (I hear two more metaphors: *get up to speed* and *feeling bruised*.) You seem close to tears when you say you feel bruised. Help me understand what you mean by this.

LARRY: Look, I am not at my best right now in life. I am not that strong, I just had my husband die after a long illness. I lost a lot of weight. I get depleted. I had to move with my son to start a new life for us. I am new here and finding my way. This is my manager, and she has a lot of feedback to give me. But it just seems like when she comes into my office at the end of the day, she is throwing punches. I can't take it. I end up getting bruised.

Expanding the Meaning

I notice that when a metaphor is accompanied by emotion or strong symbolic language, this is often my cue to explore it further. I ask the client to go a bit deeper into the symbolism. To do this, I bridge from what the client has said, using an adaptation of the "clean language" technique, from the work of Grove, that I referenced earlier. Clean language means that I respond to what has been said with the word "and" followed by the client's symbolic language. It's like a run-on sentence, one where I pick up on what the client has just said. Then I will prompt the client to say more, by asking: "What happens next?"

or "What is that like?" I keep a calm, nonjudgmental demeanor and ask these questions gently. I pace this to match the client's rate of speech. I try to help the metaphor develop easily. Possible clean language questions include:

And what happens next?
And then?
And how does that feel in the moment?
And who is with you when this happens?
And that's like what?
And is there anything else about that?
And who is that speaking?
And whereabouts is this taking place?

Here is the continuing conversation with Larry, with the clean language adaption, as the metaphor of "getting bruised" deepens. (Note: My comments and questions to deepen the metaphor are in italics.)

LG: *And when she throws a punch, and you get bruised, what is that like?*

LARRY: It's like pain. I get hurt. It literally hurts me. I just want to cry, but of course I don't. Like I said, I feel beat up, really beat up.

LG: *And when you feel beat up, what happens next?*

LARRY: That's the thing. I get confused, like rattled. I can't talk. I actually shut my eyes the other day while she was talking to me. I feel like once she starts, I can't see and I can't think. That's how I get beat up.

LG: *And what else is there to say about how you get beat up?*

LARRY: I know a little about getting beat up. I used to box a bit in high school. I hated it, and it was hard, but I did learn a few things that helped me as I got older. I could defend myself. As a gay man, that was useful. I know when a punch comes, you are supposed to turn away from the punch.

LG: *And when the punch comes at you, what happens next?*

LARRY: When the punch comes, it hurts. You are supposed to keep your eyes open and see it coming and then turn away from the punch. So that it passes through you and doesn't land too solid. If it really lands, you are in trouble.

LG: *And when the punch comes and really lands, how are you in trouble?*

LARRY: It's like I am shocked. Bam! Each time, I guess I don't see it coming. At work, I am so overwhelmed by the end of the day. She comes in to talk to me, and before I know it, bam, there it comes, the punch. She says something that is so important, it's all about numbers and analysis, and it lands hard. I am so new at the job. I am barely hanging on. I don't know all the things I am supposed to be doing, so I don't have a way to defend myself from her criticism. Maybe she is right and I am really a lousy project manager, I am thinking. I am just standing there, open, and a good target for the punch to connect.

LG: *And when you are a good target and the punch connects, what happens then?*

LARRY: It makes me feel weak, on top of everything else. I am so defenseless. I crumble, fall down on the mat. She wins. I lose.

Solutions within the Story

This is Larry's personal, symbolic metaphor that is unfolding; I don't want to impose my bias, thoughts or judgment, but shifting my role a bit to enable the solution is necessary to move this forward. The story he tells me so far leaves him crumbled on the mat. I will not leave him there, collapsed. I need to facilitate the unpacking of information in the metaphor and to help him stay on track, so that the telling doesn't veer off and in doing so, create more trauma. My role is to trust that there is a solution in the story and help him bring it to light. It's as though I hand him a flashlight at this point in the story, and with the light in his hand, together we look for a bright gem of a solution, buried right inside the deep story.

At this point, when I am looking with him for the solution, I break the "clean language" approach. I stop saying "and" to begin a sentence. I ask more directive questions to encourage Larry to bring its teachings into the present day. Simon Maryon, a coach who has written about the

Grove process, calls this stage of a client-based metaphor "turning the focus away from the client to explore the metaphor."[7] What he means is that the facilitator becomes interested in what the experience being described may hold. You can see how I do this, turning the focus away from the pain of Larry, to the subject of boxing, to help him see the possibilities. Questions to find solutions can include:

What needs to happen now?
How can this go forward?
What do you do to change this?
What would help turn this around?
What resource is hidden in this memory or story, and could help?
What is the best way through this?
Where can you look in this story for an answer?

I used some of these questions, adding in the specific details of the story Larry relates, in order to prompt him to find his own solutions. (Note: My questions to find a solution are in italics.)

LG: I want to make sure I understand what you are describing, so that I understand what happens to you. You said you crumble and fall on the mat and that in boxing, that means you lose. *What do you need to do, when you are boxing, so you don't crumble onto the mat?*

LARRY: Well, basically, I need to deflect the punch so it doesn't land so well.

LG: *How do you deflect a punch in the ring?*

LARRY: My boxing teacher was pretty clear about this. He was a real piece of work, always yelling at those of us who were not great boxers. I guess I can thank him for teaching me this one lesson, since I got bullied in school and punched a few times. I never really got hurt in a school fight, and this is why. What you do is keep your eyes open. You see the punch coming. You turn your body slightly away from

_____

7 http://www.gomentor.com/simonmaryan/blog/321-the-use-of-metaphors-in
-coaching.aspx

the punch so it doesn't really land square. You can even parry, which means that you raise your hand to swat it away. My teacher would yell, "Parry, Larry!" when I was in the ring training, his cue for me to blunt the hardest punches and swat them away.

LG: That's really instructive. Let me see if I have all of this. You stay alert, keep your eyes open. You turn away from the force so it doesn't land squarely, full on. You learn to "Parry, Larry" to blunt the force of the hardest punches.

LARRY: You got it.

LG: *Knowing this, how can you deflect a punch at the office from this manager at the end of the day?*

LARRY: That's a really good question. A really good question. Let me think about this. Let me think about what my boxing teacher would say.

LG: (I am silent while Larry goes back into his symbolic story to find his answer.)

LARRY: I need to do a few things. One thing is to keep my eyes open. I need to watch for her to come into my cubicle so I can get ready. Then I need to see it coming, as soon as she starts to talk about what I did wrong. I have to deflect the criticism so it doesn't land so hard. Like when she tells me what I did wrong, I end up feeling blamed because I take it on the chin. But she is actually talking about something I did, not who I am. It's her form of feedback. I need to keep the focus on what I did that worried her. What I did, not who I am. This is important. Because it's what I say to my son. I tell him that in my mind, there are no bad kids, only bad behavior at the moment.

LG: There is an important, deep understanding here about how to resolve getting bruised. *Deflecting the punch seems to mean many things.* How to keep standing. How to blunt the criticism by focusing on its meaning. But also, remembering that in the face of criticism, there is a difference between who you are versus what you did. This is a distinction you give to your son. *So, if you remember this message yourself . . .*

LARRY: If I remember it myself, I am walking my talk. Not taking the punch full on, but not getting out of the ring either, so to speak. I'm not going to run away or collapse.

LG: *You're still in the ring, toughening up.*

LARRY: Yes, this job is like a boxing ring. I know I am weakened by my husband's death, but I need to be strong. The manager is like a sparring trainer, trying to save me from falling flat on my butt. I can take it, I can do this and hang in. As long as I see it coming, I can deflect and parry. I am so glad I finally see this. I know how to do this.

Making it Real

Once Larry has found a solution within his symbolic boxing metaphor, I ask him to create actions to move this forward. What can be done to use the solution in current life, to address the initial problem? In this way, the metaphor is brought forward and given more concrete value. Often, because the solution is one that the client has created, he is very motivated to follow through on making it real, by developing an action plan. (Note: My questions to identify actions are in italics.)

LG: *Based on all you now see and understand, what specific actions can you take to make this situation better?*

LARRY: One is to keep alert and watch for her. She comes in at the end of my day. Be ready. Stand up from my desk, to be at eye level. Be strong in my posture. Meet her on solid ground, don't be at a disadvantage by staying in my seat. Meet her professional to professional. Second, I am not going to stay silent when she criticizes. I will ask what specifically, in my behavior, she thinks needs to be different. That's a parry. It's also a way I remind myself that this is about what I am doing, not who I am. Third, I am going to think about her as my sparring partner, so I can have a new perspective on her comments. She is training me up, not out to get me.

LG: These are very good ideas, and each one seems doable immediately. It also might be good to add in some self-talk, something to tell yourself during the week to stay strong. *Is there anything that you heard yourself say here today that you can use as a mantra or a personal slogan?*

LARRY: *I am not leaving the ring. I just need to toughen up.* I am going to tell my son about this, so he knows his dad is in training to be stronger!

LG: I like that. The more you remind yourself of your capacity to strengthen and grow, the easier this job will become.

Your Turn: Find the Metaphors that Matter

Use this exercise to master the skill.

1. *Listen for the metaphor.* In the discussion of a problem or issue, you may hear a client use symbolic language to describe a situation, especially how it feels. Pay attention to any and all references in normal conversation. The metaphor may be linked with deep emotion or a change in affect.

2. *Develop and deepen the metaphor with the client.* Respond with using clean language: Ask a run-on question beginning with "and" and then a repetition of the metaphor, to stay in the midst of the symbolic story with a client. Maintain rapport and watch your pacing so that it matches your client's. Examples of clean language questions for the therapist to ask in the midst of deepening the metaphor are:

   And what happens next?
   And then?
   And how does that feel in the moment?
   And who is with you when this happens?
   And that's like what?
   And is there anything else about that?

3. *Find the solution within the story.* Gently stop the clean language. No more run-on sentences. Turn from the client to the symbol or topic. Ask the client to explain more about the metaphor. Focus your questions on finding strategies, hidden meaning, strengths, and skills within the story to make the metaphor more concrete. See if your client can relate what is being understood through this process to the present day issue, so the solution can be brought forward. Use active listening, and pace your questions slowly. Don't bias the solution by trying to impose one. Just stay with the process long enough for your

client to generate the resolution of the issue. Questions to elicit the solution can include:

What needs to happen now?
How can this go forward?
What do you do to change this?
What would help turn this around?
What resource is hidden in this memory or story, and could help?
What is the best way through this?
Where can you look in this story for an answer?

4. *Summarize the solution.* Create action steps to make the solution more concrete. Suggest that your client find a mantra to use, as a phrase or a sentence, to capture the meaning of the solution.

Now that you know how to encourage more possible solutions, by co-creating a client-based metaphor, there is one more skill to complete this section about possibility: How to help a client look ahead and see not just a treatment plan, but a plan for a fulfilled life. Let me show you how to help clients design a satisfying future.

14

Skill #9: Design a Plan for Life

Beverly says she is done with therapy, that she has gotten all she needs. Many therapists treating Beverly would agree. Six months ago, she presented with anxiety and depression as well as stress-related health issues. In her sessions, she identified several issues: the strain of a demanding job, her husband's drinking problem, and her lack of consistent self-care. Reducing stress in her life was a focus of her treatment. By using the skills within my model, Therapy with a Coaching Edge, I helped her to set and achieve a number of goals. Beverly has evidence of progress: Her health problems are less acute and she has some specific boundaries in place to deal with the demands of work and to be less enmeshed with her husband.

She ticks off her therapy results: "My anxiety and depression are now in check. I am calmer. I sleep better. I know how to avoid the most difficult problems my boss causes me at work. I can stand up for myself when my husband is being belligerent. I think, given the way my life is, this is the best I can do. I mean, I will always have a hard job, probably these chronic health issues will still be around, and my husband will always be a drink away from a crisis. But I don't mean to say that therapy wasn't useful because I got a lot from our sessions. So, I guess I am done. Unless there is anything more you can think that I should do in therapy?"

Beverly is one of those clients I feel lucky to have gotten to know. She is resilient and has overcome many hardships. She grew up in poverty, got educated by dint of her own hard work and school scholarships, and has been the main support for her family. At 45, she works long hours in a full-time job and is a caring wife and mother, who gives much to others. She has little time or energy left for herself. As I think about her logical, yet melancholy assessment of her future, a phrase comes to my mind, one that I often heard Thomas Leonard, my teacher at CoachU, say, when he was coaching someone who had a limited outlook of the future. "What I want for you," Leonard would begin, and then fill in the rest of the sentence with an optimistic, expansive, heartfelt wish for another. For a few seconds, I think about what I want for Beverly.

What I want for Beverly is a way to reduce future sources of stress and rise above them, to have a plan over time, for optimal health and wellness. What I want for her is to continue to grow more assertive and develop stronger boundaries. What I want for her is the gift of time: time for her own endeavors, time to have fun, and even travel to those places she longs to visit, as she ages. I try to put what I am thinking into words.

"Beverly, I agree you have met your treatment goals, but sitting here, I can't help myself from thinking about what else you might want in your life, what else could be possible. I wonder if we could use this session to talk through the beginning of a life plan, one that focuses on your health and happiness. Would this be of interest to you today?"

She nods enthusiastically. I am sure, given what I know about her resources and the people in her life, that this is a unique offer. Probably no one has ever tried to help her plan for a better, brighter future, one that is focused on her well-being. Designing a life plan with a therapy client brings together all four key aspects of a coaching approach: It uses a client-centered focus, and relies on partnership, possibility, and action, in one definitive process.

In this chapter, I will show you how to design a life plan with a client, the specific steps to take, the language to use to introduce this concept, and offer you a template that gives a life plan some structure. This final skill relies on many of the skills you have learned in earlier chapters, and I will reference the previous techniques as they occur. One aspect to note about life planning with a client: If you use this as a parting process with a client, sometimes it can extend therapy sessions, since you may identify goals that clients want to tackle right away, rather than wait to achieve over time. If this extension is acceptable to both therapist and client, then anticipate that looking to the future can deepen the conversation about the present. For other clients, designing a life plan can serve to summarize and digest all that has occurred in therapy, allowing you and your clients to end therapy well, with a sense of completion and anticipation. You acknowledge the work that has been done, and see that with the preparation of therapy, a client's future direction is clear and inviting.

To me, at its best, a life plan functions like a map of what is probable and possible for a client. Imagine that you and the client are standing at the center of a valley. Your client can note her issues and challenges within the immediate landscape, but with this map she can also look out a bit further to the foothills of self-esteem, filled with possibility, self-confidence, and achievement. Raising her gaze higher, she can see further to the alluring mountain range, off in the distance, filled with self-actualization, creativity, and legacy. What she needs from you, beyond the map showing the possibilities, is a path forward.

Aspects of a Life Plan

Let me start by contrasting a life plan, which may be unfamiliar to therapists, to a treatment plan, one we know how to craft. A treatment plan has the elements of assessment, presenting problems, diagnosis, objectives, and measures of success. Whereas a treatment plan considers the past, present, and short-term future, a life plan takes these some of these same factors into consideration, but brings them into the longer-term future. It makes sense for therapists to consider the longer-term future, as part of treatment. "Action is not driven by the past, but pulled by the future," says Martin Seligman, PhD, explaining the psychology of "prospection"—the mental evaluation of possible futures. He posits that future-looking therapies could devote some of the time now dedicated to the exploration of past events to helping the patient explore possible future situations by incentivizing the future.[1] "What if we are not *Homo sapiens*, but *Homo Prospectus*?" Seligman asks.

---

1 Seligman, M., Railton, P., Baumeister, R.F., & Sripaga, C. (2013) Navigating the future or driven by the past: Perspectives on psychological science. Retrieved from https://www .prospectivepsych.org/sites/www.prospectivepsych.org/files/pictures/Seligman-et-al _Navigating-into-the-future-2013.pdf.

My skill for life planning starts with a basic three-step formulation, similar to the "what, who, and how" strategy I explained in Skill #2: Be a Strategist with a Twist. It may help you to review that chapter, because you will be using your strategic skills. Begin with these three aspects:

1. *What* is possible for my client (what is his or her vision of the future)?
2. *Who* does my client need to become to carry out the vision?
3. *How* exactly can the vision be accomplished?

The first step, the *what* of the life plan, requires that you understand how to co-create a vision. As therapists, we are familiar with goals, but a vision is bigger and broader than a single goal. A goal is a specific, realistic target that falls within one's grasp; a vision is expansive. It's limitless and does not need to be pragmatic or even rational. When stated, it can sound like a fantasy. It may look like a prophecy about what is imaginable. In his iconic *I Have a Dream* speech, Martin Luther King, Jr., envisioned a world filled with a series of ideas and dreams, where "children will one day live in a nation where they will not be judged by the color of their skin but by the content of their character." Visions are big and bold. They exist out of time. They use lofty language and broad ideals.

To find the visionary concepts and language that relate to the purpose of therapy, one place to start is with Abraham Maslow's top-tiered needs hierarchy, in the area of self-actualization. According to Maslow, self-actualization includes a need for creative expression, a quest for spiritual enlightenment, the pursuit of knowledge, the longing for beauty and goodness, or the desire to give back to society.[2] These higher-level meta-needs offer the language and ideas that help to advance a personal vision. When refining a client's vision, you can build on several skills from earlier chapters:

- Use your skill of questioning, Skill #1: Ask Effective Questions, to ask some pointed "ah-ha" questions to elicit a big vision of health and well-being from your client, including these below:

---

2 Maslow, A. H. (1943). A Theory of Human Motivation. *Psychological Review*, 50(4), 370-396.

What is the greatest possible life you could have during the next five years?

Which people do you need to cultivate in order to bring out your best?

What routine or personal habits would promote a healthy and vibrant life?

What would you love to accomplish, if time and money were not considerations?

What would describe a perfect day, perfect month, perfect year, or perfect life?

If you could design a good, healthy and happy life, without worry of failure, what would it include?

- Use your skill of collaboration for some leadership via brainstorming with your client (explored in Chapter 4: Creating Therapist-Client Collaboration).

- Use a deft touch in your conversation, as defined in Skill #3: Add Humor and Lightness, to make the process of finding a vision a safe and uplifting experience, one without demand or expectation.

- Ask your client to complete the core values survey from Skill #7: Align with Core Values to help him or her orient a future life plan based on selected values for optimal meaning and purpose.

Ben Dean, founder of Mentor Coach, a national coach training school, teaches classes on vision and encourages clients to go toward ideas that are big and bold. "Don't think about being on the Oprah show, think about being Oprah," he says. Dean call these "blue-sky visions." They will feel like a fantasy, he admits, and need an eventual concrete, material plan to make them real. "A vision on paper is not enough to bring it to reality," he says. In his Blue-sky visioning project,[3] he uses social support, via a group process, to bring brainstorming about visions into certainty. Attendees interview others who may be role models, think through a five-year plan, and then do backwards planning into the present.

---

3 http://www.mentorcoach.com/courses/blue2016.htm

The Want-for Technique

If your client is not able to think in a blue-sky manner, you can show some partnership by considering the "want-for" technique I mentioned at the start of the chapter. Articulate a sentence for a client beginning with the phrase: "What I want for you." Take the lead to lift your client to a higher level of prospection. The "want-for" sentence is offered as a well-intentioned idea, one that can be freely rejected by your client if it does not fit his preference. Examples of want-fors include these stated hopes:

- For a client focused on career who overworks and, as a result, neglects his family: *What I want for you is to know when you have done enough work each day and, leaving the office with energy and excitement, head home to be with your spouse and children.*
- For a client who puts herself last on her list: *What I want for you is to have a large reserve of spare time, more time than you think you need, to refresh and renew yourself each week without fail.*
- For a client who holds onto old grudges: *What I want for you is to completely let go of resentment and anger, to lay it all down, and finally be at peace with the past.*
- For a client who is worried that he has not provided well for his grandchildren: *What I want for you is to proudly leave a legacy of wisdom, stories, and support for those you love—which is as valuable as financial support.*
- For a client who says that retirement equals boredom: *What I want for you is to enrich yourself as you age, with continual learning and doing, so that retirement becomes the best time of your life.*

A want-for like this is usually met with a client giving me a blank look and saying something like: "Well, I want that too, but how in the world do I do that?" Or a client might say, "That is a pipe-dream and not going to happen for me." When I have formulated a possibility using a want-for that seems too far ahead of the client in scope or idealism, I expect some push-back. I welcome this kind of response. It shows me that I am out in front, taking a strong lead, and signals that I can begin a discussion about how to develop a brighter vision or a better future. You can see how this idea of leading a client towards a vision worked with Beverly in the transcript below.

Beverly Develops Her Vision

Beverly was intrigued with my offer to discuss a life plan in her session. The start of the plan, developing a vision, was unfamiliar to her, so I went slowly. With gentle encouragement, she entered into the spirit of the topic and found a vision of the future that carried personal meaning and excitement.

LG: Let's start with coming up with a picture, set into the future, of a good life—the best life you can imagine. What would be in this life, between now and when you turn 50?

BEVERLY: I guess one where no one gets hurt or dies, where I keep my blood pressure down and keep my job.

LG: I agree, that is a picture of a good life, in which the people you love stay safe, you stay healthy, and you feel financially secure.

BEVERLY: Yes, that would be good.

LG: I wonder if we could expand on this a bit, to make it even a bit bigger and brighter for you.

BEVERLY: Well, I don't know what that would look like. How would you do that?

LG: I think one way would be to spend a little more time thinking about some specific areas of life we haven't touched on in this picture yet. Is it okay if I offer you an area of life not in this picture, and then you can think about how you would like it to be in the future? Then we can add it to the vision you are building.

BEVERLY: Okay.

LG: Let's start with the area of relationships. Beyond everyone in your family being safe, what would be something you would love to see or to have, regarding relationships, in the next five years?

BEVERLY: My best friend moved to Florida, so I would love to have a friend close by.

LG: Good, let's add that to the vision. I will tweak it just a bit, in the way that I word this, if that is agreeable. I would add to the vision that you have a caring and supportive circle of friends close by.

BEVERLY: Oh, that would be wonderful. A circle of friends. That would make my life a lot more fun. I could have more people to talk to and be with.

LG: You are doing great with this. Here's another area to consider for this vision: Creativity.

BEVERLY: It's funny you mention that. I have never talked about this in therapy, but I have a project I love doing, it's scrapbooking. Do you know what this is? I never get to do it, there isn't time and I need a room for this. I collect things, tons of photos of the kids all through school, knickknacks from our holidays, things to put into the scrap-books. I would love to have a life where I had time for this on a regular basis. I would love to take a class in this, I have heard that there are even weekend retreats for this. That would be heaven!

LG: Okay, if your future could be heaven, we are going in the right direction with this vision! (She laughs.) Let me start to pull this together so far. You want to a life where people you love stay safe, you stay healthy, and you feel secure in your job. A life that includes a caring and supportive circle of friends who live close by, whom you can talk to and do things with. A life that has time for your love of scrapbooking and even attending retreats to immerse yourself in your craft.

BEVERLY: When you say this, it makes me smile, it sounds so great. But it also makes me want to cry. It seems like a fantasy, a life for someone else.

LG: Tell me what about it feels especially impossible from where you are right now.

BEVERLY: Well, let's start with the circle of friends. I want this, but I am not that kind of person who makes friends easily. I am not like that. That's why the vision just seems like a wish, like make-believe. It's a fantasy, right?

LG: I am so glad you are explaining this to me, because the thoughts and feelings you are having right now, that you want this but don't know how to get there, are exactly the right thoughts at this stage of the life plan. Let me explain why, and you will understand the next step in a life plan, an essential one for us to discuss before the session ends. It has to do with how a person needs to grow into the plan.

Ongoing Learning and Growth

As explained to Beverly, when a vision is articulated well, it will look and sound like an out-of-reach, big and bright possibility, one that is far from current reality. The fact that it feels so far away is not a problem—it is inherent to the vision. At this point of the life plan, a client may feel excited and motivated ("How do I get there?") or discouraged ("That will never occur."). The second aspect of a life plan has to do with who the client needs to become, over time, in order to achieve the vision. A big vision points the way to personal growth and development. If Beverly was already the person who could achieve this vision, she would have it in place.

Once we articulated her vision, Beverly's excitement dissipated quickly into resignation. "This is just a fantasy," she told me, meaning: I will never get to have this in my real life. I know Beverly's feeling well; that sense of excitement and then deflation. I am someone who has lived by going from vision to vision, through much of my adult life. I have often experienced this gap between seeing what would be wonderful, and then having to acknowledge the work I need to do on myself, in order to realize the vision.

When I was finished writing my first book, *Building Your Ideal Private Practice*, and waiting for it to be produced, I took a trip to Europe. I was on a train, watching out the window as the landscape rushed by, thinking about the book I had just completed. I began to see an imagining, a vision of what my professional life could become after publication of the book. I would be speaking, traveling across the country, and be an expert spokesperson for my message. I was enthralled for a few minutes, but then felt a curtain of fear and anxiety descend over me. I was an introvert, not a public speaker. I was not a university professor with a Ph.D., simply a therapist on the ground doing basic research and coming up with a program. I was not a very good traveler. As the landscape rushed by, I felt close to tears at my lack of preparation and competence that I would need, to ever make this vision a reality.

Over the next year, I had to learn and grow and develop aspects of my personality to accomplish this potential. Again, it wasn't just what I needed to do, it was who I needed and wanted to become: less introverted—someone who could connect with strangers comfortably and not get drained from the contact. Brave enough to travel—staying alert to my surroundings and making sense of spatial markers. Physically stronger—to stand in front of a room for hours conducting a workshop. My list of personal development goals was long, and I had much change to take on.

A vision points the way, but it can't do the work of getting there. That is up to the person. The good news is that, as therapists, our business is to provide the skills and tools for personal growth and change. I know what a client like Beverly may need to do, in order to get where she wants to go in her life plan. Growing toward a vision is the path of self-actualization; it helps to remember Maslow's qualities of a self-actualized person, which include:[4]

- Accepting and being open to life and self, with all their flaws.
- Being creative and spontaneous.
- A willingness to embrace ambiguity and the unknown.
- Enjoying the journey, not just the destination.
- Living in appreciation and gratitude.
- Shifting from dependency to autonomy to allow for self-direction.

Who Beverly Needs to Become

I wanted to reassure Beverly that her vision was possible, and begin to identify the qualities she might want to develop, over time, in order to manifest it.

LG: I know that this vision means that you would need to make some changes, in your words, to become someone different. But I want to

---

4 http://www.huffingtonpost.com/david-sze/maslow-the-12-characteris_b_7836836.html

remind you that you have been engaged in becoming different in therapy for the past six months. You have evidence of how you are able to change to reach your goals.

BEVERLY: That's true. But those were small steps. This vision seems huge.

LG: I understand that this vision feels very far away from who you are right now. Let's focus on a few of the qualities you would need to develop to make this vision easier to reach. You mentioned one: That you would need to become a person who makes friends more easily.

BEVERLY: Yes, I have always been very shy, and I don't open up to people I don't know.

LG: Thanks for clarifying. We could start a list of qualities you would want to develop in the future, like becoming more open with people you don't know.

BEVERLY: I don't know how to do that.

LG: I would add one word, you don't know how to do that *yet*.

BEVERLY: Do you think it is possible to learn to do this, to become a friendlier person?

LG: Do you?

BEVERLY: I don't know. Maybe for others. Not sure for me.

LG: What I want for you is that you find a way to easily make new friends over time.

BEVERLY: I want that for myself, too. Is this something we could do in therapy?

LG: Yes, we could. It takes us to the next task of your life plan: identifying the steps needed to achieve it over time.

Steps for Achieving the Plan

We took one more session to refine Beverly's vision, list the personal growth qualities she could acquire over time, and then do a quick outline of a basic plan, with goals and some markers. Using my five-year Life Planning Template (see below), Beverly made notes and came up with her own ideas. Some of this was speculative, in that it was her best guess of what she might need to do. More time and research would be required to gain clarity and flesh it out completely. But by the end of the last session, Beverly, at least on paper, had a rough five-year plan that she could look at.

At this point, Beverly asked to extend therapy for another three months, to work toward the first steps of the life plan. In the next session, she also brought in evidence of her creativity. Outside of the session, she created a "vision board," a large piece of cardboard filled with pictures, cut from magazines, that represented what she wanted and who she would need to become. Beverly was enthusiastically engaged in the next several months of therapy as she focused on her life plan. No life plan can be exact because so much is unknown about the future. For Beverly, her plan set priorities and suggested direction. It gave her a feeling of control and confidence. Even the more immediate issues she brought to the remaining months of therapy seemed to be easier to resolve, now that she had a vision in place. She ended therapy after the additional months, feeling good about her achievement of a successful therapy treatment plan, and with a map of the future—a written life plan in place—one that she could refer to and adapt as needed. Beverly said many times that it was helpful to know where she was headed and how to work towards a better future. Although therapy was over, I told her that my therapy door was left open. She could return when she wanted, to work more on her life plan or address other issues. I kept a copy of her plan in my notes, so that I could support her with what she had developed when and if she returned.

Your Turn: Life Planning

Use this exercise to master the skill. Give this template to your clients and/or use it for yourself.

The Five-Year Life Plan Template

This template addresses three stages of a five-year life plan:

- Vision
- Self-actualization
- Manifestation

Step 1: Vision

What do you see that would be possible within five years within any or all of these categories?

- Health and well-being
- Autonomy
- Self-care
- Finances
- Relationships
- Spirituality
- Creativity
- Legacy
- Work and productivity

Based on the above, summarize your five-year vision as succinctly and clearly as possible in a few sentences.

Note your feelings and thoughts about the vision above:

_____

_____

_____

_____

Add in the results of the core values survey from Skill #7, to see if your vision is based on your core values. Rewrite your vision if necessary to include important values.

_____

_____

_____

_____

Step 2: Self-Actualization

Complete the following questions:
Who do I need to become to make this vision a reality?

_____

_____

_____

_____

What personal qualities will be essential to my development?

_____

_____

_____

_____

Who do I know who models these qualities?

_____

_____

_____

_____

What can I borrow or learn from their example to make my own?

_____

_____

_____

_____

Step 3: Manifestation

Fill in each area, working backwards from year five to year one.

Year five:
Goals (what to do and who to become) and a timeframe for each:

_____

_____

_____

_____

Specific action steps for each goal:

_____

_____

_____

_____

Markers of progress and success for each action step:

_____

_____

_____

Year four:
Goals (what to do and who to become) and a timeframe for each:

_____

_____

_____

Specific action steps for each goal:

_____

_____

_____

Markers of progress and success for each action step:

_____

_____

_____

Year three:
Goals (what to do and who to become) and a timeframe for each:

_____

_____

_____

_____

Specific action steps for each goal:

_____

_____

_____

Markers of progress and success for each action step:

_____

_____

_____

Year two:
Goals (what to do and who to become) and a timeframe for each:

_____

_____

_____

Specific action steps for each goal:

_____

_____

_____

Markers of progress and success for each action step:

_____

_____

_____

Year one:
Goals (what to do and who to become) and a timeframe for each:

_____

_____

_____

Specific action steps for each goal:

_____

_____

_____

Markers of progress and success for each action step:

_____

_____

_____

Starting now:
What is my first step?

_____

_____

_____

Who can support me in this process?

_____

_____

To whom am I accountable?

_____

_____

IN CONCLUSION: WHAT I WANT FOR READERS

We are almost at the end of the book. You now understand my model, Therapy with a Coaching Edge, complete with foundational elements and nine, specific adapted coaching skills that promote more client-based control, partnership, action, and possibility. There is one final chapter for you to read, in the Addendum, that offers guidance to integrate this model of therapy into your existing work. It's a recipe for the best blending of various other methods that therapists are commonly trained to use, how to assimilate them with this model. Also, see the Worksheets for a quick review of the many checklists and exercises from earlier chapters, to help you put all the skills in this book into action more easily. All this allows you to have a full program, one that you can apply immediately or over time in your practice. Coming to the conclusion of the book brings me to thoughts of what I want for you, my readers, going forward. Here is my list of want-fors:

> *What I want for you is that you experiment with bringing a coaching approach, as I have described, into your clinical practice and allow it to help you become more flexible, proactive, and effective.*
>
> *What I want for you is to be an authentic presence in the therapy room, bringing your humor, lightness, compassion, intuition and directness to each and every session.*
>
> *What I want for you is that you combine the candor and action of a coach with the wisdom and experience of a therapist.*
>
> *What I want for you is that you take Therapy with a Coaching Edge and work with it to make it your own.*

Thank you for reading this book.

Addendum

THE BEST BLEND: HOW TO INTEGRATE THERAPY WITH A COACHING EDGE

Therapy with a Coaching Edge provides you with a working therapy model based on a foundation, nine specific skills, and additional techniques and tools to add to your existing therapeutic toolbox. However, if you are like most other therapists and counselors I know, your toolbox may already be full to overflowing. If so, how do you proceed to integrate one more method of therapy with what you already know and do?

Much has been written over the past few decades about the theory and application of integrating methods of therapy. However, many therapists approach integrating methods instinctively; for example, they go to a training, and then come back to their practice without being given a plan, assuming that what they have learned in a workshop will combine in some way with what they already know or do over time. An instinctive or informal process of integration can work, but since my model, Therapy with a Coaching Edge, has relied throughout on a strategic design, I wanted to offer you a conscious, strategic plan for its integration. One advantage of having a planned approach to integration is that it allows you, the therapist, to be more intentional about your process and outcomes.

Integrating skills as a therapist is a bit like cooking—having a refrigerator full of many ingredients, some that could work well together and others that really could not. The integration plan in this chapter is akin to a basic recipe that is based on common sense. It's a framework of how ingredients tend to blend best. Just like being in the kitchen, successful results require some testing and tweaking by each particular cook. I have found that when cooking by recipe, it's necessary to bring in common sense and to taste regularly as you go. You may not rely on recipes, but I do, since I am not a natural or gifted cook. My kitchen is filled with cookbooks that help me avoid my inadvertent mistakes when preparing a meal. I especially like finding a recipe online, because it is rated by others and often fine-tuned by a community of readers who try it and then share what worked or what didn't, and how they added other ingredients or more time in the oven to improve it.

Based on my appreciation of community-sourcing a recipe, I am also offering this integration plan with the hopes you will test and improve it, within your own practice, and share what you learn with the rest of us, a community of readers who want to bring a coaching approach into our clinical work. As you work with this model with your clientele, within your specific clinical situation, I hope you can let me know about your findings, both your successes and challenges. My request is that you will share what you learn with me, much like tweaking a recipe, so that I can use your comments to further the learning of others that I teach and supervise. (To this end, I offer my contact information at the end of this chapter.) First, let me give you the basis for this integration recipe.

The Basics of an Integration Plan

With hundreds of "schools" or models of psychotherapy in active use, integrating therapeutic methods is a topic that has been give a lot of attention in the psychological literature. Methods abound because therapists become frustrated with singular approaches. The bible of integration may be the *Handbook of Psychotherapy Integration* (2005),[1] and its authors make a strong case for the value of being eclectic as a clinician: No one school or approach can address all issues or all clients.

When you are integrating approaches, the first area of attention is to identify "common factors"—aspects of what a given model or method has

---

1 *Handbook of Psychotherapy Integration*, edited by John C. Norcross, Marvin R. Goldfried (2005).

in common. The factors in Therapy with a Coaching Edge, which need to be in common with those you use to blend well, are part and parcel of cognitive therapeutic mainstays, including: talk therapy, building rapport, active listening, asking open-ended questions, using empathy and unconditional regard, setting goals, and encouraging behavioral change. In the recipe I share for blending models, you will see some additional common factors of my model that do or don't combine well with yours. Not every model of therapy integrates well with another because there are other factors to consider, such as the philosophy, protocol, or specific techniques that may not blend or mix well with others in actual practice.

Think about cooking again. When you combine ingredients in a recipe, it helps to have some understanding of the science of food so you avoid disasters in the kitchen: A baker knows how to combine alkaline, acid, and starch to help a cake rise, not fall. A chef making salad dressing knows that oil and vinegar quickly separate and require a third element, an emulsifier, to hold them together. Here's where therapeutic combining of methods can start to get tricky: It's not always clear what we are mixing together and whether it will hold when used in a session or as the basis of a treatment plan.

As you may now understand, Therapy with a Coaching Edge is an integration in itself. I designed an adapted form of life coaching and merged it with existing methods of talk therapy, primarily cognitive-behavioral therapy. I also included some philosophy and techniques of methods of personal growth. That's a three-fold combination of life coaching, cognitive-behavioral therapy and personal growth. The integration process that I used for Therapy with a Coaching Edge is called "assimilative." This means that I started with a grounding in a familiar method of therapy (cognitive-behavioral therapy) and incorporated ideas and strategies of other less familiar methods (coaching and personal growth) in a practical way for the purposes of clinical effectiveness.[2] Since I used an assimilative process to create this model, I am recommending that we stick with an assimilative process in this recipe or inte-

---

2 Stricker, G. (2001). An Introduction to Psychotherapy Integrations. *Psychiatric Times*. Retrieved from http://www.psychiatrictimes.com/articles/introduction-psychotherapy-integration.

gration plan. I want you to stay grounded in your existing methods and then add mine into the mix, in a practical way, for clinical effectiveness. As I demonstrated in the case example of Su-Ann in Chapter 2, Therapy with a Coaching Edge is designed to add to, not replace, the skills you already have. You can shift back and forth as needed from therapy that is slower-paced, insightful, and reflective, to a coaching approach that is directive and action-oriented.

To assimilate further, you need to identify what your existing model of practice consists of too, by categorizing your primary orientation.

Find Your Primary Leaning

Although there are hundreds of existing models of psychotherapy being taught and used today, most models fit into one of five broad categories, according to the American Psychological Association:[3] psychodynamic, cognitive, behavioral, holistic, and humanistic. To simplify the assimilative integration process, I have compressed the five American Psychological Association (APA) categories into three. These are broadly drawn explanations of the three categories. You may already be combining two or all three in the way you practice, but usually a therapist or counselor can point to his or her primary leaning, a core theoretical form of clinical practice. See if you can identify your primary orientation among these three commonly used clinical models:

Psychodynamic: Starting with Freud's methods, this category of therapy includes a large variety of analytic and post-analytic models of therapy that rely on the relevance of an intrapsychic focus of mental health, including an acceptance of attachment and/or systems theory. In this category, therapists use talk therapy as the main device to explore family of origin antecedents, unconscious and conscious beliefs, behaviors, feelings, and emotions.

Cognitive-Behavioral: Models of therapy in this category are many and varied, but they agree on theories of learned behavior. Most focus on thinking and cognition, and how it influences behavior, emotions and subsequent feelings. The models of practice in this category rely on a

---

3 http://www.apa.org/topics/therapy/psychotherapy-approaches.aspx

cause and effect orientation, using a problem-solving approach, which may or may not be combined with some aspect of behavior modification.

Humanistic-Holistic: This catch-all grouping includes a wide variety of personal growth methods that place an emphasis on human potential, mind-body wellness, and self-expression. Models in this category include Gestalt therapy, art therapy, psychodrama, somatic therapy, narrative therapy, and methods of transpersonal psychology that include a mind-body-spirit focus. Techniques used may include meditation, mindfulness, breathwork, energy healing, and other approaches.

Take a moment to identify which category constitutes your main clinical orientation, the category of therapy that you use and that feels most reliable, most of the time. Then see the recipes for integrating the way you primarily work with Therapy with a Coaching Edge below, customized for your clinical orientation.

The Recipes

Orientation: Psychodynamic Therapy

Step 1: Review the common and differing factors:

- *Common factors*: Psychodynamic therapy (when used as a postmodern, contemporary approach) and Therapy with a Coaching Edge share the common factors of preference for talk therapy, some attention to the here and now in a session, and the ability to selectively use a problem-solving focus. You will find that the skills of effective questioning, strategizing with clients, and those skills from my model that focus on client-based metaphors as well as meaning and purpose can be comfortable aspects of integration, not too distinct from techniques inherent in a psychodynamic model.
- *Differing factors:* The most obvious difference is the therapist positioning. Try to preserve your existing, more neutral and distanced stance in lieu of trying to adopt a coach-like partnership or collaboration, since this may invalidate your existing approach. This may affect your results with a coaching approach, but you must go slowly and take care to respect the existing framework of the session and its routines that may offer safety and security. Don't force a newer, structured agenda, such

as Getting to Yes as outline in Chapter 5, without explanation. Watch for projection and negative transference when bringing in a more structured approach or skill from Therapy with a Coaching Edge.

Step 2: Skills to apply first:

- **Skill #1: Ask Effective Questions** can align well with a psychodynamic approach, because it is similar to other types of psychotherapeutic interventions.
- **Skill #4: Call a Client into Action** is a good first step for encouraging behavioral change and helping a client move toward readiness.
- **Skill #8: Find the Metaphors that Matter** works to help clients access inner symbolism and stories; rather than using this skill for insight, allow it to further client-based problem solving.

Step 3: Procedure:

Use a skill from the above list in a session with a "coachable" client, then observe and track results. Add other skills from the model as useful and desired. When blending or applying skills, be sure to add in time to process your client's feelings and thoughts about this, including how the client responds to your attempt to be more proactive or take the lead.

Orientation: Cognitive-Behavioral Therapy:

Step 1: Review the common and differing factors:

- *Common factors*: Cognitive and behavioral therapies are among the easiest to blend with a coaching approach, given the similarities in method: both rely on client-therapist give and take using talk therapy, with a focus on behavioral action: setting goals, finding solutions using a present-day or future orientation, and pragmatic direction. Many CBT methods use specific protocols, including a formulaic session structure, the inclusion of a white board or written materials for use in session, assigned homework and measures of progress. Therapy with a Coaching Edge also uses a structured Getting to Yes session plan, but it is less formal. For my model, shift to a more flexible position and a looser session structure; allow sessions to veer from problem-solving to include dialogue and conversation that can incorporate a range of topics regarding personal growth and possibility. Therapy with a Coaching Edge is focused on action but uses less insistence on homework; this can be helpful for those clients who prefer less rigidity in treatment and resist homework. See the chapters on action skills and specifically Skill #4: Call a Client into Action on readiness, to have additional ways to motivate clients towards behavioral change.

- *Differing factors:* While some CBT methods focus on building a warm and empathic rapport between therapist and client, others CBT methods keep the relationship more distant. If you follow a distant relationship model, consider working "closer-in" with a client for integrating this model, and review the foundational chapter about creating client collaboration (Chapter 4.)

Step 2: Skills to apply first:
- **Skill #2: Be a Strategist, with a Twist** enhances goal-setting by using a coaching approach, to extend a client locus of control in resolving problems and issues.
- **Skill #3: Add Humor and Lightness** builds an alliance with a client that may aid with homework compliance.
- **Skill #7: Align with Core Values** highlights goals based on meaning and purpose which put goals into a broader context.

Step 3: Procedure:
Use a skill from the above list in a session with a "coachable" client, then observe and track results. Add other skills as useful and desired. When blending or applying these recommended skills, allow for flexibility. Make the client "right" by validating and acknowledging any and all progress to enhance forward movement. Review chapter 5, Results in Every Session, to see how to spot and promote evidence of forward movement and the Getting to Yes agenda to focus on client needs *and* wants to boost compliance and retention.

Orientation: Humanistic-Holistic Therapy:

Step 1: Review the common and differing factors:
- *Common factors*: Humanistic and holistic methods share a broad piece of common ground with a coaching approach, within the territory of personal growth, as described in Chapter 2. If you are using

body-oriented therapy, breathwork, somatic processes, energy healing, meditation, even hypnosis, then the skills of Therapy with a Coaching Edge may be natural to adopt in order to enhance pragmatic, cognitive, and behavioral outcomes.

- *Differing factors*: To integrate models, note first the difference in the locus of control, from therapist to client. For Therapy with a Coaching Edge, the session agenda and interventions are direct and transparent, to give the client more responsibility. You may need to shift the locus of control from the therapist (for example, if you channel energy or silently impose elements of a transformative process) to make the session client-centered. Be transparent and give clients explanations about therapy in the moment, as things occur in session. Educate them to increase their control of the session goals and the unfolding process. Allow them to own the progress they make as explained in Chapter 5.

Step 2: Skills to apply first:
- **Skill #4: Call a Client into Action** encourages behavioral change, to shift a client into a state of readiness.
- **Skill #5: Add Shared Accountability** suggests steps for you to be supportive and proactive, to help clients address problems pragmatically while still feeling emotionally and energetically "held".
- **Skill #9: Design a Plan for Life** allows a client to become oriented to the future, beyond the scope of here-and-now therapy sessions, to have a longer view of how to accomplish their goals.

Step 3: Procedure:
Use a skill from the above list in a session with a "coachable" client, then observe and track results. Add other skills as appropriate and desired. When blending or applying these recommended skills, allow time for education and verbal transparency. Work with the client to look for evidence of results, validating and acknowledging any and all progress to enhance forward movement. Allow the session to have a structure so that you have time to accomplish the goals of this model. Review Chapter 5, Results in Every Session, to set up a session for this purpose.

Customizing the Integration Process

The best cooks know how to use a recipe as a guide, but then improvise to make the recipe better. The key to successful assimilation of methods is to use a similar framework of experimentation: Your clinical work is an ongoing laboratory for developing a cohesive model of integration, one that works for you and your clients. Think of this recipe as a hypothesis you are testing Apply your best judgement and application, observe the process in sessions and note the results for further review.

On the front end of adding a skill or technique from Therapy with a Coaching Edge to a session, communicate with your client. Letting a client know what you intend for a session is a way to further a coaching approach aspect of client-based control. When I bring in a skill from my model, I might say the following:

> *"This session, I want to offer you something different. I would like to add a skill I have found helpful, a process for you to consider to aid your goals. I think this can make our work together more effective. Are you comfortable with me adding this to our session today?"*

Then I leave time at the end of the session to debrief, asking the client for feedback to help me assess its usefulness. I might ask the client to tell me what he or she will take from the session and how to measure what we did. After the session, as I write my notes, I track the session and any missteps or results using the following questions:

- What skill did I bring into the session and why?
- How was it received?
- What occurred as a result?
- Does it need to be repeated?
- What might I do differently next time?
- What is my next step in the treatment plan?
- How can I follow up with the client in future sessions to track effectiveness of this skill over time?

Tracking My Results with You

Just as I hope you will be tracking your effectiveness and results from this integration process with your clients, I am eager to do some tracking of my working model with you. As you integrate the foundational elements, concepts, and skills from this book into your practice of therapy or counseling, I am open to your feedback. My goal is to build a community of therapists who are testing out this model and helping to improve and shape it, to make it useful in their specific situations or with their client populations. I believe that a rising tide lifts all boats. We, as a community of therapists, counselors, helpers, and healers, need to keep each other viable and our work informed by the larger wisdom of all. For this reason, I offer my contact information, my office email and websites, so that you can reach me if you want to let me know about your experience.

Please know that anything you send me to read will be kept confidential, and I will not share your email or contact information with others. Your feedback is requested solely for purposes of research and teaching, not for any marketing or promotion. It may interest you to know that I have made this same offer within my earlier books, and it helped to add value to the community of readers over time. Much of what I am able to teach with confidence is due, in part, to thousands of readers whom talk back to me, those I have met at conferences, workshops, and presentations, or who have taken the time to tell me via email or phone calls what does and doesn't work for them and in doing so, have helped me improve my content and message.

Again, I thank you for reading and responding. I can be reached at:

Email: *info@privatepracticesuccess.com*
Book website: www.therapywithacoachingedge.com
Business coaching website: www.privatepracticesuccess.com
Counseling and life coaching website:
www.counselingsilverspring.com

Worksheets

A. Guidepost for Client Suitability

B. Strategies for Collaboration

C. The "Getting to Yes" Session Plan

D. List of Effective Questions

E. Stages of Strategic Partnership

F. Therapeutic Alliance

G. Client Readiness

H. How to Lend a (Limited) Hand

I. Steps to a Coaching Edge

J. List of Core Values

K. Client-Based Metaphors

L. The Five-Year Life Plan

A. GUIDEPOST FOR CLIENT SUITABILITY

From Chapter 3: Who's Coachable in Therapy

In Chapter 3, you learned how to determine suitability for this model, using a series of client questions and then reviewing the responses with a checklist. Suitability is based on three factors:

- Client Preference (what your client wants out of therapy)
- Client Challenges (presenting issues, short history of mental health problems, diagnosis)
- Client Capacity (overall functionality, ability to work with a proactive, collaborative therapist)

Questions for Clients

Here are questions to use in session with individual adult or mature adolescent clients to determine suitability, along with any other assessments you currently use. Use some or all in each category, in conversation or written form, to help you and your clients decide if Therapy with a Coaching Edge is a good approach for them, given each category:

Client Preference:

Are you seeking short-term or long-term therapy?

For example, would you prefer a slower-paced, longer-term method that would allow you to spend more time talking and processing memories and developing insight? Or would you prefer a faster-paced therapy which results in taking action and making decisions?

Do you have trouble expressing thoughts and feelings and would you like therapy to help with this?

Do you want therapy sessions that focus on the present and future, or more on the past?

Do you want therapy that results in behavioral change?

Are you interested in using therapy to set and achieve goals in order to make concrete change in your life?

Do you want a therapist who primarily listens and lets you talk, or one who voices thoughts and opinions?

Do you like to have homework, reading or action steps to take between sessions?

Client Challenges:

Why did you decide to come to therapy now?

Are you in danger or in a crisis that needs immediate attention?

Are you able to make good decisions for yourself and those dependent upon you?

Do you think your issue can be resolved by focusing on your own feelings, behavior, or thinking?

Are you interested in changing yourself and your situation?

Do you need something or someone outside of you to change first, before you can address your own problems?

Can you think of a possible first step that would begin to resolve one of your problems?

What would a successful outcome in our work together be?

Client Capacity:

What gives you energy and what drains you?

What is a typical day like?

What is going well?

What is not?

Are you worried about physical or personal safety or immediate survival?

Of all the problems you face, which need attention immediately?

Which are low priority that can be corrected over time?

What are you proudest about in regards to your life/ and or work?

Where would you like to see yourself (in life, relationships, work, career) by the end of therapy?

What would you want from me, as your therapist, to help you reach your goals?

For Therapist Review: After conferring with your client on the above, review the answers along with any other assessments you may have used. The following checklist is to help you confirm suitability. Unchecked items need to be evaluated on the basis of anticipated progress from early stages of treatment that might resolve the issue quickly.

The client who is right for this approach:

☐ prefers therapy or counseling that is short-term.
☐ likes between-session homework, reading, and/or moving forward to complete action steps.
☐ wants a therapist who is collaborative, interactive, and verbal during a session.
☐ appreciates conversation that is pragmatic and optimistic.
☐ is willing to focus more on present-day issues than on the past.
☐ desires therapy that involves planning for the future with goals and action steps.
☐ fits the presenting criteria above and suffers from mild to moderate symptoms.
☐ is not in physical danger or mental/emotional crisis, including active addiction or relapse.
☐ is dealing with issues that can be resolved with a collaborative discussion, goal setting, and an action plan.
☐ likes problem solving as a way to resolve challenges.
☐ has access to internal and external resources to make any problematic situations (debt, living conditions, career) quickly resolvable.
☐ can tolerate and participate in conversations with a therapist who is proactive and cooperative.
☐ is struggling with only moderate or mild symptoms of depression, anxiety, loss, stress-related, relationship, parenting, or workplace issues.
☐ has a lifeline or some type of support system in place.
☐ has sufficient energy or vigor to stay with an approach of therapy that is faster-paced than traditional talk therapy.
☐ is employed or employable and/or functions in a safe way in the world.
☐ can (with help) identify, set, and begin to follow through on goals.
☐ can relate to the therapist without undue projection or transference.
☐ can allow and utilize the therapist's support to stay on track with treatment.

Determining Therapist Suitability

This model of Therapy with a Coaching Edge is appropriate for a therapist, if:

☐ You naturally tend to use a proactive, personal-growth, behaviorally focused approach of therapy.

☐ You like to work short-term and see clients make change quickly.

☐ You are comfortable with the give and take of a behavioral, solution-focused therapy.

☐ You like tangible results, to see evidence of change, even in a single session.

☐ You like treatment to have a beginning, middle and end, when possible.

☐ You favor a client-based model of responsibility in therapy.

☐ You are comfortable ceding some control in a session, including veering from a strict protocol, to allow your clients to have the ability to drive the direction of a session.

☐ You know how to gracefully retain your expertise and adhere to a treatment plan, but still share power with a client.

☐ You know how to set and maintain clear boundaries in terms of session management. You can start and stop a session on time, bill for sessions appropriately, don't carry large debt of unpaid client bills, and run your practice in a professional manner.

☐ You are a model of the services you are offering and careful to maintain your professional policies.

☐ You adhere to the ethical requirements of your licensure. You don't befriend clients inappropriately, have dual relationships, or get enmeshed with clients inside or outside of therapy sessions.

☐ You are self-aware; you have spent time in your own therapy.

☐ You can recognize transference and countertransference as it occurs in a session. (It is important that you have a way to recognize and contain countertransference to promote the results of this model.)

☐ You are drawn to therapy with a coaching approach.

☐ You want to expand your therapeutic skills to be more proactive, but are not trying to be your client's coach.

B. STRATEGIES FOR COLLABORATION

From Chapter 4: Creating Therapist-Client Collaboration

In Chapter 4, you learned the steps to adopt a partnership position. The following checklist is a guide to collaboration in a therapeutic relationship. Therapy with a Coaching Edge requires that a therapist shift toward the following behavior to be:

☐ Natural (versus neutral)
☐ Proactive (versus nondirective)
☐ Supportive (versus diagnostic)
☐ Curious (versus quiet)
☐ Responsive (versus deflecting)
☐ Questioning (versus interpreting)
☐ Leading (versus following)

Note the items that are part of your normal client interactions and those that may require more exploration or supervision to achieve.

Demonstrating Collaboration

Therapy with a Coaching Edge recommends that a therapist implement collaboration and partnership in four specific steps:

1. **Take the lead:**
   - Be willing to help shape a session agenda.
   - Keep a client on task.
   - Take responsibility to make the session relevant.
2. **Reduce negative transference:**
   - Observe and discuss any transference that interferes with therapy.
   - Refocus on the objectives of the session.
   - Maintain a cooperative stance.
3. **Use appropriate self-disclosure:**
   - Self disclose for the benefit of the client, not for your own purposes.

- Only disclose material that you have fully processed, emotionally and psychologically.
- Be willing to repair the therapeutic alliance when broken by speaking openly and honestly about your experience as the therapist.

4. **Increase the use of self:**
   - Be a model of your services.
   - Be fully present in every session. If you feel bored or distracted, quickly find a way to refocus and re-engage.
   - Stay authentic, to bring all of who you are into your therapeutic role.

Review the chapter to see the explanation of these steps and points, as demonstrated through a full case example. Given your therapeutic orientation, you may need to slightly modify this approach to make your work congruent: Use interventions in ways that follow your training and work within your existing methods. Review the previous material on integration of methods and see Chapter 4 to understand how to best protect therapeutic boundaries while still maintaining a collaborative stance.

C. THE "GETTING TO YES" SESSION PLAN
From Chapter 5: Results in Every Session

Therapy with a Coaching Edge recommends that you implement a three-step session plan to address client satisfaction and retention. The three steps in the plan are as follows:

1. **Find the purpose**—set a shared agenda during the beginning phase of the session with the client (this may take up to the first 10 minutes of a session) by asking questions such as these:

   What should we focus on today?

   Is this the most important topic for you?

   What is it about this that would make a difference in your life?

   Is it vital for us to explore and address this now, or can it wait?

   What might be even more immediately central to your wellbeing?

   What aspect of this topic would create the biggest impact on your life or work immediately?

2. **Work it through**—advance the agenda topics during the middle phase of the session by use of any appropriate skills, methods, and techniques using this model or others

3. **Consolidate gains**—leave time for a good ending (at least the last 5 to 10 minutes before the end of a session) to summarize progress by asking questions such as these:

   What will you take away from our session today?

   What did you learn?

   How can you use what you learned in your life this week?

   What does this lead us to do in our next session?

   May I share what I think was important about today, what I observed as progress?

   Would you like to know what I will be highlighting in my notes about today's session?

Tracking Client Progress Over Time

In Chapter 5, I offer several ways to track progress with a client over the time of treatment. I suggest that this tracking be done every three to six months. One method is to ask a series of questions such as these with clients, in order to check in on the level of satisfaction:

How do you feel about continuing to come to therapy?
Do you feel understood and listened to in here?
Is there more about you—your history or your current situation—that I should know?
Do our conversations make sense to you?
Are you satisfied with the results you are getting?
Is there anything I can do better, as your therapist, to help you stay involved with your treatment?

D. LIST OF EFFECTIVE QUESTIONS
from Skill #1: Ask Effective Questions

In Chapter 6, you are introduced to a key skill in this model: How to ask a powerful, pointed question, one that gives you the leverage to:

- Create sudden insight.
- Challenge existing beliefs.
- Prompt new options.

The steps to asking this type of question are:

1. **Find a question you could ask** from the lists that I have compiled, or add an effective question of your own choosing to the lists.
2. **Keep a question or two in mind** during a therapy session to use when needed.
3. **Ask the question clearly,** making eye contact, and then stay silent to let the client respond. Allow the question to land and be absorbed.
4. **Ask a question you don't know the answer to.** Listen and learn from your client's response. Maintain rapport without bias..
5. **Don't stack questions.** Don't interrogate your client. Ask one at a time and buffer with some statements of active listening, validation and/or acknowledgement.

Here is a list of questions for each category.

Questions to Create Sudden Insight:

Is that really your truth?
What makes you so certain?
What might be equally true?
What or who is missing from the way you tell this story?
Does the way you tell the story of your childhood do you justice?
In the big picture of your life, what or who matters most?
Who is in control of your life today?

Who are you when you are at your best?

Do you love yourself conditionally, unconditionally or not at all?

If you could love yourself more, would it make a difference in your life?

If you had no fear, what would you want to accomplish before you die?

What do you need to accept, once and for all, about your life?

How do you know if you are seeing all sides of this issue?

What are you not saying that needs to be voiced right now, once and for all?

What childhood story or message can you let go of forever?

What new connections are you making as we talk about this?

Questions to Challenge Existing Beliefs:

Who taught you to believe this?

Whose opinion matters now?

Is your belief based on fear or on love?

Could your belief be an excuse for bad behavior?

What if the opposite of what you believe is true?

Was there ever a time you took your own side first?

What do you gain by repeating your old pattern of behavior, and what do you lose?

If you were (braver, smarter, richer, etc.) what would you do differently?

Are you strong enough to fail?

Would you rather be right or be loved?

What question—if answered correctly—would help you change your mind?

Is there anyone's opinion on this issue that matters to you more than your own?

Based on what you believe, can you to act with integrity?

How will you measure your life in 20 years?

Questions that Prompt New Options:

Are you ready to take a risk?
What is possible for you in this regard?
What is impossible for you in this regard?
What is the easiest way to move forward on this goal?
Can you try another way entirely?
What resources do you need to make this a success?
Can you add more passion to the plan?
What is a win-win solution for all involved?
What are you waiting for?
Is this goal based on your head or your heart?
What is the biggest step you could take?
What is the safest step you could take?
What is the best possible outcome?
Who would you need to be in order to take this to the next level?
How can you bring more of your essence, (creativity, talent, spirit, total commitment) to this plan?
Who will you become after you have accomplished this goal?

Your Favorite Effective Questions:

Keep a list of questions that you like to use for these same purposes, as a way to enhance your skill level in this regard. What are the questions that have the biggest impact when you use them?

1. _____

2. _____

3. _____

4. _____

E. STAGES OF STRATEGIC PARTNERSHIP

From Skill #2: Be a Strategist with a Twist

If you can listen and think strategically, it's not a big step to add the elements of a coaching approach, and ensure that your client has control when it comes to personal plans Your job is not to give advice or take over the planning process for a client. Instead, use a strategic mindset and further a coaching approach of partnership, action, and possibility. Remember these steps:

1. **Listen strategically.** Detach slightly from the emotion and complications of a difficult client issue to hear its basic elements.
2. **Think strategically**. Think about the following (what, who, how) questions as you talk with your client about a problem:
   What is the problem, stated simply and clearly in the present?
   Who is the client, in terms of strengths, assets, and resources?
   How can the client start to see options to get to the goal?
3. **Use a coaching approach.** Make sure that your role as a strategist gives your client control over any personal plan. Don't get ahead of the client or get overly attached to any aspect of a plan. Be encouraging for all progress. Use therapy sessions for accountability as needed, to support action steps.
4. **Focus on asking questions geared to strategy.** See a list of additional questions below that can help a client become more proactive.
5. **Encourage your client to use a written, goal-based format** to track and measure goals such as Doran's S.M.A.R.T. goals.

Effective Questions for Strategizing

If you rise above the emotional complications, what is the truth about your present situation?
How can you state the problem at its core?
Now that you see the heart of the issue, what do you really want?
What would it take to make this happen?

Who do you need to become to make this happen?
What are five existing opportunities you can spot?
Which of those opportunities hold the most hope for you?
How could you bring that opportunity within your grasp?
What are five new possibilities you could imagine?
If your goal was already true and present, how would you live, from this moment forward?
Who, besides yourself, would you be helping or benefitting with this goal in place?
How long would you be willing to persist to see results?
How can you confidently and happily take a first step?

F. THERAPEUTIC ALLIANCE

From Skill #3: Add Humor and Lightness

An additional skill to enhance partnership involves the use of humor and lightness, to build the therapeutic alliance. Although therapy and counseling are serious endeavors, the therapist must be able to engage a client on many levels to maintain rapport. In coaching, this ability to be light on one's feet and responsive is known as "dancing" with a client.

A checklist to aid this skill of flexibility includes knowing how to:

☐ **Build the therapeutic alliance.** Use humor to aid partnership. Don't immediately judge a client's attempts to bring humor into therapy as resistance or obfuscating. It may be a valid way of communicating. Consider how it can be used to develop warmth and trust, as appropriate.

☐ **Be thoughtfully spontaneous.** Using the metaphor of dancing, being on your toes, by allowing your role as a therapist to have plasticity. Be flexible. Be prepared to listen, brainstorm, question, celebrate, and even bring in a joke or funny story.

☐ **Respect all ethical boundaries.** Protect the principles of your licensure so that humor is healing and helpful, not harmful.

☐ **Remember the formula:** Humor = Pain + Distance. Give difficult issues and memories a chance to fade first, before bringing in humor.

☐ **Track your results.** Take notes and observe how and when this skill aids or increases therapeutic alliance.

If you have unchecked items, consider these steps to help develop your capacity for humor and lightness:

1. **Build rapport.** Get to know the client before using humor in a session.
2. **Use humor in a timely way.** Wait for an opening or the right moment. Let your client initiate humor when possible.

3. **Enjoy a laugh with a client** as an expression of a healthy defense mechanism.
4. **Let an appreciation of the occasional expression** of life's normal absurdity be part of an ability of you and your client to also accomplish the painful work of therapy.
5. **Allow the things your client says and does,** the natural incongruity of humans, to surprise you.
6. **Cultivate "thoughtful spontaneity,"** a willingness to think about being more flexible in a session.
7. **Consider nonclinical resources** to help you develop more expressions of humor: listen to comedy; take an improv class; find a way to laugh every day; learn to tell a funny joke.

G. CLIENT READINESS

From Skill #4: Call a Client into Action

To help a client take the initial steps forward toward a desired goal, use the three-step skill to advance readiness (explained in Chapter 9, with a full case example).

Steps to Client Readiness:

1. **Lower the bar.** Find a way to make the action easier to begin. Small steps always count. Build on a client's existing ability or interest as a starting place.
2. **Make action steps relevant.** Don't forget the overall vision as a motivator for action. Any and all forward movement can be relevant to the end goal. See action steps as building blocks, that are helpful in developing a person's capacity.
3. **It's an experiment.** Set a framework of experimentation. Lighten the mood of any attempt. Help a client stay in process while they are taking action. Ask questions that put the focus on learning and improving, instead of on the outcome.

Debrief with Clients

After a client leaves a session with a goal or action step to take, in the next session, debrief to focus on process more than progress. This helps to reduce shame and blame and keep the therapeutic relationship collaborative, instead of isolating the client for a lack of achievement. Ask questions that invite connection, including:

What did you learn?
What do you need to do more of? Less of?
What will be different the next time?
How was this experiment useful?
What are you most proud of?
Was any of this fun or interesting?
What is the next step to take, given your experience?

H. LEND A (LIMITED) HAND

From Skill #5: Add Shared Accountability

You can extend partnership by offering a limited helping hand to clients who need support in accomplishing their goals. Calibrate any support you extend to also preserve essential therapeutic boundaries.

Shared Accountability Checklist

Use this checklist of action steps in order to find the best balance:

- ☐ **Clarify the goal.** Ask your client to define the goal, tasks and action steps. Participate in this conversation so that the parameters of the goal are well understood by your client and yourself.
- ☐ **Extend limited partnership.** Offer some shared accountability, with appropriate limits, in the process of a task. Ask:
  What is my role in this task and what is yours?
  What specifically will you do and how can you be accountable to me?
  What can I offer to keep you on track?
  What should we do if you fall off track?
  How would you like me to check in with you at the next session?
  How can I support you to succeed?
- ☐ **Check your boundaries.** Find an expression of support that feels appropriate to you, as the therapist, and meaningful to your client. Follow through with your end of the agreement. Don't promise or agree to anything that is not within your ethical principles or that would jeopardize your licensure. Get supervision or advise if needed to maintain your boundaries.
- ☐ **Focus on process, not just progress.** Check in each session with your client, not just about what has been done, but what has been learned, experienced, and opened up in the process of committing to a goal. Continue to extend shared accountability as appropriate until the goal is complete.

For any items that seem difficult to accomplish, reread Chapter 10 to see how these are applied in the case example. Shared accountability is a process and may require some time and adjustment in your practice, to find your comfort level and effectiveness. In this skill as in others, while you are learning, small steps count.

I. STEPS TO A COACHING EDGE

From Skill #6: Deliver a Coaching Edge

An important skill for a therapist with a coaching approach is the ability to offer direct, unvarnished feedback. Also known as using a coaching edge, this can be a tool to challenge, encourage, inspire, and when needed, to confront clients in a session. Using a coaching edge can also be a wake-up call, helpful when a therapist needs to quickly get a client's attention. This skill does not come naturally for many therapists, so use this guide to develop your ability to be direct when necessary and appropriate.

Delivering a Coaching Edge

1. **Speak up to benefit the client, not yourself.** Giving strong feedback is not an ego trip, to make the therapist look good or strong in a session. It is done to benefit a client who needs honest feedback, a strong message to start or stop an action, to highlight a critical moment in therapy, or as a caution about what is needed to survive or succeed. Be clear about why you are using this and what you are going to say. Examples of direct statements to give a wake-up call to a client include:

   That step is too small to get you where you want to go.

   You need to do more.

   You are running out of time and are at a critical point.

   Please don't take that next step until you think hard about the consequences.

   What you do next could change your life.

   I think you are better than what you are demonstrating.

   What you are describing is a very good way to lose a job (or a spouse, etc.).

   Like the Nike slogan, I want to challenge you to "just do it!"

2. **Use a neutral tone of voice.** You are not a drill sergeant, barking out orders. You are a therapist, and it is best to use a coaching edge from a place of calm confidence. In my coach training, this was called "charge

neutral"—no positive or negative charge, just a natural tone of voice without judgment, anger, or bias in the statement.

3. **Step over nothing.** Address what you observe. Don't hold back on what a client needs to know or hear. If you don't have the courage or will to say what is needed to your client, who will? As one of my social work teachers used to say, ironically, about the need to be honest and direct with a client, even when the topic was uncomfortable: "This is why we therapists get paid the big bucks."

4. **Make strong requests.** Establish that a client has the right to say yes, no or maybe to any request that you, the therapist make and then ask for what you would like to see. Look at the wording that is offered in this chapter to make sure that your requests fit within appropriate bounds for your session and your therapeutic relationship. Examples:

   Please rate your progress this month.

   I need you to pick up the pace. Are you game?

   I request that, instead of self care, you add extreme self-care to your action steps.

   Can you stop and recognize what you have done so far, before you go further?

   How will you top this?

   I'd like you to double that goal, how about it?

   Do. Or do not. There is no try.

5. **Validate and acknowledge all forward movement.** Once a client responds to your coaching edge, it's important to appreciate any and all willingness to correct the situation.

J. LIST OF CORE VALUES
From Skill #7: Align with Core Values

Helping clients understand how to align with their core values can be an antidote to a low-level depression, hopelessness, or boredom. It can bring urgency and resolution into decisions and help to shift the perspective on intractable issues and problems.

Steps to Enhance Meaning and Purpose

The steps to take to introduce a discussion about core values includes showing clients how to:

1. **Identify core values.** To bring the topic of values into therapy, offer a client a core-values list similar to the one offered below. Ask a client to target no more than three core values for this process.

2. **Align action with values.** Use therapy sessions to help your client talk about his or her top three values. Allow your client to talk about how these values have influenced earlier choices and decisions. Ask questions, hear stories from the past. Listen, acknowledge, and be curious. Suggest that your client select one value to focus on. Then ask your client to consider how to orient some problem, challenge or goal in life to highlight this core value.

3. **Design a value-based plan.** Help your client orient a goal based on one specific core value. Ask:
   How does this plan honor the core value?
   What steps will bring this value into play?
   Is there a way to make sure that the solution to the problem, challenge, or goal allows this value to shine through?

4. **Develop a plan with measurable action steps**. Once your client is satisfied with a plan that is based on the selected value, commit the plan to paper. Track progress toward the goal. Celebrate any wins. Use sessions to overcome obstacles. Continue to process how the core value changes the level of meaning and purpose in your client's life.

Here is a list of core values that you can share with your clients. If important values are missing from this list, ask clients to add to this or adapt and adjust it for their needs.

List of Core Values

accomplishment	duty	influence	power
action	economy	inspiration	quiet
adventure	encouragement	integrity	respect
advocacy	enlightenment	intuition	risk
altruism	excellence	invention	rules
assurance	experience	joy	sacredness
awareness	expression	justice	safety
beauty	fairness	kindness	security
diversity	faith	leadership	sensuality
optimism	family	learning	service
challenge	freedom	literature	attraction
change	friendship	love	spirituality
children	frugality	loyalty	stability
cleanliness	fun	mastering	strength
community	goodwill	nature	support
compassion	grace	novelty	trust
connection	gratitude	nurturing	truth
contribution	growth	openness	understanding
courage	happiness	organization	vitality
creativity	home	partnership	wholeness
daring	honesty	patience	winning
decency	honor	peace	wonder
democracy	humility	persuasion	youthfulness
discovery	imagination	perfection	playfulness

Values not in the list but important to clients:

1._____

2._____

3._____

4._____

5._____

K. CLIENT-BASED METAPHORS
From Skill #8: Find the Metaphors that Matter

You can help your clients find their own solution through a process of eliciting metaphors that originate with a client's own symbols and stories. Using client-based metaphors allows your clients to see more possibility for themselves, since they have the healing solutions inside their own minds. This skill is a new one for many therapists, who know how to impart a metaphor of their own making, but not how to elicit one from a client. To begin, use the checklist below:

Metaphor Skill Checklist
Take these steps to elicit and expand client-based metaphors.

☐ **Listen for the metaphor.** In the discussion of a problem or issue, you may hear a client use symbolic language to describe a situation, especially how it feels. Pay attention to any and all references in normal conversation.

☐ **Develop and deepen the metaphor with the client.** Respond with using clean language: Ask a question beginning with "And" to stay in the midst of the symbolic story with a client. Maintain rapport. Examples of clean language questions for the therapist to ask in the midst of deepening the metaphor are:

And what happens next?
And then?
And how does that feel in the moment?
And who is with you when this happens?
And that's like what?
And is there anything else about that?

☐ **Find the solution within the story.** Gently stop the clean language. Ask the client to explain more about the metaphor. Focus your questions on how to make the story relate to the present day, so the solution can be brought forward. Use active listening and pace your questions slowly. Don't bias the solution by trying to impose one. Just stay with the process long enough for your client to generate the resolution of the issue. Questions to elicit the solution can include:

What needs to happen now?
How can this go forward?
What do you do to change this?
What would help turn this around?
What resource is hidden in this memory or story, and could help?
What is the best way through this?
Where can you look in this story for an answer?

☐ **Summarize the solution**. Create action steps to make the solution more concrete. Suggest that your client find a mantra to use, as a phrase or a sentence, to capture the meaning of the solution.

If you need more help, review the case example from Chapter 13 to see how each step works in a session. Helpful additional resources include the "clean language" work of David Grove and those books written by others, explaining its use in therapy and coaching.

L. THE FIVE-YEAR LIFE PLAN

From Skill #9: Design a Plan for Life

A life plan functions like a map of what is probable and possible for a therapy client over time. Co-creating a life plan in therapy can serve to summarize and digest all that has occurred in treatment. It may also extend therapy or counseling, since it offers new goals and challenges to work through in order to move it forward.

Introduce the Life Plan

First, use some open-ended questions in sessions with a client to introduce the topic of a life plan in sessions, such as:

What is the best possible life you could have during the next five years?
Which people do you need to cultivate in order to bring out your best?
What routines or personal habits would promote a healthy and vibrant life?
What would you love to accomplish, if time and money were not considerations?
What would describe a perfect day, perfect month, perfect year, or perfect life?
If you could design a good, healthy and happy life, without worry of failure, what would it include?

When a client expresses interest in this process, copy and use the template below.

The Five-Year Life Plan Template

This template addresses three stages of a five-year life plan:

- Vision
- Self-actualization
- Manifestation

Step 1: Vision

What do you see that would be possible within five years within any of all of these categories?

- Health and well-being
- Autonomy
- Self-care
- Finances
- Relationships
- Spirituality
- Creativity
- Legacy
- Work and productivity

Based on the above, summarize your five-year vision as succinctly and clearly as possible.

_____

_____

_____

Note your feelings and thoughts about the vision above:

_____

_____

_____

List your top 3 or 4 core values (from Skill #7.) Does your vision incorporate any of your selected core values? If not, align your vision with your values to make sure the vision is filled with meaning and purpose.

_____

_____

_____

Step 2: Self-Actualization

Complete the following questions:

Who do I need to become to make this vision a reality?

_____

_____

_____

What personal qualities will be essential to my development?

_____

_____

_____

Who do I know who models these qualities?

_____

_____

What can I borrow or learn from their example to make my own?

_____

_____

Step 3: Manifestation

Fill in each area, working backwards from year 5 to year 1.

Year 5:

Goals (what to do and who to become) and a timeframe for each:

_____

_____

_____

Specific action steps for each goal:

_____

_____

_____

Markers of progress and success for each action step:

_____

_____

_____

Year 4:
Goals (what to do and who to become) and a timeframe for each:

_____

_____

_____

Specific action steps for each goal:

_____

_____

_____

Markers of progress and success for each action step:

_____

_____

_____

_____

Year 3:
Goals (what to do and who to become) and a timeframe for each:

_____

_____

_____

Specific action steps for each goal:

_____

_____

_____

Markers of progress and success for each action step:

_____

_____

_____

Year 2:
Goals (what to do and who to become) and a timeframe for each:

_____

_____

_____

Specific action steps for each goal:

_____

_____

_____

Markers of progress and success for each action step:

_____

_____

_____

Year 1:
Goals (what to do and who to become) and a timeframe for each:

_____

_____

_____

Specific action steps for each goal:

_____

_____

_____

Markers of progress and success for each action step:

_____

_____

_____

Starting now:

What is my first step?

_____

_____

_____

Who can support me in this process?

_____

_____

_____

To whom am I accountable?

_____

_____

_____

Index

accountability
  in achieving behavioral change,
    137
  in coaching, 133–43
  defined, 136
  described, 136
  external, 137–38
  internal, 137
  personal trustworthiness and, 136
  sense of failure and, 136
  shared, 133–43, 236–37. *see also*
    shared accountability
  in therapy, 133–43
  understanding, 136–38
  willpower and, 135
  worksheet, 236–37
achievement
  as hallmark of coaching, 22
action
  boosting of, 49
  call client into, 119–32. *see also* call
    client into action
  in coaching approach, 22, 23, 119
  as experiment, 129–31
  path to, 121–25
  readiness for, 119–32. *see also* call
    client into action
  shared accountability in, 138–41
  skills for, 11, 117–57. *see also spe-*
    cific types and skills for action
agenda for session
  case example, 69–71
  identify, 68–71

agreement
  session, 66–67
aligning decisions and values, 168–70
align with core values, 161–74. *see*
    also core values
  aligning decisions and, 168–70
  beyond medical model of, 162–63
  bringing core values into therapy,
    165–66
  case example, 165–72
  exercise, 172–73
  prioritizing values, 166–68
  understanding core values, 164–65
  value-based plan, 170–72
  worksheet, 240–42
Allen, W., 9, 21
American Psychological Association
    (APA), 19, 212
American Psychologist, 19
Andreas, S., 65
anxiety
  case example, 189–90
APA. *see* American Psychological
    Association (APA)
ask effective questions, 81–94
  challenge existing belief, 87–89,
    92–93
  create sudden insight, 85–87, 92
  exercise, 91–93
  how to ask, 84–85
  powerful questions, 83–84
  prompt new options, 89–91, 93
  worksheet, 228–30

ask for more
   case example, 151
   in delivering coaching edge, 150–51
   wording examples, 150
assimilative integration process,
      211–12
attitude(s)
   "the client knows best," 17

balance
   life, 163
Baumeister, R., 135
behavior(s)
   maladaptive, 35
behavioral change
   external accountability in achieving,
      137
   skills for promoting, 117–57
belief(s)
   challenge existing, 87–89, 92–93, 229
best blend
   described, 11
bias
   defined, 179
biological dysfunction
   as client challenge, 35
blatant(s), 145–46
"blue-sky" visions, 193
boundary(ies), 64–75
   case example, 60–62
   between therapist and client, 59–60
   upholding, 60–62
boundary crossings
   boundary violations vs., 59–60
boundary violations
   boundary crossings vs., 59–60
Bruckman, E.S., 111
Building Your Ideal Private Practice,
      xv, 197
Burns, D., 136–38
buyer-beware market
   coaching as, 15–16

call client into action, 119–32
   in coaching, 119
   exercise, 131–32
   as experiment, 129–31
   make it relevant, 128–29
   path to action, 121–25
   readiness within therapy, 125–28
   worksheet, 235
category(ies)
   in guidepost development, 31–38
   ranking of, 38–39
"cause and condition," 99
CBT. see cognitive behavioral therapy
      (CBT)
Celente, G., 162
challenge existing beliefs
   case example, 87–89
   questions to, 87–89, 92–93
   worksheet, 229
change(s)
   behavioral, 117–57
   in CBT, 121
   coaches as facilitators of, 22
   in coaching approach, 21–22
   in cognitive methods of therapy, 22
   in gestalt practices of therapy, 22
   stages of, 120–21
   willingness in, 120–21
clean language questions
   examples, 182
clean language technique, 179–81
client(s)
   call into action, 119–32. see also call
      client into action
   design life plan for, 189–207. see
      also design life plan; life plan
   difference between therapy and
      coaching, 15–17
   merging needs and wants of, 67–75
   needs vs. wants of, 66–67
   questions for. see question(s)
   tracking progress of, 77–78

client action, 119–32. *see also* call client into action
client-based control
in coaching approach, 21–23
client-based metaphors, 176, 178–80.
see also metaphor(s)
examples, 178–79
worksheet, 243–44
client capacity
checklist in, 38
as guidepost, 36–38
in guidepost for client suitability, 221
questions in, 37
client challenges
case example, 42
checklist in, 36
in guidepost for client suitability, 221
questions in, 35–36
types of, 34–35
client communication
transference as form of, 54
client disappointment
noticing, 64–75. *see also* noticing
client disappointment
client dissatisfaction
described, 65
noticing, 64–75. *see also* noticing
client disappointment
client dropout, 65
client functionality
as guidepost, 36–38
client noncompliance
homework-related, 137
client notes
tracking progress in, 77–78
client preference
case example, 42
checklist in, 33
as guidepost, 32–33
in guidepost for client suitability,
220–21
questions in, 33

client readiness, 120–21
worksheet, 235
client retention
defined, 63
client satisfaction
in measuring successful treatment
in Therapy with a Coaching Edge,
63
poor, 63–64
poor retention tied to lack of, 63–64
"close in"
motivation stimulated by working,
49
coach(es)
certified, 16
educational training of, 16
as facilitators, 16, 22
lack of data on, 16
life. *see* life coach(es)
as optimistic, 22–23
posture in therapeutic work, 5
reliance on "the client knows best"
attitude, 17
sessions with, 17
trained, 16
unlicensed, 15–16
untrained, 16
voice in therapeutic work, 5
voice of, 5
coachable
uncoachable *vs.*, 29–44
coaching. *see also* life coaching
accountability in, 133–43
achievement as hallmark of, 22
action in, 119
aim of, 18
as buyer-beware market, 15–16
coaches use of term, 16
cognitive proactive therapy and, 18
described, 13–14, 20
external accountability in, 137–38
feedback in, 145

coaching (*continued*)
  formalized, 19–20
  functional client presumed in, 22
  humor in, 107–16. *see also* humor
  life. *see* life coaching
  needs *vs.* wants in, 66–67
  as programmatic, 20
  purposes of, 18–20, 67
  as relating, 20, 21
  of "reluctant entrepreneurs," 46
  settings for, 17
  solution-focused counseling and, 18
  sports, 18
  strong feedback in, 145
  style of, 20–23
  suitability for, 29–42. *see also* guide-
    post
  therapy *vs.*, 13–20. *see also* therapy
    vs. coaching
  Therapy with a Coaching Edge and,
    211
  as trendy and new, 32
  who benefits from?, 29–44. *see also*
    guidepost
coaching approach
  action in, 22, 23
  client-based control in, 21–23
  described, 21–23
  factors in, 21–23
  how to deconstruct and adjust in, 24
  locus of change in, 21–22
  partnership in, 22, 23
  possibility in, 22–23
  suitability for, 28
  in therapy, 23–24
coaching collaboration
  example, 45
coaching curriculums
  "core competencies" in, 16
coaching edge
  benefits to client, 146
  deliver, 144–57. *see also* deliver
    coaching edge

  softening of, 146
  when health depends on, 153–56
  worksheet, 238–39
coaching experts
  therapy experts *vs.*, 15–17
coaching questions, 83
coaching relationship
  described, 16
coaching sessions, 17
coaching style, 20–23
  defined, 21
CoachU, 29, 46, 190
cognitive behavioral therapy (CBT)
  change in, 121
  described, 212–13
  orientation to, 214–15
  session agreement *vs.*, 66–67
  Therapy with a Coaching Edge and,
    211, 214–15
  unwillingness with homework
    related to, 137
cognitive distortions
  as client challenges, 34
cognitive methods of therapy
  locus of change in, 22
cognitive proactive therapy
  coaching and, 18
collaboration
  coaching, 45
  therapist–client, 45–62. *see also*
    therapist–client collaboration
  worksheet, 224–25
Colvin, S., 97
common factors
  in integration plan, 210–11
communication
  transference as form of, 54
competency(ies)
  core, 16
confrontation
  in therapy, 145, 146
connection
  humor in building, 112–13

consolidate gains
  case example, 74–75
  in getting-to-yes session plan,
    73–75
contemplation
  described, 121
contemporary therapy
  metaphors in, 177
  purpose of, 18–19
control
  client-based, 21–23
conversation
  therapeutic, 162
core competencies
  in coaching curriculums, 16
core values
  align with, 161–74. *see also* align
    with core values
  bringing into therapy, 165–66
  identifying, 164
  list of, 173–74, 241
  prioritizing, 166–68
  understanding, 164–65
  worksheet, 240–42
counseling
  client's lack of clarity about, 64–65
  couples, 145–46
  solution-focused, 18
counselor(s)
  educational training of, 15
couples counseling
  "full throttle marriage" style of,
    145–46
create sudden insight
  case example, 86–87
  questions to, 85–87, 92
  worksheet, 228–29
curriculum(s)
  coaching, 16

Dean, B., 193
decision(s)
  aligning with values, 168–70

deliver coaching edge, 144–57
  ask for more, 150–51
  described, 145–46
  exercise, 156–57
  expect evidence, 152–53
  step over nothing, 147–49
  worksheet, 238–39
depression
  case example, 189–90
  design life plan, 189–207
  case example, 189–90
  want-for technique, 194
  worksheet, 245–51
directness
  therapeutic, 145–46
disappointment
  of client, 64–75. *see also* noticing
    client disappointment
dissatisfaction
  client, 64–75. *see also* noticing client
    disappointment
distance + pain = humor, 115–16
distortion(s)
  cognitive, 34
dropout
  from therapy, 65
Duncan, B., 77

effective questions, 81–94. *see also* ask
  effective questions
  ask, 81–94
  favorite, 230
  for strategizing, 231–32
  worksheet, 228–30
Emotional Intelligence, 21
entrepreneur(s)
  coaching reluctant, 46
erotic transference
  therapist defusing, 54
ethics
  situational, 59–60
  of therapist–client collaboration,
    59–60

evidence
    in delivering coaching edge,
        152–53
expect evidence
    case example, 153
    in delivering coaching edge,
        152–53
    wording examples, 152
expert(s)
    difference between therapy and
        coaching, 15–17
external accountability
    in achieving behavioral change,
        137
    in coaching, 137–38
external stressors
    as client challenges, 34

facilitator(s)
    coach as, 16, 22
failure
    sense of, 136
feedback
    in coaching, 145
*Feeling Good: The New Mood Ther-
    apy,* 136–37
find metaphors that matter, 72, 175–
    88. *see also* metaphor(s)
    case example, 180–87
    client-based metaphors, 178–80
    exercise, 187–88
    expanding meaning, 181–83
    listening for metaphor, 180–81
    making it real, 186–87
    solutions within story, 183–86
    worksheet, 243–44
Fisher, 67
flexibility
    humor in, 108
formalized coaching
    history of, 19–20

foundation
    described, 10
    of Therapy with a Coaching Edge,
        1–78. *see also* Therapy with a
        Coaching Edge
Freud, S., 107, 176–77, 212
"full throttle marriage" style of cou-
    ples counseling, 145–46

gain(s) of session
    consolidating, 73–75
GAL scale. *see* Global Assessment of
    Functioning (GAL) scale
George Washington University Cancer
    Institute Office of Survivorship, 125
gestalt practices of therapy
    locus of change in, 22
Getting to Yes, 67
getting-to-yes session plan, 67–75, 78
    consolidate gains, 73–75
    find purpose, 68–71
    in merging needs and wants, 67–75
    work it through, 71–73
    worksheet, 226–27
Global Assessment of Functioning
    (GAL) scale, 37
goal(s)
    accomplishment of, 134
    defined, 192
    failure in fulfilling, 134
    S.M.A.R.T., 104–5
goal accomplishment
    in therapy, 134
Goleman, D., 21
Greenberg, R., 67
Grodzki, L., xv, 9, 21, 121–25, 197–98
group therapy
    humor in, 108–9
Grove, D., 179–81
    protocol for symbolic modeling,
        179–80

growth
  ongoing, 197–98
  personal, 211
guidepost
  in action, 39–42
  case example, 39–42
  categories in, 31–38
  client capacity as, 36–38
  client challenges as, 34–36
  client preference as, 32–33
  in incorporating coaching approach
    into therapy sessions, 30–42
  ranking categories in, 38–39
  suitability for therapist, 42–44
  worksheet, 220–23
guidepost for client suitability
  determining therapist suitability,
    223
  questions for clients, 220–22
  for therapist review, 221–22
  worksheet, 220–23

habit(s)
  happiness promoted by, 137
*Handbook of Humor: Clinical Appli-
  cations in Psychotherapy,* 111
*Handbook of Psychotherapy Integra-
  tion,* 210
happiness
  feeling lack of, 161–62
  habits promoting, 137
harmony
  universal needs of, 163
"head-on collision"
  in intensive short-term dynamic
    psychotherapy, 146
healing
  humor in, 108–10
health
  dependence on coaching edge,
    153–56

Hicks, R.F., 129–30
hierarchy
  needs, 163, 192, 198
  reducing friction of, 45–46
  reduction in, 49
homework
  client noncompliance with, 137
  internal accountability and, 137
  unwillingness in CBT, 137
humanistic-holistic therapy, 213
  orientation to, 215–16
  Therapy with a Coaching Edge and,
    215–16
humanistic psychology, 163
human needs
  hierarchy of, 163, 192, 198
humor, 107–16. *see also* lighthearted-
    ness; lightness
  in aiding partnership, 108
  in building connection, 112–13
  case example, 108–9, 112–16
  in coaching, 107–16
  contraindications in therapy, 110
  example, 107
  exercise, 116
  in flexibility, 108
  in healing, 108–10
  pain + distance =, 115–16
  in therapy, 111–12
  thoughtful spontaneity and, 113–14
  thoughts and tips about using,
    111–12
  worksheet, 233–34

idealized transference
  therapist defusing, 54
I Have a Dream speech, 192
inner strength(s)
  identify, 101–3
insight
  creating sudden, 85–87, 92, 228–29

integration of methods of therapy, 209–18. *see also* integration plan
integration plan, 209–18
  assimilative process in, 211–12
  basics of, 210–12
  CBT, 214–15
  customizing process for, 217
  find your psychotherapy model in, 212–13
  humanistic-holistic therapy, 215–16
  identify common factors in, 210–11
  psychodynamic therapy and, 213–14
  recipes, 213–16
  Therapy with a Coaching Edge–related, 209–18
  tracking my results with you, 218
intensive short-term dynamic psychotherapy, 146
internal accountability
  therapy homework and, 137
internal struggles
  as client challenges, 34
International Coach Federation, 16, 21, 108

Johnson, S., 50–51
Jung, C., 176–77

King, M.L., Jr., 192
knowledge
  universal needs of, 163

language
  clean, 179–81. *see also* clean language
latent(s), 145–46
learning
  ongoing, 197–98
Lend a (Limited) Hand
  worksheet, 236–37
Leonard, T., 19–20, 190

life balance, 163
life coach(es), 16. *see also* coach(es)
  non-hierarchical position of, 22
  verbal techniques of, 20
life coaching. *see also* coaching
  purposes of, 18–20, 67
  style in, 20
  therapy *vs.*, 21
  as trendy and new, 32
life plan. *see also* life planning
  aspects of, 191–93
  described, 191
  design, 189–207. *see also* design life plan
  introduction, 245
  steps for achieving, 192, 199–200
  treatment plan vs, 191
  want-for technique in, 194
  what of, 192
  worksheet, 245–51
life planning. *see also* life plan
  developing vision in, 195–97
  exercise, 200–6
  ongoing learning and growth in, 197–98
  three-step formulation in, 192
  want-for technique in, 194
  who one needs to become in, 198–99
life plan template
  five-year. *see* The Five-Year Life Plan Template
life-threatening diagnoses
  as client challenges, 35
lightheartedness. *see also* humor
  exercise, 116
  in therapy, 107–16
  worksheet, 233–34
lightness, 107–16. *see also* humor
  exercise, 116
  worksheet, 233–34

listening
    for metaphors, 180–81
    strategic, 98–105. *see also* strategic
        listening and thinking
list of core values
    worksheet, 240–42
list of effective questions
    worksheet, 228–30
locus of change
    in coaching approach, 21–22
    in cognitive methods of therapy, 22
    in gestalt practices of therapy, 22
    in therapy, 22
locus of control
    shifting, 24–28

"making the present perfect," 99
maladaptive behaviors
    as client challenges, 35
manifestation
    in The Five-Year Life Plan Tem-
        plate, 203–6, 247–51
Marin, R., 110
Maslow, A., 163, 192, 198
    top-tiered self-actualization of, 192
Master Certified Coach, 16
meaning
    metaphors in expanding, 181–83
    therapeutic conversation about, 162
medical methods of therapy, 22
    beyond, 161–74. *see also* align with
        core values
    to Therapy with a Coaching Edge,
        162–63
memory(ies)
    traumatic, 179
Mentor Coach, 193
merging needs and wants, 67–75
    of clients, 67–75
    getting-to-yes session plan in, 67–75.
        see also getting-to-yes session plan

"metaneeds," 163
metaphor(s)
    case example, 177
    client-based, 176, 178–80
    in contemporary therapy, 177
    defined, 175
    in expanding meaning, 181–83
    in expressing traumatic memory and
        PTSD symptoms, 179
    finding, 72, 175–88. *see also* find
        metaphors that matter
    how they help, 176–78
    listening for, 180–81
    in shifting perception, 177
    usefulness of, 176–78
    use in therapy, 175–88
    worksheet, 243–44
"metavalues," 163
Miller, S., 77
"miracle" question, 83
modern therapy
    aim of, 18
motivation
    stimulated by working "close in,"
        49

need(s)
    harmony, 163
    hierarchy of, 163, 192, 198
    knowledge, 163
    life balance, 163
    merging with wants, 67–75
    universal, 163
    wants *vs.*, 66–67
needs hierarchy
    described, 192, 198
negative transference
    case example, 54–56
    therapist defusing, 53–56
negotiation
    merging needs and wants in, 67–75

noncompliance
    client, 137
note(s)
    tracking progress in, 77–78
noticing client disappointment, 64–75
    getting-to-yes session plan in, 67–75.
        see also getting-to-yes session plan
    merging needs and wants, 67–75
    needs vs. wants–related, 66–67

One Thousand and One Nights, 113
ongoing learning and growth
    in life planning, 197–98
optimism
    of coaches, 22–23
option(s)
    prompting new, 89–91, 93, 230
    seeing, 103–4
outcome resistance
    defined, 137

pain + distance = humor, 115–16
partnership
    in coaching approach, 22, 23
    humor in aiding, 108
    skills for, 10–11, 79–116
    strategic, 231–32
partnership position
    in therapy, 48–50
path to action, 121–25
perception
    metaphors in shifting, 177
personal growth
    Therapy with a Coaching Edge and,
        211
personality disorders
    as client challenges, 35
personal trustworthiness
    accountability and, 136
plan for life
    design, 189–207. see also design life
        plan; life plan

possibility
    in coaching approach, 22–23
    skills for, 11, 159–207. see also
        specific types and skills for pos-
        sibility
"post-modern" therapy
    therapist's changes with, 51
post-traumatic stress disorder (PTSD)
    metaphors in expressing symptoms
        of, 179
potentiality
    therapeutic conversation about,
        162
powerful questions
    categories of, 83–84
practice
    difference between therapy and
        coaching, 17–20
precontemplation
    described, 121
Premature Termination in Psycho-
        therapy: Strategies for Engaging
        Clients and Improving Outcomes,
        67
preparation
    described, 121
problem(s)
    see options, 103–4
    identify inner strengths, 101–3
    questions forming basis of strategic
        skills in solving, 98–104
    stating, 99–101
process of therapy
    defined, 19
process resistance
    defined, 137
Prochaska, J., 121
professional(s)
    difference between therapy and
        coaching, 15–17
programmatic
    coaching as, 20

prompt new options
  case example, 89–91
  questions to, 89–91, 93
  worksheet, 230
prospection
  defined, 191
  psychology of, 191
psychoanalysis
  sports coaching *vs.*, 18
psychodynamic therapy, 212
  orientation to, 213–14
  Therapy with a Coaching Edge and, 213–14
psychology
  humanistic, 163
  of prospection, 191
psychotherapy
  client's lack of clarity about, 64–65
  intensive short-term dynamic, 146
  purpose of, 19
  types of, 212
psychotherapy model
  in integration plan, 212–13
Psychotherapy Networker, xi, xiii, xv
PTSD. *see* post-traumatic stress disorder (PTSD)
purpose
  difference between therapy and coaching, 17–20
  in getting-to-yes session plan, 68–71
  therapeutic conversation about, 162

question(s)
  ask effective, 81–94. *see also* ask effective questions
  clean language, 182
  in client capacity, 37
  in client challenges, 35–36
  in client preference, 33
  coaching, 83
  to create sudden insight, 85–87, 92
  effective. *see* ask effective questions; effective questions
  in forming basis of strategic skills in defining what, who, and how of problem, 98–104, 106
  in guidepost for client suitability, 220–22
  "miracle," 83
  powerful, 83–84
  "stack," 85
  for strategizing, 106

readiness
  for action, 119–32. *see also* call client into action
  client, 120–21
  within therapy, 125–28
  worksheet, 235
Real, T., 145
Reamer, F., 59
relating
  coaching as style of, 20, 21
relationship(s)
  coaching, 16
  collaborative, 45–62. *see also* therapist–client collaboration
  therapist–client, 15
  therapy based on, 56
relationship issues
  as client challenges, 34
relevance
  in therapy, 128–29
"reluctant entrepreneurs"
  coaching of, 46
resistance
  early stages of, 121
  outcome, 137
  process, 137
result(s)
  defined, 76

retention
  defined, 63
  poor, 63–64
Richarde, P., 46–48
Rousmaniere, T., 77
Rubin, G., 137
"rule of the worst," 89

Satir, V., 56
satisfaction
  client. *see* client satisfaction
self
  sense of, 57
  use of. *see* use of self
self-actualization
  in The Five-Year Life Plan Tem-
    plate, 202, 247
  growing toward vision as path of, 198
  list of, 163
  qualities of, 198
  top-tiered, 192
self-control
  willpower and, 135
self-discipline
  willpower and, 134–35
self-disclosure
  case example, 58–59
  in heightened use of self, 57
  by therapist, 57
  use of, 57–59
Seligman, M., 19, 191
sense of failure
  accountability and, 136
sense of self
  therapeutic, 57
session(s)
  agenda for, 68–71
  coaching, 17
  difference between therapy and
    coaching, 17
  ending it well, 73–75

gains of, 73–75
  spotting results in, 76–77
  three-step plan, 64–75. *see also*
    three-step session plan
session agreement, 66–67
  CBT *vs.*, 66–67
setting(s)
  difference between therapy and
    coaching, 17
shades of gray
  in situational ethics, 59–60
shared accountability, 133–43
  in action, 138–41
  add, 133–43
  case example, 138–41
  exercise, 142–43
  therapist's limited role in, 141–42
  worksheet, 236–37
shifting locus of control
  case example, 24–28
  in Therapy with a Coaching Edge,
    24–28
significant traumatic experiences
  as client challenges, 35
Simon, R., xi–xiii
situational ethics
  shades of gray in, 59–60
skill(s). *see also specific types, e.g.,* ask
    effective questions
  for action, 11, 117–57. *see also
    specific types and* skills for
    action
  integration by therapist, 209–10
  for partnership, 10–11, 79–116. *see
    also specific types and* skills for
    partnership
  for possibility, 11, 159–207. *see also
    specific types and* skills for pos-
    sibility
  for promoting behavioral change,
    117–57

in refining of client's vision, 192–93
in Therapy with a Coaching Edge, 79–207. *see also specific types, e.g.,* ask effective questions
skills for action, 117–57
add shared accountability, 133–43
call client into action, 119–32
deliver coaching edge, 144–57
described, 11
skills for partnership
ask effective questions, 81–94
be strategist with twist, 95–106
described, 10–11
humor, 107–16
skills for possibility, 159–207
align with core values, 161–74
described, 11
design life plan, 189–207
find metaphors that matter, 175–88
S.M.A.R.T. goals, 104–5
Soderquist, R., 177
solution-focused counseling
coaching and, 18
solutions within story, 183–86
spontaneity
thoughtful, 113–14
sports coaching
psychoanalysis *vs.,* 18
spotting results in session, 76–77
"stack" questions, 85
stages of change model, 121
stages of strategic partnership
worksheet, 231–32
step over nothing
case example, 148–149
in delivering coaching edge, 147–49
wording examples, 147, 148
steps to coaching edge
worksheet, 238–39

story
solutions within, 183–86
strategic listening and thinking, 98–105
see options, 103–4
case example, 99–105
identify inner strengths, 101–3
state problem in present, 99–101
strategic partnership
stages of, 231–32
strategic plan
for Therapy with a Coaching Edge integration, 209–18
strategies for collaboration
worksheet, 224–25
strategist(s)
listening as, 98–105. *see also* strategic listening and thinking
questions for, 106
thinking as, 98–105. *see also* strategic listening and thinking
with twist, 95–106. *see also* strategist with twist
way of, 96–105
strategist with twist, 95–106. *see also* strategist(s)
exercise, 105
questions related to, 98–104, 106
strategic listening and thinking, 98–105. *see also* strategic listening and thinking
worksheet, 231–32
strategizing
effective questions for, 231–32
strength(s)
inner, 101–3
stressor(s)
external, 34
strong feedback
in coaching, 145
struggle(s)
internal, 34

style(s)
  of coaching, 20–23
  of relating, 20
  of therapy, 20
  of therapy *vs.* life coaching, 21
suitability
  for coaching approach, 28
  for therapist, 42–44, 223
  for Therapy with a Coaching Edge,
    29–42. *see also* guidepost
Swift, J., 67
symbolic modeling
  Grove's protocol for, 179–80

The Business and Practice of Coaching:
  Finding Your Niche, Making Money,
  and Attracting Ideal Clients, 9, 21
"the client knows best" attitude
reliance on, 17
"The Coaching Edge," xiii
The Five-Year Life Plan Template,
  199–206, 245–51
  manifestation in, 203–6, 247–51
  self-actualization in, 202, 247
  vision in, 201, 246
  worksheet, 245–51
The Happiness Project, 137
The New Private Practice: Therapist-
  Coaches Share Stories, Strategies,
  and Advice, 9, 21
The Portable Coach, 19–20
The Psychology of Humor, 110
therapeutic alliance
  worksheet, 233–34
therapeutic conversation
  about meaning, purpose, and poten-
    tiality, 162
therapeutic directness
  models of, 145–46
therapeutic sense of self
  developing, 57

therapist(s)
  being more "coach-like" in stance
    and collaborative positioning,
    45–62. *see also* therapist–client
    collaboration
  criteria for using Therapy with a
    Coaching Edge model, 43
  defusing negative transference, 53–56
  educational training of, 15
  increased use of self by, 56–59
  integrating skills by, 209–10
  as model of your services, 57
  "post-modern" therapy impact on,
    51
  private setting of, 17
  professionalism of, 15
  role in shared accountability, 141–42
  role in therapist–client collabora-
    tion, 50–51
  self-disclosure by, 57
  shifting persona of, 50–51
  suitability for, 42–44, 223
  taking lead, 51–53
  verbal techniques of, 20
therapist–client collaboration, 45–62
  boundaries in, 59–60
  clients looking to therapist as model
    of your services, 57
  creating, 45–62
  described, 48–50
  ethics of, 59–60
  shifting persona of therapist, 50–51
  therapist defusing negative transfer-
    ence in, 53–56
  therapist increased use of self in,
    56–59
  therapist taking lead in, 51–53
  upholding boundaries in, 60–62
  worksheet, 224–25
therapist–client relationship
described, 15

therapy. *see also* contemporary
   therapy; psychodynamic therapy;
   specific types, e.g., cognitive
   behavioral therapy (CBT)
   accountability in, 133–43
   aim of, 18–19
   based on relationship, 56
   boosting action within, 49
   bringing coaching approach into,
      23–24
   bringing core values into, 165–66
   client's lack of clarity about, 64–65
   cognitive behavioral. *see* cognitive
      behavioral therapy (CBT)
   cognitive methods of, 22
   cognitive proactive, 18
   confrontation in, 145, 146
   contemporary, 18–19, 177
   contraindications to humor in, 110
   described, 13–14
   dropouts from, 65
   gestalt practices of, 22
   goal accomplishment in, 134
   group, 108–9
   humanistic-holistic, 213, 215–16
   humor in, 108–9, 111–12
   integrating methods of, 209–18
   life coaching *vs.*, 21
   lightheartedness in, 107–16
   locus of change in, 22
   metaphors in, 175–88. *see also*
      find metaphors that matter;
      metaphor(s)
   modern, 18
   partnership position in, 48–50
   "post-modern," 51
   process of, 19
   as process-oriented, 20
   psychodynamic, 212–14
   purposes of, 18, 19, 67
   readiness within, 125–28

   relevance in, 128–29
   with something extra. *see* Therapy
      with a Coaching Edge
   style of, 20
   success of, 19
therapy experts
   coaching experts *vs.*, 15–17
therapy homework. *see* homework
therapy *vs.* coaching, 13–20
   how (style), 20
   what (practice and purpose), 17–20
   where (sessions and settings), 17
   who (professionals and populations),
      15–17
Therapy with a Coaching Edge, *e.g.,*
      see also specific components, ask
      effective questions; call client into
      action, 23
   as adaptive, 8
   add shared accountability, 133–43
   align with core values, 161–74
   ask effective questions, 81–94
   benefits of, 7–8
   be strategist with twist, 95–106
   call client into action, 119–32
   case example, 3–7
   CBT and, 211, 214–15
   client-focused control of, 30
   coaching and, 211
   criteria for therapists using, 43
   deliver coaching edge, 144–57
   described, 7–9, 209
   design life plan, 189–207
   development of, 7–9, 23–24
   directive nature of, 30
   find metaphors that matter, 175–88
   foundation of, 1–78
   guidepost in, 30–42. *see also* guide-
      post
   humanistic-holistic therapy and,
      215–16

humor, 107–16
indications for, 7
as integration, 211–12
integration with therapy methods,
    209–18. *see also* integration plan
measuring successful treatment in,
    63
from medical model to, 162–63
personal growth and, 211
psychodynamic therapy and, 213–14
purpose of, 8
results in every session, 63–78
skills in, 79–207. *see also specific
    types, e.g.,* ask effective questions
suitability for, 29–44
therapist–client collaboration in,
    45–62
three-step session plan for, 64–75
treatment measurement in, 63
where therapy and coaching meet,
    13–28. *see also* therapy *vs.* coaching
Therapy with a Coaching Edge inte-
    gration
    strategic plan for, 209–18
thinking
    strategic, 98–105. *see also* strategic
        listening and thinking
thoughtful spontaneity
    humor and, 113–14
three-step session plan, 64–75
    described, 64
    noticing client disappointment,
        64–75
    spotting results in session, 76–77
    tracking client progress, 77–78
top-tiered self-actualization
    Maslow's, 192
tracking client progress, 77–78
trained coaches, 16
transference
    erotic, 54
    as form of client communication, 54
    idealized, 54
    negative. *see* negative transference
traumatic experiences
    significant, 35
traumatic memory
    metaphors in expressing, 179
treatment plan
    described, 191
    life plan *vs.,* 191
Trends 2000, 162
trustworthiness
    personal, 136

uncoachable
    coachable *vs.,* 29–44
untrained coaches, 16
unwillingness
    with homework in CBT, 137
Ury, 67
use of self
    described, 56
    self-disclosure in heightened, 57
    therapist's increased, 56–59

value(s)
    core. *see* align with core values; core
        values
    prioritizing, 166–68
value-based plan, 170–72
verbal techniques
    of therapists and life coaches, 20
vision(s)
    "blue-sky," 193
    case example, 195–99
    described, 192
    developing, 195–97
    in The Five-Year Life Plan Tem-
        plate, 201, 246
    growing toward, 198
    refining of, 192–93
voice
    coach's, 5

want(s)
merging with needs, 67–75
needs *vs.*, 66–67
want-for(s)
examples, 194–95
want-for technique
in life planning, 194
Way, M., 180
Weiss, A., 122–25
"What I want for you," 190
where therapy and coaching meet,
13–28
shifting locus of control in, 24–28
WHO-DAS. *see* World Health Organization's Disability Assessment
Schedule (WHO-DAS)
willingness
in change, 120–21
willpower
accountability and, 135
described, 135
limits of, 134–35
self-control and, 135
self-discipline and, 134–35
working "close in"
motivation stimulated by, 49

work it through
case example, 72–73
in getting-to-yes session plan, 71–73
worksheet(s), 219–51
client-based metaphors, 243–44
client readiness, 235
described, 12
The Five-Year Life Plan Template,
245–51
getting-to-yes session plan, 226–27
guidepost for client suitability,
220–23
lend a (limited) hand, 236–37
list of core values, 240–42
list of effective questions, 228–30
stages of strategic partnership, 231–32
steps to coaching edge, 238–39
strategies for collaboration, 224–25
therapeutic alliance, 233–34
World Health Organization's Disability Assessment Schedule (WHO-
DAS), 37
"worried well"
defined, 161

Zur Institute, 59–60